Caste System and Social Change

Caste System and Social Change

Edited by
Virendra Prakash Singh

Commonwealth

Caste System and Social Change

ISBN : 81-7169-238-9

Edition : 2026

Published by :
COMMONWEALTH PUBLISHERS (P) LTD.
4831/24, Govind Lane,
Ansari Road, Darya Ganj,
New Delhi - 110002
Ph. : 23272541, 23242541
e-mail : commonwealthpublishers2016@gmail.com

Distributed by :
ARJUN PUBLISHING HOUSE
4831/24, Govind Lane,
Ansari Road, Darya Ganj,
New Delhi - 110002
Ph. : 23272541, 23242541
e-mail : arjunbooks2001@gmail.com

Laser Typesetting by :
Dimple Computers
Delhi

Printed at :
Divine Digital Printers
Delhi

"Dedicated to the people's
Who lost their lives in
The struggle against
Caste System."

PREFACE

The dynamics of the much discussed caste system in India has had profound and far-reaching effects on the very ethos and character of development efforts in the country. The division of society into four castes on inherently religious grounds is a theory of class which, on deeper insight, contains many more levels of reasoning related not only to an understood order in nature but also the mechanics of occupation, place in the hierarchy, the ordained structure of human endeavour and, not the least, the economic viability of the entire social and economic structure of nations. The caste system in relation to class structure and cultural change has over the years become the subject of a vast amount of literature, a large part of which can be termed as the Sociology of the Caste System.

The division of people into distinct classes with understood functions and place in overall society are not a phenomenon peculiar to India. The Japanese have their *bura-kumin*, the "untouchables", and ethnicity in South-East Asia has also bred many so-called sub-cultures and race distinctions. It is accepted, nonetheless, that in traditional society, particularly villages such as those in India and other Asian countries, there are even more subtle variations of the easte system. In fact, "caste" is, in other contexts, a purely social division based on such misconceptions as racial superiority, the arrogance of wealth and the much-vaunted educational advantage. But, at this point we may take a quick look at the dynamics of the caste system in India.

The ancient Hindu pattern of social organisation aimed at the value of *Dharama*, *Artha*, *Kama* and *Moksa* by the individual through his physical, psychological and social evolution. This evolution was calculated to be effected through the process of the Varna-asrama system. It was a comprehensive scheme of individual fulfilment with social purpose through concrete institutions. It has been regarded as the basic concept of Hindu culture and the pivot of Hindu social structure throughout the ages. At the same time it cannot be denied that the Varna Dharma has been equally the target of vehement attack by saints and scholars alike from time to time.

It would be necessary to look into the meaning of the Varnasrama Dharma. The protagonists of this system maintain that the Varna Dharma aimed at the classification of society into four Varnas—the Brahmin, the Ksatriya, the Vaisya and the Sudra, respectively, in the order of precedence and on the basis of the element of Sattva, Rajas and Tamas in the nature of human beings to fulfil the multitudinous needs and purposes of society at large. The Asrama Dharma my be best described as the vision of normal life for the individual in his social mileau. It refers to the main stages of life through which the normal individual is expected to pass—student, householder and hermit (in two stages) in the process of evolution and fulfilment of his personality. So far as the Asrama Dharma is concerned, it has been appreciated by all but what is regrettable is that with the passage of time it has been observed more in breach than in practice.

As far as the subject of Varna Dharma, it has been the most controversial theme since long and particularly of late, scholars, sociologists and politicians have held diverse opinions about the origin and usefulness of this institution. Its advocates maintain that the genesis of this fourfold classification of society is to be found in the 'Purus Sukta' of the Rgveda. We also find similar references in the Satapatha and the Taittiriya Brahmana. The Puranas and the Smritis in particular give an elaborate account of it. The Mahabharata and the Gita are also full of several references about this institution. The other school of scholars maintain that there is no mention of the four Varnas in the Vedic literature. The Veda speaks only of the Arya and Dasa Varna. The third school of scholars stress that the concept of Varna Dharma is not only eternal but also universal and it does and did exist in one form or the other in all climes, times and species. They say that the classification of society on the basis of Guna-Karma (nature and work) exists not only in the human or animal world but also in the world of inanimate things. A peep into the ancient history of Egypt, China, Japan, Persia, Greece and Rome shows that there did exist three or four distinctive classes of the priests, the warriors, the businessmen and the artisans and the agriculturists or the slaves resembling more or less the Brahmins, the Ksatriyas, the Vaisyas and Sudras of ancient India.

The next important question, although a very controversial one, that engages our attention is: What is the basis of this fourfold classification of Varnas? Whether it is Janmona (by birth) or Karmana (by work or occupation)? The Sanatana (orthodox) school of Hindu theologists regard Janmana as the basis of the Varna classification while the scholars of the reformist school emphasise the Karmana aspect. The late Dr. Bhagwan Das propounded the Karmana theory. His three-volume study of Indian social organisation has been regarded as a pioneering work in the field of Hindu sociology in modern times. The progressive school of Indian sociologists maintain that the fourfold classification of Varnas was merely a poetic concept of the ancient Hindu sociologists and it did never have a practical existence. They say that it can be proved from history that the theory of the Varna Dharma remained divorced from practice. The name of Sardar K.M. Panikkar may be cited as a representative scholar of this school. His book *Hindu Society at Crossroads* deserves careful study by students of Hindu sociology. He has tried to prove that the Brahmins alone may be regarded as illustrations of the theory of Varna Dharma while the same thing cannot be said about the other three Varnas, *i.e.*, the Ksatriyas, the Vaisyas and Sudras. But at the same time, Sri Panikkar states that slthough the concept of four Varnas is merely an imaginary creation of ancient Hindu sociologists, yet the Hindu social life is inspired and pervaded by this concept. Thousands of castes and sub-castes that comprise the Hindu society try to establish their origin from one or the other of the four Varnas. So we may say that the original concept of the four Varnas either did never find a practical form or if it ever existed in the practical world, that must have been only partially evolved. With the passage of time the original concept might have degenerated into the practical form of the castes and sub-castes that we see with all their glaring absurdities even in the present day Hindu society.

What are the cardinal principles underlying the Varna concept? The following three principles are regarded as the quintessence of the Varna Dharma:

1. Unchangeable inequality based on birth.
2. Classification of occupations and their disparity.
3. Prohibition of marriage outside one's own Varna.

The first and the third may be noted to be prevalent even doday while the second has never been observed in practice. From the Vedic times upto the present day works of history and literature provide several illustrations which show that persons born in lower castes took up occupations theoretically belonging to the higher castes and *vice versa*. Example of inter-Varna or inter-caste marriages are also cited from the ancient literature. A certain class of scholars maintain that Varna is changeable but not caste. The principle underlying the Varna theory, according to them, is Guna-karma while that of caste is birth. So one may change one's Varna but not caste. They cite illustrations from the old literature to prove their contention. But whatever they might believe about the practicability of the Varna concept, it has to be conceded that it played an important role in the evolution and development of Hindu social organisation.

The principal underlying the religious and secular activities of the Hindus has been spirituality. That one cardinal value is the realisation of unity in diversity. Hierarchy will exist as long as diversity remains in the world and without diversity there can be no world; but spiritual equality was regarded by the ancient seers of India as a permanent safeguard against the hierarchy breaking up into an anarchy of ego-centric individuals. Except in periods, according to an eminent thinker, when it displayed a downward curve, Indian culture has been a harmonisation of the individual and the collectivity. In the Mahabharat it is said that if an untouchable happens to be virtuous, even the Gods would recognise him as a Brahmin. This harmonisation of the individual and the collectivity has been regarded by many as a marvel of Hindu sociology, but there are others who lay their accusing finger on the intolerant and exclusive priestcraft and petrified social hierarchy, and conclude that it has disfigured Indian history and caused the general impression of a repression of the individual under a system of hidebound orthodoxy. Prof. A.R. Wadia has taken this stand in his *Contemporary Indian Philosophy*.

A certain section of scholars maintain that the concept of fourfold Varnas was really a novel and useful device of the Hindu sociological brain to maintain the purity and solidarity of the society but later on what caused the decay and disintegration of society was not the Varna classification but its gradual degeneration into innumerable castes and sub-castes. Not only that but the caste system, despite their glaring drawbacks, did play a very significant part in maintaining the purity and solidarity of Hindu society at the time of external aggressions and alien rule. According to these scholars, it was the caste system of Hindus that saved their culture from the onslaughts of Islam and Christianity and kept undefiled the original content.

Now we come to a very perplexing problem that poses itself before every student of Hindu sociology and that is; What is the future of the Varna and caste system after the promulgation of the present constitution of India which does not recognise any sort of disparity or inequality on the basis of caste, colour, creed, sex or religion. The concept of the modern welfare or socialistic state with authorised powers to inerfere in every sphere of human activity and to make or amend laws to fulfil its declared aims has also posed a challenge before the Hindu society which must be answered.

Sardar K.M. Panikkar's approach deserve consideration in this respect. He proves by his penetrating analysis that the various social institutions of the Hindus are not a part of religion and that they are based on laws, customs and traditions and hence they are secular. Thus he tries to establish and conclude that since these social institutions are based on laws and customs, it is desirable that the constitution or the constituted authority should re-interpret or amend them whenever the necessity arises to do so. This he has tried to establish on the basis of the amendments and reforms made in the various Smritis from time to time.

This view is not very far from truth and carries much weight. Varna and caste have now outlived their utility. It is time when we should recast our social structure on the basis of complete equality. History has proved that man is a highly individualistic and group-minded creature who is apt to divide and separate even where perfect unity and equality is intended. A concept or a system based on a view to divide may only aggrevate the division. Man's natural separatism should not be assisted by social separatism; it should rather be fought by social equalism, on all levels and at all fronts. Then only we can hope to acquire the minimum equality needed to harness human energies for progress, material and spiritual.

The inspiration for this collection of papers, articles and comments, from a wide variety of both published and unpublished sources, is drawn from the character that has marked the Indian peoples-always hospitable, adapting, loyal yet not blind and most willing to be swept off by the tumultuous changes that mark the present age. It is hoped that the anthology of reference and source material, some as old and precious, as six decades, will be useful for the student and scholar as well as sociologist and economist. Class and culture are relative terms and caste is inherent. All interact and effect in various ways the economic and social development efforts of the government. This too has become a part of our planning process, evident from the special component for Scheduled Castes and Scheduled Tribes. The Mandal Commission and the Reservation issue are just behind us. Atrocities on a caste basis contiaue to hamper growth and development. Caste is also an integral part of our political ethos. One hopes for change and change brings pain and suffering. India is on the move and in the midst of change.

In this effort at compilation, the publishers and I wish to thank all the librarians, assistant librarians, research scholars and academicians who assisted in identifying and also at times providing copies of the papers and articles. Due thanks are due to all of them.

EDITOR

CONTENTS

PREFACE vii

1. Theory and Psychology of Caste 1
2. Resurgence of Social Change 45
   —*B. Ryan*
3. Social Integration of Scheduled Castes 59
4. Causes and Consequences of Individual Change in Six Developing Countries 83
   —*A. Inkeles*
5. Social Reform Through Education 112
6. Dr. Ambedkar on Caste System 138

APPENDIX I 164
APPENDIX II 188
APPENDIX III 224
APPENDIX IV 241
APPENDIX V 272
APPENDIX VI 286
APPENDIX VII 302

INDEX 310

1

THEORY AND PSYCHOLOGY OF CASTE

Theory of Caste

Hindus believe that all men in the world are divided into four castes: Brahamans (priests), Kshatriyas (warriors), Vaishyas (common people), and Shudras (servants). The precedence of these castes is in the order of enumeration. All other castes are produced by intermarriage either with pure or the mixed. These differences in the castes are innate and can not be obliterated or concealed.

If there are any tribes or communities or nations like the old Greeks and English people where caste is not found, it is because those people neglected the rules of marriage and conduct, and have consequently merged into barbarism, and caste among them is destroyed by indiscreet intermixture (fusion of vernas).

The caste system does not decide the position of the Hindus only; it decides the position of non-Hindus in society, *e.g.*, the Mohammedans and Christians have a certain definite status according to Hindus social theory.

Abstract from Ketkar, *History of Caste.*

Caste is due to the occupation which a man's forefathers were in.

Nobody can raise his caste in the Kali age, the age of discord, while it was possible to do this in the good old Krita age, the age of virtue.

The precedence given to a caste is not given by man; it is absolute, and the order is supposed to be known and fixed, and it ought not to be otherwise.

Though no man can raise his caste, he can degrade it by neglect of the ceremonials or by connection with the "low and barbarous". In such case he may either degrade himself completely or hold an intermediate position.

As a man may lose his position in the caste, so a caste may lose its position in the society. Taking a low trades is one of the things which may cause such a degradation.

There are certain occupations considered higher than others. Among the occupations assigned to the people, the occupation of a writer is superior to that of a merchant; that of a goldsmith superior to that of a copper-smith, and so on.

Certain animals also have several degrees of status varying from sacred and clean to unclean and foul. And the castes which serve these animals are graded accordingly.

A case is again degraded by giving up or not having the traditional rules of purity of the surrounding dominant castes and by irregular conduct from their standard. In Western India, some castes are degraded by the use of wine and meat and even by that of tobacco. Many Brahmin castes in certain localities have lost in status by using meat, which is used in those localities only by non-Brahmins. Though the use of meat is generally not approved, yet the eating of beef and of pork and of vermin is considered most degrading. Many castes have been lowered in the social scale by the custom of polygamy, and by the custom prevailing among them of the purchasing the bride. They also gain or lose status according to the higher or lower form[1] of marriage which they use. Moreover, if at the time of the marriage the bridge is already of age, that fact is considered as degrading to the caste. It is preferred that a girl should marry before she comes of age. The reasons for such a belief will be given later on.

These examples of the ceremonial law of purity, which tend to raise of lower the caste, are neither complete nor universal. The law differs according to the locality. The principles of ceremonial purity which in some parts form a hard and fast rule may be simply a sentiment elsewhere. When a question of precedence between two castes came before the colleges of Pundits in Benares, or Poona, it was decided, not by the observation of actual social conditions, but by the authority of old books. When they did not find any reference to the caste in the old book, they would either identify it with some old caste, or might invent some explanation regarding its origin. When they admitted the pretensions to a higher status of a few castes, they depended not on the actual conditions, but on some fiction which was supposed to be misunderstood till then.

The underlying theory was that the laws which define caste status are fixed and known. They are given by the gods. It is the duty of the Pundits to explain the laws.

The question referred to the colleges of Pundits was usually this: Is the claim of a certain caste to being Brahmana or Kshatriya a true claim or a false one?

But every caste decides for itself whether certain members who have been guilty of irregular conduct should be allowed to remain in the caste, and also whether another caste is fit for intercourse with them and to what extent it is. Consequently, whatever opinion the colleges of the Pundits may give, the actual precedence depends on what a caste can exact. The Sarasvat Brahmins in Maharashtra, however, succeeded in proving their claims to Brahminship in the Peshwa's court; but since public opinion was against them, they did not get the status equal to that of other Brahmin castes.

But what does the precedence amount to? This precedence means simply a public opinion that one caste is better than another. It is this public opinion which is fought for even to-day. At present this caste precedence means very little tangible good. But under native rulers it may have been a tangible good. The country is now falled into the hands of "casteless barbarians," and only formal precedence has remained.

The ways in which this precedence is manifested are worthy of notice, especially because, if we want to understand *de facto* and not *de jure* precedence, these ways are the only means to understand it.

How is the precedence manifested? As Brahmin is at the head of society holiness is the standard. A caste is pure or impure as much as it is high or low. This purity is not the outside purity, which is apparent to the "bodily eye," but it is some mystic, innate purity. If the pure and impure are brought together, the pure become impure. For this reason the holy and pure castes should keep as little connection with impure castes as possible. The purer the substance, the more easily it is soiled. So a caste should define its relation with another caste, in so far as the latter is pure or impure.

It should be remembered that there is a wide range of substances which are polluted by the touch of low-castes. The higher caste may not take them when polluted. What substances are pure and what are impure, what substances are easily polluted and what are not depends on the local customs. In the Maratha country a Brahmin will regard water touched by any other caste but his own as polluted. In Gujarath and Bengal, a Brahmin may take water touched by a Shudra. In the Maratha country, it is only the touch of the lower castes which pollutes food. But soldiers from many northern castes are known to throw away their food simply because the shadow of an English officer falls on it. The pretensions of Madras Brahmins go father than that: their food is polluted if a man of low caste looks at it.

The theory of purity and pollution would require a whole volume to treat at length; but what a have already said will enable the reader to understand the justice of some of the rules which can be inferred, in order to understand the status of the caste. The rules are as follows:

(a) Where a certain caste cannot eat food cooked by another caste, while the latter permits food to be eaten which was cooked by the first caste, then the first caste is superior to the second.

(b) If a Brahmin or other high-caste Hindu keeps more connection with one caste than another, then the former is superior to the latter. For example:

   (i) If a Brahmin accepts water from another caste, that caste is considered as clean in Bengal.

   (ii) If he accepts food cooked in oil, then the caste is better.

   (iii) If he accepts food cooked in water, then the caste is still better.

(c) The amount of pollution that a caste carries with it makes the caste low or high. If a caste pollues some substances, but not the rest, that caste is better than one which pollutes all substances. All three classes of castes stated under (b) are clean castes, which do not pollute water; but below them are castes who pollute water, and below them there are the following castes in the descending order of status:

   (i) Caste which pollute an earthen vessel.

   (ii) Caste which pollute a brass vessel.

   (iii) Castes which pollute the courtvard of the tample if they enter.

(iv) The castes which pollute the town if they live in it, and are consequently required to live outside.

There is another shade of distinction regarding the grades of castes whom a Brahmin can touch or from whom he may, as in some parts, accept water witnout pollution.

1. If a caste can give water to a Brahmin or touch him, that caste is pretty good.
2. If a caste can give water to a Brahmin lady or touch without polluting her, that caste is better still.
3. A caste from whom a Brahmin window may accept water, or one whose members she can touch without being polluted, is the best of all.

I know that what I say looks very ridiculous; but if I explain the reason for these shades of distinction, then I think it will not look so ridiculous.

The harder the rules of ceremonial purity, the more easily they are broken. The more extravagant the notions of purity are, the more easily is the purity defiled. The castes are good in proportion to the hardness of the ceremonial rules of purity of the people they can touch without polluting them. The ceremonial rules of purity of a Brahmin lady are harder than those of men, and of widows harder than the ordinary women; and castes could be graded accordingly.

The Indian method of excommunicating a man also must be understood in order to understand the propriety of some rules regarding the treatment of the low classes.

If a man is excommunicated by his caste-fellows, nobody in the caste will marry with him or will accept water from his hands, or will invite him to dinner. Sometimes, if the offense is very bad, as the killing of a cow, the whole village will outcaste him. The priests will not attend any ceremonial in his house. The barbers will not shave him, and the washerman will not wash his clothes. These are the methods of bringing pressure on the man.

These ideas have their influence in manifesting the status of a caste. With these principles in view, the castes in some parts may be graded as follows: The castes served by good priests are superior to the castes served by degraded priests. Again, the castes served by a barber and a washerman are superior to those who are not. Even among the castes served by a barber, a distinction may be drawn based on the question whether the barber pares the nails or not; among the latter, whether he pares the toe nails or not. Nonperformance of service on the part of this powerful class implies inferiority in every case.

Psychology of Caste

What human feelings lie at the basis of the mystery deserve to be considered. These social differences of caste have become so firm in the mind of the Hindu that he regards it as a very natural institution. An outsider regards it is foolish, harmful, unjust, and artificial. He thinks that the constitution of the Hindu's mind is different from that of all other people in the world.

How this caste distinction came into existence will be dealt with in the History of Caste. At present I confine myself to making a few remarks on whether there are any passions common to all human beings at the root of the caste system, or whether it is due to certain abnormal traits of character peculiar to a strange and unspeakable people, the Hindus.

I do not care to inquire into the reason of all the phenomena that are supposed to be a part or result of the Indian caste system. I make a few remarks regarding those I consider most important. There are two important elements in the Hindu caste system; for example, endogamy and hierarchy. The classes, races, and occupations exclude themselves from other groups while there is an understanding that one group is superior to the other. Of these two let endogamy be singled for consideration.

I think that I should begin the discussion regarding the psychology of endogamy by quoting Westermark. He says: "Affection depends in a very high degree upon sympathy. Though distinct aptitudes, these two classes of emotions are intimately connected: Affection is strengthened by sympathy, and sympathy is strengthened by affection. Community of interest, opinions, sentiment, culture, mode of life, as being essential to close sympathy, is therefore favourable to warm affection. If love is excited by contrast it is so only within certain limits. The contrast cannot be so great as to exclude sympathy."[2]

Human affection is generally restricted to those who are similar to them in these respects. People differing in race, religion, civilization and customs are also different in those essentials of close sympathy, and human affection is always guided by race and religion, customs or social position.

It is not true that these factors always restrict man's choice. Marriages do take place where these factors are not considered. But they are so rare as to be regarded as a romance, and people feel like writing a novel or an invective when such a case may occur.

The greatest number of castes which do not marry with each other are simply tribes converted into castes. The tribes when they were converted into castes were often fighting with each other in the early days, when the seed of caste distinction was sown. At present the various tribes and castes feel strong repulsion against one another, and this fact is a clear manifestation of our present savagery. What I say is very humilitating but it is nevertheless true. One subdivision of a caste feels strong repulsion to another subdivision, because among the latter the use of tobacco is customary; two sections of one caste do not intermarry and feel strong repulsion for each other because they use different kinds of shoes; two castes refuse to marry with each other to-day because their forefathers at one time quarreled over the boundaries of the village or over certain other questions, important or foolish. The primitive nations always have a very strong dislike for one another. "Savage nations are subdivided into an infinity of tribes which, bearing a cruel hatred toward each other, form no intermarriages, even when their language springs from the same root and only a small arm of a river, or a group of hills, separates their habitations".[3]

The castes are not simply developed tribes. Classes are converted into castes by becoming endogamous. Sometimes a section of the society becoming a hereditary class like the Brahmins and desiring to become exclusive does not design to marry outside the class. Endogamy in this case is due to vanity and want of affection between the different layers of the society. This feeling is coupled with the desire for keeping the blood pure when the pretensions of the upper layer sufficiently increase.

Nowhere are the different orders of society more distinctly separated from each other than in the South Sea Islands. In the Mariami group it was the common belief that only the nobles were endowed with an immortal soul and a nobleman who married a girl of the people was punished with death. In Polynesia the commoners were looked upon by the nobility as a different species of being. Hence in the higher ranks the marriage was concluded only with persons of corresponding positions; and if in Tahiti, a woman of condition chose an inferior person as a husband the children he had by her were killed.

But let us not take all the instances from barbarous times and barbarous peoples. Let us take the case of civilized nations in Europe. In Sweden in the seventeenth century marriages outside the class were punished. According to the German civil law the marriage of a man belonging to the high nobility with a woman of inferior birth is still regarded as disparaging and the woman is not entitled to the rank of her husband nor is the full right of inheritance possessed by her or her children.

Another characteristic of the caste system is hierarchy. The feeling of superiority and inferiority either is a cause of endogamy or even a result thereof. A race of people which regards itself as superior to another will not intermarry with one that is thought inferior. Conversely i, two races of people come together and do not intermarry, one would have to assume inferiority to the other. When the Chinese first came to the United States they were filled with prejudice against the white people and therefore did not intermarry; the whites and the yellows are two mutually exclusive communities, and the yellows are compelled to assume an inferior position. In South Africa, when the Hindus migrated there, and on account of their caste notions did not intermarry with the English settlers, a feeling of superiority and inferiority of race which did not exist before that time came into existence. When two people come together and do not intermarry freely, a feeling of superiority and inferiority is sure to come into existence.

One interesting feature in the hierarchy of caste is the preeminent position which the priests hold. I intend to write a special treatise on the question as to how the Brahmins attained such a high position in Hindu society and managed to maintain it for so long a time. At present I only remind the readers that this supremacy of the priests is not confined to India. The extravagant claims which the priest makes are always coexistent with the primitive character of the people. In ancient Persia, as well as ancient Egypt, the priest was always at the top. In Europe, till the nations were emancipated from the temporal control of the Pope and clergy was always superior to temporal authority. Even to-day I have known of Christian missionaries in India who are not much behind the Brahmins of olden times in making pretenses to occult superiority and omniscience and exalted position over the ignorant masses that came in contact with them. The scholar holds the highest position in the society of China, and this is probably due to the same feeling of respect for learning.

The sectarian castes in India owe their existence to the same mental attitude which people of different religions have regarding intermarriage. Mohammedans and Christians do not intermarry. Even the adherents of different churches have been prohibited from intermarrying. In the Roman Catholic Church the prohibition of marriage with heathens and Jews was soon followed by the prohibition of marriage with Protestants. Protestants also originally forbade such unions.

If the psychological reasons for caste are the same for the Hindus as for other peoples, why is it, we may ask, that the people of India have so tenaciously held to those customs and other people have dropped them?

We must remember that India, unlike other countries, has kept the custom of early marriage still in vogue. There is no choice in the marriage arrangements. If young men and young women were to marry for themselves, the caste restrictions would become much shaken. The feeling of love would have become an incentive to break the rules. But at the marriages are arranged by the parent, the force of this feeling is not available. The feelings, notions, and calculations of the parents being the controlling factors in the Indian marriages, the custom of marrying within the caste is retained.

Something must be due to the nature of the people themselves. The people of India were for many centuries unprogressive and trying to live up to the ideal past. For their guidance they do not depend on their own intelligence but on the intelligence of the people who are dead and gone. They will not break a custom because they see no sense in it as an Englishman or an American of strong individuality will do, but will blame their own frail intelligence that they do not see the sense in it. They have almost the same respect for what is old as Christians might have for the words of Jesus.

In the theory of caste the reason why certain occupations

should be considered as pure and certain others as impure is very easy to understand; but why certain castes which have early marriage should be preferred to the castes with late marriages is a matter not so very easy.

The Philosophical Theories

In order to understand the spirit of the ages which upheld caste and varna, one must take pains to understand the philosophy which justified this system. For without proper comprehension of the philosophy we shall unjustly condemn people for doctrines which appear to our eye as unjust, cruel, and monstrous. The philosophy may be wrong, it may have vitiated the ideas of people regarding justice and charity; but the devout people of those ages were not wanting in ideas of those virtues. They thought that they were doing only right by observing and maintaining the rules of four varnas and four ashramas.

Our writer believed that four varnas are created, and to each varna a proper duty is assigned to prevent social dissolution (i, 87). He also believed that dharma for every individual is determined by his origin, because the nature of every person is originally determined.[4]

> "But to whatever course of action the Lord at first appointed each (kind of beings), that alone it has spontaneously adopted in earn succeeding creation."
> "Whatever he assigned to each at the first creation, noxiousness or harmlessness, gentleness or ferocity, virtue or sin, truth or falsehood, that clung (afterward) spontaneously to it," (i, 28-29).

Our writer probably did not know what great disaster would follow if the fusion of varnas should take place, but he knew that some great disaster would follow.[5] Probably the fusion of varnas itself began to be looked upon as a great disaster. He had knowledge of a legend of a period when confusion of castes took place (ix, 67), but probably did not have any idea of such a condition. To see Brahmanas and Shudras mixed was something the very thought of which they abhorred.

The dharma writers wanted order in the society. If people who are meant for servitude be allowed to give it up, then there would be no servants left, and who then would perform their functions? Shudras will begin to rule, who are unfit to rule, and this social order would be completely destroyed. They quite thoroughly believed that castes and varna are natural things associated invariably with specific qualities. A Shudra connot be of noble quality; servitude is his nature. If there be any doubt regarding the varna of any individual it would at once be revealed by his nature or by actions which are due to his nature (x, 57).

But a question will be asked,

> "Why it is that one man should be compelled to be a servant all his life, and another man be a Brahmana all his life, simply because his father was a servant or a Brahmana? This is sheer injustice."

Our writer would say, "No!" for he firmly believed in the theory of Karma, three gunas, and transmigration of soul. All these three theories, as they applied them, justified the entire system. In the concluding chapter our author has given all those theories. There he says to the following effect:

> By Karma (action) are caused the various conditions of men, the highest, the middling, and the lowest. In consequence of many sinful acts committed by one's body, voice, or mind, that individual in the next birth will become a bird, or a beast, or a low caste person respectively. There are three gunas[6] (qualities), satva (goodness), rajas (activity), and tamas (darkness). When one of these three qualities predominates, the body becomes distinguished by that quality. The study of Vedas, austerity, and knowledge, and purity, etc., are marks of the quality of goodness. Delighting in adventure, want of firmness, indulgence in

sexual pleasure are marks of the quality of activity. Cruelty, covetousness, evil life, etc., are marks of dark quality.

Through each of these qualities man obtains various transmigrations. It is preponderance of various qualities that determines the birth of man as a Brahmana or a Shudra. Those who commit sins go into inferior existences or wombs; those who do good actions pass into superior wombs; and those who lead an ideal life obtain cessation of birth and death.[7]

Thus it will be noticed that Hindus of that period who upheld caste did not do so out of disregard for justice, but only out of regard for it. They held that the varna order is ordained for justice and human betterment. The mere statement of their belief in this matter sounds like a satire to a person who is unacquainted with their system of thought. They did not hold that a man should not have a chance to better his condition. They only denied him such a chance in that particular life which is after all a small portion of the entire human existence. To a Shudra they gave distinct grounds to hope for a better life and an inducement to better his condition. For our text says: "A Shudra who is pure, the servant of his betters, gentle in his speech, and free from pride, always seeks a refuge with Brahmanas and attains in his next life a higher caste" (ix, 335).[8]

The Theory of Purity

The caste system was supported not only by theological doctrines like Karma and the Transmigration of Soul, but also by ideas like those regarding purity and pollution which had a practical bearing on life. The precedence of caste is always manifested by ideas of purity and pollution, and for this reason the ideas of the period as they are reflected in our text deserve careful examination.

Our work reveals the ideas on this subject in its various

relations. The articles of food were divided into pure and impure by degrees. The various sections of the country differed greatly in sacredness and impurity. A principle that actions that are holy and sacred ought not to be done with impure associations appears to have been well recognized. Purifying agencies and ceremonies for purification existed. Purity was closely associated with good omen, *i.e.* Those things which were pure were supposed to bring good result or fortune, by their association, as good omens do, and impure things would bring misery. Various substances were graded on the principle of purity. But how far the various castes were graded is less clear.

The most conspicuous field in which the Hindu notions regarding purity and pollution manifest themselves is their treatment of the important question of food.[9] In order to determine whether anything is estable or not the first question to be answered is, How is the food obtained? The food obtained by begging was not considered impure food; but there also were various restrictions, under which alone a Brahmana considered it eatable. They would inquire, Who is the giver of the food? Here not only the ideas of morality came into play but also the ideas of ceremonial purity. The food given by a thief, a prostitute, a cruel man, a liar, or a criminal was prohibited side by side with the food given by a musician, physician, hunter, by men of Ugra, Nishada and Shudra castes, by goldsmiths, stage players, deals in weapons, basket-makers, washermen, dyers, carpenters, and money-lenders. A supposition seems to have prevailed that a person's intelligence and desires will be like those of the man whose food he has eaten, and it was also supposed that the people engaged in the occupations mentioned above were not quite moral people.

The restrictions did not end here. The food, even if it be given by a proper person, may not necessarily be eatable. It may be rendered impure or it may be polluted. Impure food is intrinsically not pure, while polluted food is intrinsically pure, but considered impure by the people out of prejudice.

Food that has turned sour, stale food, leavings of another person, food in which hair or insects are found, which had been pecked at by birds, on which anybody has sneezed, may be considered as impure food; food may be considered polluted when it is touched with the foot intentionally by anybody, or touched by a menstruating women or by dogs. Our next does not distinguish between these two ideas of impurity and pollution, but classes both of them together.

Of these rules regarding for the most important were those which explained what substances should be consumed and what not. There were various rules regarding the use of meat, although it was considered meritorious to abstain from meat altogether. Again, a distinction was drawn between the food for Shudra and that for twice-born. The twice-born, whose code of conduct was stricter than that of a Shudra, was forbidden the use of a good many kinds of meat, like pork and chicken, and of vegetables, like onions, garlic, and mushrooms. Again, some sort of distinction was drawn between Brahmana and the rest of the twice-born.

Penances also were prescribed to free a person from the guilt of eating food that he ought not to have eaten.

Some places were considered more scared than others, while some were actually considered foul and polluting. The summary of the opinions of our writer has already been given where his locality is discussed. The writer is silent regarding the necessity of expiation for migrating into countries like Anga, Vanga, Kalinga, Sauvira, and Deccan, while his predecessor, Baudhayana insists on it. This fact, as I have said, shows greater liberality of the age regarding migration, or may probably hint something regarding the locality of the writer himself. There is one reference to show that falsely denying a Brahmana's claim to nativity of his particular country[10] was regarded as an offense somewhat like defamation, punishable with fine (viii, 273). But besides this there is not much in our text where purity or impurity of the country is made a matter of any consequence. The writer had a good opportunity to do so had he wished. He could have said that Dravidas, Shakas, etc., lost their status as a Kshatriya because they lived in Deccan.

Let us now find out of there was anything else to which purity or impurity was supposed to be attached. The part of the body above the navel was considered pure and the part below it was considered impure. Some animals were pure while others were impure. Those which were impure were not only not fit to be eaten, but even their touch or look would make other things impure. Death or birth in the family would make the relatives and associates impure; and a long, elaborate code of rules existed which governed these matters. A menstruating woman was extremely impure; her touch, her look, and her voice carried pollution along with it.

Side by side with impure articles there existed two other kinds of articles, which may be called pure and purifying. Pure are those which are somewhat socred in themselves but which would be polluted by associating with impure. Purifying are those which could not be polluted themselves and had the capacity of purifying others which may have been polluted. Also there were some things which could never be polluted, although they had no capacity for purifying others.

Pure actions ought not to be done with impure associations. For example, the study of Veda should not be done on any evil day or during the days of impurity due to the death or birth of a relative; nor should it be done in the presence of a Shudra or a menstruating woman, or in impure places.

When it is said that some things are impure it should not be cousidered that all the impure things are equally impure, Things which a Snataka may regard as impure other Brahmanas may not so regard. Again, one impure thing would be polluted by contact with things more impure; *e.g.*, a Shudra, who is more impure than a Brahmana's corpse, may not carry ı though the corpse is an impure thing.

The purifying agencies were control of mind, austerities, fire, holy food, water, earth, the wind, the sacred rites, the sun, liberality, sacred text, etc. These agencies would purify from pollution or impurity, as the case may be. Our writer has given methods of purifying various inanimate things, like vessels made of gold, silver, and copper.

The purity or pollution of a Brahmana was much more than what we may call physical purity and impurity. We may distinguish contamination or pollution from physical impurity, but our writer did not care to differentiate them sharply. If a Shudra touches the food of a Brahmana feels that by some occult process the whole food has been spoiled and in rendered impure. Such food if eaten would make his body impure, at least just as much as food mixed with dirt or with articles that ought not to be eaten would do. As such ideas we can trace in the author before us.[11]

The theory of purity and pollution will remain incomplete unless mention is made of the sacraments which held such an important place in the systsm. These sacraments were about sixteen ceremonies, from the conception of a man in his mother's womb until after the end of his life. These sacraments sanctify the body and purify from sin a person in this life and after death (ii, 27). By the Maunji bandhana ceremony the taint derived from both parents is removed. By great sacrifices and Shrauta rites the human body is made fit for union with Brahma. Thus the various sacraments were meant to remove the sin from the body and to purify it. The arays or the twice-born distinguished themselves sharply from a Shudra, not so much on racial grounds, but on the grounds of purity, which was largely due to sacraments done for generations.

A question may be asked, What is the purpose of going into details regarding the ideas of the writer concerning purity and pollution when we are considering the questions of castes? The answer is a very simple one. I have pointed out elsewhere that the chief principle on which the entire system depend is that of purity and pollution. The Brahmana is at the top of

society because he is more pure and sacred than other castes, while Mahar and Paraiyan are at the bottom because they are impure. Thus purity is the pivot on which the entire system turns. Rank, social position, economic condition have no direct effect on the gradation from the stand-point of caste. They are simply aids to establish the status. Caste in India is strong and rigid because the ideas of the people regarding purity and pollution are rigid.[12]

We find in our text that various articles, hours, conditions, and places, almost everything that can be imagined, were graded according to their supposed purity and impurity. The status of a caste or a tribe always depended on the karma[13] which in various degrees might be pure or impure. The wide range and the minute gradation of substances and actions with regard to purity and pollution is the condition which made the gradation of castes a possibility. To sum up, in short, the caste system sought its justification in the theories of karma and transmigration of souls. The various gradations were simply a natural result of wild and monstrous ideas regarding purity and pollution. The chief objection to the fusion of varnas was that it would lead to the discontinuance of oblations. This discontinuance would lead the forefathers to hell and would cause the destruction of everything, evidence gleaned from them of considerably greater importance.[14]

There is another factor which we should consider in examining the truth of any of the statements. If any rule given by our text is also given by writers before him like Vashishtha, Baudhayana, Guatama and reasserted even by later writers and works like Yajnavalkya, Vishnusmriti, Parashara, Narada and Brihaspati, then the rule is more likely to be respected.

The Chinese travelers also supply something which is reliable, but it is very little. The Arabic traveler Alberuni, who traveled in the land during the eleventh century, gives us something on the subject.

It is true that all these sources, the literary data, the niti writers, foreign travelers, and the inscriptions, belong to dates considerably different from that of our author; but they have one thing in common—the priority to Mohammedan conquest, a matter of considerable importance to the history of civilization to India.

Religious and Ceremonial Discriminations

Let us first pay attention to the rules relating to religion and ceremonial, where the varna of men is made by tbe writer a matter of discrimination.

First of all, the first three varnas were sbarly distinguished from the last by the fact that the first three had a right to sacraments with Vedic texts, and consequently had a right to be called twice-born. The Shudra had no such rights.

But it should not be supposed that the rules regarding the sacraments of all twice-born varnas were the same. The method in which persons of different varnas received sacraments differed greatly, according to their varna. Our text gives manifold directions regarding sacraments. It tells what kind of name soould be given to a child, what the first and second half of the name should mean, what the proper age for initiation should be, how early the initiation may be performed, and how long it may be postponed. It also gives detailed rules of what colour the garment of the student should be, of what material the upper and the lower garments should be made, of what grass the girdle around the waist should be made, of what material the sacred string (Yajnopavita) should be, of what wood the student (Brahmacharin) should make his staff, of what height the staff should be, and what formula should be used for begging. I do not care to give the detailed injunctions regarding the different varnas in these matters; I only say that the rules differed in each and every matter, as above enumerated, according to the varna (ii. 31-49).

But the difference in the ceremonial did not end here. For the ceremony of clipping the hair different ages were prescribed for different varnas (ii, 65). Our text refers to a belief that for the sake of purification, the higher the varna the farther should the sacred water reach when sipped; *e.g.*, "a Brahmana is purified by water that reaches his heart, a Kshatriya by water reaching his throat, a Vaishya by water taken into the mouth, and a Shudra by water touched with the extremity of his lips." (ii, 62).

There are various other places where a line a drawn between Shudra and the twice-born; but the ceremonies where the first three varnas differed are mainly those enumerated above.

The rules referred to above appear to be of considerable antiquity,[15] and most probably they were followed. The proper observance and the maintenance of the rules rested with Brahmanas themselves, and this is one of the strong reasons for its proper maintenance. Even to-day there is not much departure from these injunctions, though often disputes arise regarding the eligibility of certain peoples to be called Kshatriya or Vaishya.'[6]

Treatment of Different Varnas at Court

Let us turn our attention to the rules of our text regarding the treatment of different varnas at the court. It prescribed different formalities for different varnas.

" 'Speak,' thus let him (the judge) ask a Brahmana. 'Speak the truth,' thus let him address a Kshatriya. A Vaishya should be admonished by (mentioning) his kine, grain, and gold. A Shudra by threatening him with the guilt of every crime."

"Saying whatever places of torments are assigned by the stages to the slayer of Brahmana, to the murderer of women and children, to him who betrayed a friend, and to an ungrateful man, those shall be thy portion if thou speakest falsely" (viii, 88 ff).

Our author does not stop here. He devotes twelve more verses in order to advise Shudra of his responsibility as a witness, and to picture the graveness of the variety of sins that would fall upon his head in case he spoke a lie. But the way, I may say here that our writer or the dharma writers in general did not make this provision to insult the Shudra purposely. Shudras in general were ignorant people and did not understand their responsibility as witnesses as well as the more lettered classes did. The formality of asking the witness to swear is intended to make him more serious on the occasion. It is a common experience that the more educated classes need less formality than the ignorant ones.

Our text also provides: "Let the judge cause a Brahmana to swear by his veracity, a Kshatriya by his chariot or the animal he rides on or by his weapon, a Vaishya by his kine, grain, and gold, and a Shudra by (imprecating on) his head the guilt of all grievous sins" (viii, 113).[17]

Again, in the law of evidence, our writer prescribes: "Women should give evidence for women, twice-born men for the twice-born of the same kind, virtuous Shudras for Shudras, and men of the lowest caste for the lowest." He permits that on failure of a qualified witness evidence may be given by women and others. But here he warns that such evidence should be accepted with great consideration. In cases of violence, theft, adultery, and defamation the (eligibility of) witness should not be examined too strictly (viii, 68 ff). He admits the eligibility of all varnas as witnesses. He says truthful speakers from all varnas ought to be made witnesses (viii, 63), but in the next following verses exempts some persons from the duty of giving evidence and also denies the eligibility of giving evidence to some. But he mixes together people belonging to both the classes. He says: "The king cannot be made a witness, nor a workman (like a cook), nor dancers, nor Shrotriya, nor a student of Vedas, nor one (an ascetic) who has shaken off connection with the world."

"Nor one wholly dependent, nor one of bad fame,

nor a Dasyu, nor one who follows forbidden occupations" (viii, 63 ff).

Regarding the appointment of the officers of justice our text lays down the rule, "But if the king does not personally investigate the suits let him appoint a learned Brahmana to try them" (viii, 9).

It also recommends that the assessors should be Brahmanas (viii, 11). Moreover, it says: "A Brahmana who subsists only by the name of his jati, or one who merely calls himself a Brahmana (though his origin be uncertain) may at the king's pleasure interpret the dharma to him, but never a Shudra. The kingdom where the monarch looks on while a Shudra settles the law will sink like a cow in a morass" (viii, 20, 21).

It is here that we have great reason to doubt as to whether this rule was actually observed. The writers on niti do not appear to be completely in sympathy with these ideas.

Shukra-niti says: "If a king cannot decide, he should appoint a Brahmana learned in Vedas, of good family, self-controlled, impartial, pleasing, firm, afraid of the next world, calm, and acting according to dharma. If a learned Brahmana could not be obtained, then a Kshatriya should be appointed or a Vaishya who knows the dharma science, but the Shudra should be avoided with care."

"A king should always appoint one born of the same varna as the king himself, for generally the people of the same varna have the necessary qualities" (iv, sec. 5, 12-15).

Thus we find that both dharma and niti writers agree in recommending a Brahmana. Our writer is silent regarding the eligibility of Kshatriya and Vaishya. The work on niti makes a very strong remark in favour of a Kshatriya. It is not vehement in condemning eligibility of Shudras for the office of judge. Evidently a Brahmana judge was preferred, but not greatly.

Kshatriyas and Vaishyas also acted as judges. The strong language which our writer has used condeming the appointment of Shudras suggests that he might personally have known of cases in which even Shudras acted as judges.

Our writer advises that the assessors also should be Brahmanas. Shukra-niti indorses this opinion. It says: "A king who wishes to examine the cases should enter the assembly with learned Brahmana assessors (iv, sec. 5, 43).

We have in Mrichchakatika a scene of trial (Act ix), where the judge is assisted by Shreshthis. The word "Shreshthis" implies that the assessors were chiefs of guilds, and they are again represented as men speaking vernacular which implies that they were not Brahmanas. The case in the Toy-Cart (Mrichehakatika) may simply be local or belonging to a period different than that of our writer, but it may at the same time suggest that the claims of Brahmanas revealed by Manava-dharma-shastra were not always admitted.[18]

Economic Privileges and disabilities

Let us now consider the economic privileges and disabilities of different varnas as our text implies.

Let us first consider the occupational privileges. The occupations open to Brahmana were various. He could become a priest, an occupation which was considered proper for his caste, or he could become a soldier, an officer of the state, a money-lender, or even a farmer. But he was not to become a domestic servant. The upper castes always had the privilege of following the occupation of their inferiors but not of their superiors. Shudra was allowed a considerable margin of occupations. All the trades, like carpenter, physician, barber, elephant trainers. and probably those of goldsmith, etc., were allowed to a Shudra, but he was supposed to show preference to service in the house of Brahmana. Unless there were any restraints imposed by the trade guilds this varna appears to have a considerable margin of the choice of occupations. And if different occupations were becoming a monopoly they certainly were not becoming so through an injunction of dharma. Dharma writers put restrictions on only one occupation—priesthood. And they left the other occupations almost entirely free. Even the lower castes were not prevented from following occupations of Kshatriya. For any person or tribe which might be strong enough to exact obedience, will make himself or themselves Kshatriya. Success in war did not depend on the mercy of the Brahmanas or of the dharma writers. A man who is strong enough to rule will rule, whether Brahmins call him Kshatriya or not. It is possible that the low castes were not entirely kept off from a king's army. Kiratas and Shabaras were freely employed for fighting when necessary.[19]

Regarding the law about inheritance our text advises: "If there be four wives of a Brahmana in the direct order of varnas, the rule for the division of estate among the sons born of them is as follows:... Let the son of the Brahmani wife take three shares, the sons of Kshatriya two, the son of the Vaishya a share and a half, and the son of the Shudra may take one share... Or the Brahmana son shall take four shares, the son of the Kshatriya wife three, the son of Vaishya shall have two parts, the sone of Shudra may take one share. Whether a Brahmana have sons or have no sons (by wives of the twice-born castes) he should, according to law, give to the son of a Shudra no more than a tenth part of his estate[20] (ix, 149-155).

Our writer does not give any rules regarding the division of property of a Kshatriya and Vaishya among sons by wives of different grades.

A Shudra could marry a wife of his varna only. But he could have slaves and sons from them. Our writer has held that these sons deserve some share in the inheritance (ix, 179).

Our writer gives another very peculiar rule: "Whatever property may have given by her father to a wife, the daughter of a Brahmani wife or her issue shall take that property" (ix, 198), *i.e.*: If a Brahmana has wives of Brahmana and

Kshatriya varnas the daughter of the Brahmani should succeed to the property of the Kshatriya woman.

Now let us see how far the evidence of our text regarding inheritance can be corroborated from other sources. Niti literature and the literary works which I have examined are silent on this point. I could not find any references to substantiate or to nullify the statements made here. There is not much on this subject in the inscriptions which I have read so far. But in the dharma literature there is a good deal on this subject.[21]

The regulations which provide for the division of property among the children from the wives of different castes appear to be quite old. Older works like those of Gautama, Vashistha, Baudhayana, make provision very similar to those of our text, but with very slight variation.[22] Even later Smritis, like Yajnavalkya and Vishnu, also affirm the same rules. The principle involved in these rules is in accordance with human nature and can be traced almost everywhere in the world where similar conditions have arisen; and I think we can safely say that the rules given by our text in this matter were generally observed in his times.

But very different is the case of the rule given by our writer regarding the succession of the daughter of a Brahmani (woman) to the property of her stepmother of different caste (ix,198). This peculiar rule cannot be traced in any of the earlier or later writers on dharma. The only place where a parallel passage occurs is in Mahabharata (xiii, 47, 24, 6). At that we can say regarding this rule is that it reprents the claim of the Brahmanas of the period, in the matter of inheritance. Whether this rule was actually maintained by the rulers or not is a matter which needs more evidence before we come to any decision.

Our text also provides that on the failure of all heirs the property of the deceased may be taken by the king. But if the deceased be a Brahmana the king should not take his property, but it should be distributed among Brahmanas.

Like different rules which I mention this rule also appears to be quite old, and can be traced in some later writers[23] Though I do not have any evidence from literature other than dharma, to corroborate the rule, I think the very persistence of the claim made by Brahmana writers on dharma might have had some effect in rendering it sacred and inviolate.

We shall now turn our attention to another very peculiar claim of the Brahmanas represented in the following verses:

"From the man who shall truly say with respect to treasure-trove 'This belongs to me', the king may take one-sixth or one-twelfth part.

"When a learned Brahmana has found treasure deposited in former times he may take even the whole of it, for he is master of everything. When the king finds treasure of old concealed in the ground, let him give one-half to Brahmanas and place the other half in his treasury.

"The king obtains one-half of ancient hoards, and metals (found) in the ground by reason of his giving protection and because he is lord of the soil" (viii, 35-39).

Here also our means to find out how far this claim of the Brahmanas was accepted are restricted to the dharma literature itself. The older writers, like Gautama and Vashistha, make the same statement.[24] The later writer, Yajnavalkya, repeats the same rule, but Vishnu-smriti, another late work, gives long, elaborate rules regarding the distribution of treasure-trove among different varnas.[26] Even though this writer differs considerably from the other writers in the number of details the principle underlying is essentially the same as in the rules found in our text.

There is very little in our text which advises a king to make distinction by castes in the matter of taxation. It advises that a king, even though dying with hunger, must not levy tax on a Shrotriya, and no Shrotriya, and no Shrotriya, residing in his kingdom, should perish from hunger (vii, 133).

Further on it says: "Let the king make the common inhabitants of his realm who live by traffic, pay annually some trifle which is called tax. Mechanics and artisans, as well as Shudras who subsist by manual labour, he may cause ro work for himself fore one day in a month" (vii, 137-8).

The taxes are something which change very often, and it is vain to expect that all the kings would follow the rules given herein. In a case like this if we find a rule from ancient books repeated in new works on dharma, it becomes an evidence against its acceptability for fact. It shows that the writer, while laying down the rule, did not depend on the actual condition but on old books. Such a course was permissible to him, as he was laying down a rule on the question of how the taxes ought to have been. In the verses quoted above there are two points to be considered:

1. exemption of a Shrotriya from taxes; and
2. that Shudras, mechanics and artisans should be compelled to work for one day, in the place to taxes.

Both these statements are made by earlier writers like Gautama (x, 11, 31), Vasishtha (xix. 23), and Apastamba (ii, 26, 10). And it is very likely that our writer derived his statements from some work on dharma, and as these writers were guided by the principle that the more ancient the rule the greater is the authority as regards propriety. But whether the kings held the same attitude toward such practical matters is much to be questioned. Of works on niti. we have Shukra-niti which discusses the subject of taxes (Book iv, sec. ii, 105-130). This work is silent on the question of exempting a Brahmana and exprecses the opinion that the king is entitled to two days' labour in a month from artisans and mechanics (121). This work differs from our text in some other places.

Wherever in the world, phenomena resembling caste are found, there is always a tendency toward maintaining a strong barrier shutting the men of the lower group from the women of the higher group. This barrier often consists of laws, public opinion and perverted ethics.[27] Sentiments maintaining such a barrier are clearly expressed in the rules which all writers on dharma, including our text, give, regarding marriage, courtship illicit intercourses, and outrage on the woman.

Our text generally approves of a marriage with a person of the same varna, but noes not entirely forbid a marriage outside the varna, as later writers have done.

"A Shudra woman alone (may be) the wife of n Shudra. She and one of his own (varna, the wives) of a Vaishya. Those two and one of his own (varna, the wives) of a Kshatriya. Those three and one of his own (varna) wives of a Brahmana.'

"A Shudra woman is not mentioned even in any ancient story (Vrittanta) as the first wife of a Brahmana or of a Kshatrîya, though they lived in great distress."[28]

"The twice-born men who in their folly wed wives of the low castes soon degrade their families and their children to the status of Shudra."

"A Brahmana who takes a Shudra wife to his bed will (after death) sink to hell. By begetting a child by her, he loses Brahmanahood."

"The manes and the gods will not eat the offering of that man who performs rites in honour of the gods, and of manes, and of guests, having a (Shudra wife) to assist him, and such a man will not go to heaven."

"For him who drinks the moisture of Shudra woman's lips, or is tainted by her breath, and who begets a son by her, no expiation is prescribed" (iii, 13-19).

He tells us in the rules regarding the shraddha ceremony that a Brahmana who marries a Shudra female should not be invited to a shraddha (iii, 155).

Marriage between men of lower ca tes and women of higher castes was positively forbidden. The marriage regarded as the greatest horror was the marriage of a Brahmana woman to a man of Shudra varna. Such marriages are condemned severely by calling their progeny equal to the Chandalas. Such marriages must have been really rare and the object of the fiction is to prevent them. Neither our writer nor any other law-writer found it necessary to make the children by "marriages against the grains" (marriages of women of higher castes with men of lower castes) a topic in the discussion of inheritance. But it seems probable that men of higher castes might have married women of lower castes, especially Shudras. Our writer wishes to condemn such practices strongly.

The rules regarding marriages, which made distinctions, with reference to the varna or the bride and bride-groom; did not end here. Dharma writers always have taken into account the varna distinction when they approved or disapproved forms of marriages. They also tried to draw the line in the ceremonies that were to be performed at the time of marriage. I have told already that the always took into consideration the varnas of father and mother of a man or woman when they laid down rules regarding inheritance.

The Scriptures distinguish eight forms of marriages. Out of these eight forms some were approved and some were disapproved form of marriages, like Asura (purchase of the bride) and Paishachya (appropriation of a woman when she is unconscious), were tolerated in Shudras.[29] The form called Rakshasa consisted of the seizure of the bride. It was approved for a Kshatriya though condemned for Vaishya and Shudra (iii, 20-40).

When a man married a woman of an inferior varna, he took her, by a ceremony different from that which was used when he married a woman of his own varna. Our text says:

"The ceremony of joining hands is prescribed for marriages with women of equal varna. Know that the following rule applies to weddings with females of different castes."

"On marrying a man of higher caste a Kshatriya bride

must take hold of an arrow (the bridegroom taking hold of the other end of the arrow instead of her hand), a Vaishya bride, of a goad, and a Shudra female, of the hem of the bridegroom's garment" (iii, 44-5).

Regarding the position of wives of different varnas in the family our text advises:

> "If twice-born men wed women of their own and of other (lower castes) the seniority, the honour, and the habitation of those wives must be settled according to the order of the varna."
>
> "Among all twice-born men the wife of equal caste, alone, and not a wife of a different caste by any means shall personally attend her husband and assist him in his daily sacred rites" (ix, 85, 86).

From this meagre information it should not be inferred that a free marriage existed between people of the same varna. Our text simply tells us that the writer did not have any objection to one of the Shudra tribe marrying with another Shudra tribe. It is just possible that one caste may not marry with another caste though they both may be called Shudra by the Brahmanas. Even to-day there are hosts of castes which the Brahmanas called Shudras intermarriage between which will cause the former no unhappiness. There are differences and distinctions between various castes which Brahmanas call Shudras, but Brahmanas never recognized these differences.

Varna and Illicit Intercourse

A strict barrier between varnas and castes is sure to result in the stringent rules regarding adultery. Adultery itself was a heinous offense in India since very ancient times. This offense becomes of very great magnitude in a society where pretensions of purity of blood grow very great. Sentiments against adultery are found in various works, ancient and modern, but the sentiment in our text is not so strong as may be found in older works.

Our writer explains why adultery should be considered as a very grievous offense.

> "For by adultery is caused a mixture of the varnas among men, thence (follows) sin, which cuts up even the roots, and causes destruction of everything" (viii, 353).

The commentators explain the verse as follows: "If a mixture of the varnas takes place, the sacrifices cannot be offered properly, because duly qualified sacrificers are wanting. If sacrifices are not duly offered, no rain will fall and everything will perish" (Medh. Gov. Kull Raghavananda).

In order to bring out clearly the distinction made by our writer, as regards adultery between different varnas, it is necessary for us first of all to determine the magnitude of the offense committed by a man with a woman of the same varna, as reflected in the punishment, and it is not an easy task. Regarding the punishment for adultery he says: "Men who commit adultery with the wives of others, the king shall cause to be marked by punishments which cause terror and afterward banish" (viii, 352).

But later on he says:

> "If a wife, proud of the greatness of her relatives or (her own) excellence, violates the duty which she owes to her husband, the king shall cause her to be devoured by dogs in a place frequented by many."
>
> "Let him cause the male offender to be burnt on a red-hot iron bed; they shall put logs under it" (until the sinner is burnt to death (viii, 371-72)).

Now the question before us is how this incongruity is to be construed. To get some light on the question, I have consulted more ancient works on dharma like those of

Baudhayana, Apastamba, Gautama and Vashishtha, but even there one finds the same contradictions. For example, Apastamba says: "He who has had connection with his teacher's wife shall cut off his organs together with his testicles, take them into his joined hands and walk toward the South without stopping, until he falls down dead. Or he may die embracing a heated meral image of a woman" (i, 26, 1-2). But again he says: "He who has had connection with his teacher's wife shall eat every fourth meal-time a little food, bathe at the time of three libations, passing the day standing and the night sitting. After the lapse of three years they throw off their guilt" (i, 26, 101). He has further on described various small or great punishments and penances for adultery with different kinds of women. Baudhayana shows the same contradiction. To the violater of the Guru's bed he prescribes the same punishment as Apastamba does in i, 26, 1-2 (see Baudh; ii, 1, 13-15), but later on he expresses his opinion that if a person lives as on outcast for three years his guilt is removed (ii, 2, 14). Such contradictions on this matter appear everywhere in the literature. The meaning of all this appears to be that the dharma writers in order to impress the gravity of adultery prescribe one very severe punishment first; then another punishment which is generally a milder one. It is the latter which they really mean to impose. The statement of the severe punishment side by side is intended to make the offender feel that he is really suffering a very mild punishment in proportion to what he really deserves. When a person approaches a Brahamana to-day in India to seek atonement for some sin it is quite customary among the Brahamanas to tell the man how grave his offense is, in superlative language, and show how serious a punishment he deserves, and to explain to him how by taking various things into consideration the Brahamana is prescribing only a small penance. When this custom is taken into account those rules would not be very hard to interpret. When two punishments are prescribed, and if one of them is unreasonably severe, we should know it is the milder one that was followed and the mention of the greater punishment had only educative value.[30]

In order to get the correct idea of the attitude of dharma writers in this matter I must draw attention to some more of their remarks. In order to condemn attempts towards adultery our writer has defined adulterous acts, and includes therein actions like addressing other men's wives in lonely places, offering them presents, romping with them, touching their ornaments and dress, sitting with them, touching them improperly, or allowing women to touch them thus. All such acts done with mutual consent are adulterous acts. And then in the next verse he says that for these adulterous acts a man who is not a Brahmana ought to suffer death, for the wives of all the four varnas must be carefully guarded (viii, 356-9).

Narration of these vagaries would make one thing certain that the punishment for adultery depended more of less on the whim of the king. Dharma allowed him the widest possible margin. The actual punishment for the offense must have been much more moderate.

Now we should find out whether the magnitude of this offense became great or small in proportion to the high or low caste of the man who committed the offense. We find that in the treatment of this question in many cases our text is very vague. It contrasts cases that cannot strictly be compared, *e.g.*: "He who violates an unwilling maiden deserves death at once, but a man who enjoys a willing maiden shall not suffer that punishment if his caste be equal to hers" (viii, 364).

Here there are two elements to be considered in determining the magnitude of the crime—the status of the woman and the force used. Our writer has not analyzed them:

He again says:

"If a man of lower varna seeks a woman of the higher varna he deserves death. But if her caste be equal to his, then he should pay the father the price of the bride."

"But if a man through insolence forcibly contaminates a maiden, two fingers deserve to be instantly cut off and he shall pay a fine of six hundred panas."

"A man of equal varna who contaminates a willing maiden shall not suffer this amputation, but shall pay a fine of two hundred panas in order to deter him from the repetition of the offense" (viii, 366-8).

This carelessness of our writer is a very clear example of indefiniteness in this matter. We are not so much concerned with the details of punishment as with the principles. The indistinctness of the rules does not prevent us from knowing those principles. These rules explain to us clearly that the element of caste of the guilty man was considered in deciding cases of fornication and outrage of unmarried girls.

When the limits of varna were crossed the consent of the woman was of very little importance. When a man of low caste has intercourse with a woman of high caste, the matter, whether the intercourse was committed with her consent or against her will, became of very little significance. This spirit can be traced in the rules just mentioned and is plainly illustrated in the following rules:

"A Shudra who has intercourse with an adulteress of a twice-born varna, married or unmarried, shall be punished in the following manner: If she was unmarried he shall lose the part (offending) and all his propetry. If she was married he shall lose everything, even his life.

"For intercourse with a Brahmani, a Vaishya shall forfeit all his property after imprisonment for a year; a Kshatriya shall be fined one thousand panas, and be shaved with urine."

"If a Vaishya or a Kshatriya has connection with an unmarried Brahmani adulteress, let him fine the Vaishya five hundred panas and the Kshatriya one thousand."

"But even even these two, if they offend with a married

Brahmani adulteress, shall be punished like a Shudra, or be burnt in the fire of dry grass."

"A Brahmana who carnally approaches a married Brahmani adulteress against her will shall be fined one thousand panas, but he shall be made to pay five hundred if he had connection with a willing one."[31]

"If a Vaishya approaches a married Kshatriya adulteress, or a Kshatriya a married Vaishya adulteress, they both deserve the same punishment as in the case of an unmarried Brahmana adulteress."

"A Brahmana shall be compelled to pay a fine of one thousand panas if he has intercourse with married (females of) the two (varnas); for offending a (married) Shudra adulteress a fine of one thousand panas shall be inflicted on a Kshatriya or a Vaishya."

"For illicit (intercourse with) an unmarried Kshatriya woman a fine of five hundred panas shall fall on a Vaishya, but (for the same offense) a Kshatriya shall by shaved with urine or pay the same fine."

"A Brahmana who approaches unmarried females (of) Kshatriya or Vaishya (varnas) or a Shudra female shall be fined five hundred panas; but for intercourse with a female of the lowest caste (Antyaja) one thousand" (viii, 374-386).

Let us see what all this means to us. In these different rules there are various elements which determine the punishment. First, what is the varna of the woman who is contaminated? In general, the higher the varna of the woman contaminated the greater should be the punishment to the guilty man; the lower the varna of the man, the more severely he is to be treated. The writer considers the element of consent only in case the Brahmana holds intercourse with a woman of his own varna; he again draws a distinction between fornicatian and adultery. In these verses he does not consider fornication with a girl of equal varna, but only considers adultery with equal varna, for fornication with equal varna may result in marriage and the offense need not be treated severely. He prescribes a fine of one thousand coins for adultery by Brahmana with a woman of all varnas, and for that by Kshatriyas and Varishyas with women of all varnas except Brahmana. For adultery by a Shudra with a twice-born woman, or by any varna with a Brahmana woman, is punishable with death. Fornication is treated less severely than adultery, because adultery is more likely to cause aconfusion of varnas than fornication will. Though adultery is a graver offense than fornication, and rape greater than adultery, he recommends the same punishment for a fornication with a Brahmana girl by a Kshatriya as he does for rape by a Brahmana of a married woman (of bad character) of his own varna. For a Brahmana to commit adultery with an Antyaja (a person of the outcast tribe) woman is in his opinion an offense twice as great as an intercourse with a woman of one of the four varnas.[32]

The regulations where women are concerned to not end here. Regarding making love, our text prescribes the following rules:

> "From a maiden who makes advances to a man of high caste he (the king) shall not take any fine; but her who courts a (man of) low (varna) let him force to live confined in the house."
>
> "A (man of) low (varna) who seeks a maiden (of) the highest (varna) shall suffer death. He who seeks one of equal (varna) shall pay the nuptial fee if her father desires it" (viii, 315-16)."

REFERENCES

1. The Hindu Scriptures distinguish eight forms of licit marriage.
2. Westermark's History of Human Marriage (1981), chap. xvi, 362.
3. Humboldt Personal Narrative, vol. iii, 26, as quoted by Westermark, chap. xvi, 365.

4. One reason why they believed in a doctrine like this is that the word "dharma" had various senses in which it was used, and the different ideas carried by the word were not clearly differentiated. "Dharma" meant nature also. It was also believed that every being is endowed with a certain nature at the primary creation which could not be changed. Whatever deeds people do, those they do according to their dharma or swabhiva, which was originally assigned to them by the Creaker or Manu. They for example believed that Manu allocated to workers love of their bed, of seat, of ornament, passions, wrath, maniface, and bad conduct (ix, 17). The qualities determined their dharma. Servitude is innate in Shudra. It is a part of his nature (viii, 414), which nobody could take away from him, and this is the reason why servitude is his duty.

   These ideas have not entirely disappeared to-day. When the present ruler of one Maratha state was chosen for Gadi (the throne), he was chosen for adopt on the principle of innate royalty among the different little boys who were the candidates. Some holes were made in the trousers of different boys without their knowledge. When the boys noticed the holes, all of them, excepting one, wanted their trousers repaired, while the boy who was the exception wanted a new pair of trousers. Thus he displayed his innate kingly quality.

5. Some idea regarding the probable dangers of varna intermixture may be gathered from the treatment of adulterers in the text and from what Arjuna said to Krishna (Bhagavdgita, chap. i).

   "In consequence of the predominance of impiety, O Krishna, the women of the family become corrupt O, descendant of Vrishni, intermingling of Varnas results; that intermingling necessarily leads the family and the destroyers of family to hell; for whom the ceremonies of offering the cakes of food and water (to them) fail, their ancestors fall to hell."

   Compare with this the objection of Artistotle to communal marriage as advocated by Plato. It was this: Unholy acts done against fathers and mothers are more likely to be committed if the relationship is unknown and who would make atonement for them (Artistotle's Politics, ii, c. 4).

6. I have translated the word "guna" by quality for the sake of convenience. In fact the Sankhya philosophy which used these terms does not regard them as qualities merely, but regards gunas as substances. "Goodness" and "darkness" were something like substances which dwelt in various objects.

7. I have avoided here to explain how the doctrines of Heaven and Hell, and Transmigration of Soul were reconciled, as this explanation is not necessary for our purposes.

8. It should not be considered that a hope of this kind is no hope at all. Such an assertion would show the ignorance of the capability of the human mind. I know for certain that such ideas and hopes regarding happiness in the next birth cheer the mind and control it. In the Toy-Cart (Mrichchkarika, act viii), Skakara, the king's brother-in-law, asked his slave to kill the damsel Vasantasena. The slave refused the order flatly in the following words:

   "Beat me if you will. Kill me if you will. I cannot do what ought not to be done. Fate has already punished me with servitude, for the misdeeds of a former life, and I will not incur the penalty of being born again a slave."

   I once met a Mahara, who, fearing that I was going near him and that my purity might then be defiled in case I touched him, and that he might incur the sin of defiling my purity, cried out at once and made his caste known to me. I got into conversation with him. I found that Mahar, though illiterate, could repeat many verses of Tukaram, Namdeo and Chokhamela. He appeared to be well acquainted with the theories of Karma and Bhakti, and of transmigration of soul. He believed that though he was a Mahar in that birth, by some misdoings in his past life, he was a going to become a Brahmana in the next birth, as he felt the desire for learning Sanskrit, and reading Gita and Puranas. He conceived that these desires were clear indications of the better birth which he was going to get in his next life.

   I do not know how far such sentiments exist in other members of the tribe. But it is not improbable that very many of the low castes believe, or are made to believe, that they justly suffer in this condition as a retribution for the sins which they did in the past life.

   How much better it would have been for the whites in the United States, had they taught the negroes the doctrines of Transmigration of Soul and Karma instead of Christianity!

9. I have not given here reference to every statement, because those who care to look it up in the original can easily do so with the help of the index attached to the translation of our text by Dr. Buhler.

10. This is I suspect to be an evidence for the locality of the author. The importance of the country of a Brahmana is greater in Bengal than anywhere else. Though the Brahmanas of Brahmavarta claim

superiority over Brahmans of other parts. this superiority appears to be acknowledged in Bengal only; so much so that many Brahmana tribes which have settled in Bengal for centuries would refuse to be called natives of province.

11. The Brahmanas have very strong ideas regarding the purity of their blood, which scarecely have a parallel anywhere else. Their purity of blood is not the same idea which ethnologists understand by these words. The racial purity is only a part of the purity to a Brahmana. The purity of Brahmana's blood is acquired by generations of pure conduct, which consists of doing actions that are pure, eating pure food, by increasing his own personal sacredness, by the study of Vedas, and by marriage only with people who have kept pure conduct. Their abstaining from marriage with other castes does not come so much from their pride of birth, but is due more to their pride of purity, which would be contaminated by less sacred connections. How far other Hindu asstes have a corresponding feeling I am unable to say. But I would not be surprised to find any such feeling amongst the other high castes toward the lower castes, and against the foreigners.

12. Gautama is very often barbarously complimented as a man who fought against caste, and his creed is very often called a revolt against caste system. The disproof of this matter is needless here, but I may take the liberty of reminding advocates of this creed that pretensions of the Buddhists regarding, purity and pollution were at least as extravagant as those of the Brahmana, and Gautama is not free from the guilt of promoting such pretensions. In cases he has shown much greater stupidity in these matters that of all Brahmanas put together.

    Mr. Rhys Davids has shown the fallacy of complimenting Buddha for breaking caste in his various introductions to the Dialogues of Buddha. Robert Chalmers also exposed the attitude of Buddhism toward caste in his article "Madhura Sutta on Caste." (J.R.A.S, April, 1894, pages 360-366.)

13. The word "karma" was used in various senses. In philosophy it was used as a term expressive of the idea of "motion" as Spencer has used it. Here karma was supposed to operate on matter to produce various things. It was also used to denote that action by animate objects which governed their fate. In popular usage it was also used to denote occupations and other various actions. When applied to the topic of caste it was indiscriminately used in its philosophical as well as popular senses.

14. Here I confess that my examination of inscriptions to find material

to corroborate or nullify the injuuction of dharma is restricted to *Corpus Inscri. Indi.* vol. iii.

15. See Ashv. Grihya Sutra, I, 16; 17, '1; 18; Paraskara, i, 17, 5; 19, 1-6; ii, 1. Apasramba, i, 1, 5, 8-32; i, 2, 33-43 also given by Baudhayana and Vashishtha. The rule regarding the naming of the child does hot appear to be very ancient. It is repeated only in Vishnusmriti (xxvii, 6-9) which is a very late work but cannot be traced in any of the early texts. The proper observanee of the rule presumes a condition of society where the Brahmanas are numerous enough ta be consulted. The negligence of the observance of the rule is not associated with penance of any kind and therefore the chances of the rule being observed become much less. It is also vain to suppose that a Shudra would have the first part of the name of the child mean something contemptible even if he be a contemptible Shudra. Again, our text prescribes that the last part of Shudra's name should mean service, and this rule itself prevents the first one being followed. It is not impossible that Shudras would have names like Dwija-dasa.

16. In Uttararamacharita, act iv, the guests at the hermitage of Valmiki discovered that Kumara Lava was a son of Kshatriya from his signs, which an initated boy of Kshatriya varna bears. Notice also in Raghuvamsha three verses regarding the bringing up Raghu.

17. Shukranti, which treats the procedure of the court, is silent on both the points mentioned above.

18. H. H. Wilson in his edition of Mrichchakatika has said that the king might be a Buddhist who did not care to pay any attention to Brahmanical claims and for this reason Brahmanas may have plotted against him. But this inference dose not seem to be warranted by facts. Shakara, who was brother-in-law of the king, has said that he bends his head to gods and Brahmana alone. Again, the whole city was more or less Buddhistic, as they did not bear even an animal being killed (Shakara in Act viii). A plot by a few Brahmins against a Buddhist king would not have succeeded. In order to defy the claims of the Brahmans the king need not necessarily be a Buddhist.

19. It should also be noticed that in Mrichchakatika, Chandanaka and Viraka, who were officers of the army or police of King Palaka, call each others barbers, leather workers.

Chandanaka—(making a sign to Viraka saying that he was a barber) you were wont to carry a dead jackal in your hands, to replace dislocated joints, to flourish a pair of shears, and you are now o general—a pretty general. . . .

Viraka.—(making a sign, reminds Chandanaka that the latter is a tanner by caste) No doubt (your caste is) vastly pure, when your mother was a tabor, your father a kettle-drum, and your brother a tambourine, but you—you are a general.

20. Evidently our writer has contradicted himself. According to the first rule given above the son of Shudra wife could claim two-thirteenths of the property.

21. In connection with this verse, Dr. Hopkins writes to me that we should take this verse to cover the case where a woman dies without issue, and that dying without issue may be supplied from the preceding verse. There is one objection to such construction that the verse ix, 198, occurs in Mahabharata without ix, 197.

22. Gaut. xxviii. 35-39; Vasi. xvii, 48-50; Baudha. ii, 3, 10; Vishnu, xviii, 1-33, 38-40; Yaj. ii, 125.

23. Apas. ii, 14, 5; Gaut. xxviii, 42; Vasishtha, xviii. 83; Baudh. i, 13, 15-16.

24. Gautama, x, 43-45; Vasishtha, iii, 13-14.

25. Yajnvalkya. ii, 34-35.

26. Vishnu-smriti, iii, 56-64.

27. In India a woman of Brahmana caste living as a mistress of a man of the same caste would not be so much condemned and ostracised as a woman who marrics a Shudra. In the United States, a white woman who marries a negro would be more severely condemned than a woman who would become a prostitute.

28. One of the sources of determining dharma was to follow the conduct of persons virtuous and learned in Scriptures. The knowledge of the conduct of the virtuous which existed in the form of stories was a part of the popular lore. Some of these stories have been incorporated in Mahabharata.

29. Only the first four forms of marriage were recommended for a Brahmana. The Brahmanas who took a wife by a less approved from were looked down upon. For "The Veda declares, 'The quality of the offspring depends on the quality of the marriage rite' (Bau. i, 21, 1; Apas. ii, 5, 21, 4.)

30. Some writers very often are found in the habit of discovering analogies and regard that what once prevailed among ancient Jews, must have prevailed among the ancient Hindus. In the Jewish Scripture stoning a woman to death is prescribed as a punishment for an unmarried woman who goes astray (Dr. 22, 20-21), and sinaitic law directs that a priest's daughter shall be burned for

fornication (Iv, 21, 9). Often those engaged in comparative study of institutions seeing words which carry a meaning similar to the Jewish law, have failed to take enough care to discern the real meaning of the Indian document. I do not know how far the punishment of stoning in the Jewish Scripture was one actually in vogue or whether the mention had simply an educative value. We often find very extravagant punishments mentioned in the Scriptures of different peoples, and they cannot be real punishments. In the Scriptures of the Parsis eight hundred stripes are prescribed for involuntary emission of the seed, and the sin of the voluntary emission of the seed was so grave that it could not be atoned at all Vendidad, Fargand, VIII, v).

31. If she be unmarried he will pay the bride-price as told before.

32. I have taken the verses viii, 374-385, in a sense different from that of the Sanskrit commentators and the modern critical students. The difference of opinion lies in the translation of the words "*gupta*" and "*agupta*." These words are translated by the commentators as women "guarded and unguarded by relatives," and their interpretation is adopted by the modern critics. This interpretation, if adopted, would mean that if adultery is committed with a woman not guarded by relatives the offense is smaller, and if she is guarded by the relatives the offense is greater. I hope that by the words "guarded woman" the commentators and the modern critics do not mean a woman "having her relatives witn her to guard" when the offense was committed!

We cannot take the words *gupta* or *agupta* to refer to the question whether the woman is properly secluded or allowed to move freely. It must be admitted that our writer was not a believer in the complete freedom of women as he has emphatically asserted the doctrine that woman does not deserve entire removal of guardianship (v, 148; ix, 2-3), still he was by no means an advocate of the institution of *purda* (segregation of the sexes) which is so strong in the valley of the Ganges (ix, 10-12).

Again, in the order to estimate the gravity of the offense, the consideration whether a woman was guarded or unguarded does not appear to be made by any dharma writer. There is an aphorism (sutra) of Gautama which may give us some reason to think otherwise. While discussing the punishment to a Shudra who commits adultery with an arya woman, Gautama says:

"If a protector he should be executed" (xii, 3). Buhler has taken the aphorism to mean, "if the woman has a protector then the Shudra offender should be executed." I interpret the aphorism differently, I think that Gautama means that if an arya woman is confided to the care of a Shudra and the Shudra abuses the trust then he should be executed.

I have taken the word *gupta* to mean a married woman and *agupta* to mean an unmarried woman and have taken the verses viii, 374-385 to mean a discussion on the offenses of fornication and adultery. The word *gupta* is defined as a married woman who indulges in secret amours in Rasamanjari, 24 (See the word *gupta* in Apte's Practical Dictionary).

The words *gupta* and *agupta* may also with propriety be taken to mern adulteress and prostitute respectively.

I venture a suggestion to explain the corruption of original sense by the commentators, and it may be taken for wnat it is worth. Most of the commentators wrote their commentaries during the Mohammedan regime, a period during which the *purda* in Northern India became much more strict.

2

RESURGENCE OF SOCIAL CHANGE

B. RYAN

In 1953 Bert Hoselitz opened an essay with the words, "of all branches of economics, none has made such rapid again in popularity during the postwar period as the analysis of long run economic growth."[1] How paradoxical that this same period had brought to sociology a zenith in structural theory and a nadir in historical, temporal, orientations. While the opening up of long buried traditional societies impressed us mightily, it did rather little to ameliorate a theoretical orientation which was centered upon sociocultural structures and their functioning. Since 1953 there have been insistent qualifications, criticisms and defenses of structural and functional orientations. And related to many criticisms have been reawakenings of life in the analysis of social change. As the title of this paper intimates, you are about to hear homage

Presidential address delivered at the annual meeting of the Southern Sociological Society in Atlanta, April, 9, 1965. I am indebted to Professors C. Arnold Angerson and Aaron Lipman for their critical reading of this manuscript. Adequate documentation and acknowledgements supporting the arguments developed in this paper might well be longer than the paper itself. Footnotes have been held to a sometimes arbitrary minimum.

paid this movement and a polemic in its support. It will be argued that our generation largely rejected the concepts essential for the study of change while frequently essaying to comprehend change through an elaboration of structuralism. The tragic aspect of Sorokin's *Social and Cultural Dynamics*, published a quarter of a century age, was neither its methodology nor its conclusions, but that it failed to reawaken our interests in long range societal growth processes.

The Constriction of the Idea of Social Change

Several half century or longer trends contributed to the virtual strangulation of social change theory and research among American sociologists. By 1973 Talcott Parsons could easily begin. The Structure of Social Action with the laughable query, "Who now reads Spencer?" Already we had been firmly assured by Malinowski that we have nothing to learn from genetically oriented inquiries. As David Bidney observed, logic became the substitute for history in the study of social origins.[2] It must be confessed that many earlier evolutionists had treated historical data with as much contempt as the father of functionalism. But the correction came not through the reformation of theories of change but in the retreat from studies of change. The way out was through or useful fad of structuralism cum functionalism; cross-sectional organizational analysis with the time dimension removed. Let it be clear that no voice is being raised against this type of analysis—except as it purports to provide conceptual foundations for the study of social change. Social change as conceived in that orientation was redefined so that it became the study of the disequilibriating effects of innovation. As Wayne Hield observed in a cantankerous essay in 1954, sociology as the science of change was transformed into the science of social pathology.[3]

In the origins of functionalism, the organic model was frequently adduced, although a mechanical one also served, contemporary functionalists seem to pay lip service to the organic one while working as if human relationships were more mechanistic. People who are concerned with organization, formal and informal structure, equilibrium etc., are the kind of people who want to understand—if I may bs permitted—" how the motor works" or "how the organism maintains life." (Curious that we built so strongly on organicism in the sense of life processes and became so scornful of organicism as a developmental, evolutionary process). We have since learned greatly as to how the motor parts work together. But the engine is a stationary one. We cut short the analogy. We learned how the carburetor operates and of the need for bearings in the drive shaft but we paid very little attention to the road map. We know the motor pretty well but have little more than speculation on where the highway leads and how far it goes in which direction. That leaders in the field of contemporary structural theory are beginning to use the word evolution politely, is hopeful but it should not suggest that structural-functional theory can circumscribe evolutionary realities.

In some recent arguments, it is observed that a theory of change is simply part of the theory of society. One must be suspicious of this broad-mindedness. For 30 or 40 years the dominant theory of society has been in terms of structure and functioning. If a rising theory of change is in fact to be part of a general theory of society, let us be sure that some neglected concepts raise their now unmodish heads. I am thinking of terms like "evolution," "lineality," "tentative social process," "telesis," "perseverative pattern," "schismogenesis," "syncretism," "accommodative process," "genetic sequence," and even, "social progress." These concepts find no equivalence in the language of stress, strain, dysfunction, equilibrium, role complementation. The old-fashioned terms were largely discarded, not conceptually improved. Nor does the idea of dynamic equilibrium help much, so long as change is conceived as pathology arising from the infection of invention. Micro-change, the term used by Alvin Bertrand at this rostrum two years ago, is not social change.[4] It is the process of organizational adjustment to an upsetting innovation. And his contribution to structural theory was a brilliant one. George Homans recently observed that we seem to keep talking of equilibrium even as a group moves over the brink of disintegration.[5] Long ago a functionalist as thoroughgoing as Radcliffe-Brown, warned up against confusing change within a social structure with change toward a new structure. Why not call the one what it is—structural adjustment—and the other what it is—social change.

Throughout its life as a discipline, sociology has been polarized around two central issues, the problem of social order and the problem of social evolution. Some theorists like Durkheim—and even Spencer—sought to deal with both problems simultaneously. Others were more devoted to evolution, while still others could care mainly about order. If each generation does not forget its masters, it at least rewrites them. Secondary treatments of Durkheim surely maximize his contributions to the theory of order and deprecate or neglect his theory of evolution. The predominance of the problem of order in contemporary sociology is no dubt eufunctional, except for the myopia which fails to see the study of sequential, directional change as a core issue of our discipline, and one requiring different concepts from those involved in the science of order.

In pursuit of organic and mechanistic analogies we forgot the full dimensions of the analogues. If, by some sociological transubstantiation, homeostasis becomes social equilibrium why was not the physiological analogy completed? That functionalism in physiology was worthwhile was no sufficient cause for the demolition of the science of biological genetics, neglect of speciation, nor disinterest in fossil primates. There is no either-or proposition in biology or sociology. That genetic and functional studies are reciprocal should be obvious in either area. That they require different concepts and differing orientations should be equally obvious. There are real conceptual differences between the sociology of genesis, becoming, and direction and the sociology of structure maintenance.

Perhaps William F. Ogburn more than anyone else influenced students away from social process and sequence, toward ideas of equilibrium and adjustment. It is paradoxical that his great work on cultural mechanics held as its main title, *Social Change*.[6] Probably most change studies since his time have been concerned with cultural adjustments to innovation when they have not been concerned with the accumulation and communication of cultural items. This science of change was no less a science of social statics than was outright structuralism.

The cultural bias is deeper than concern with inventions and their spread. Beginning at least with Professor Ogburn we have undergone a basic confusion of the social and the cultural in the realm of change. One must look aside from his monumental work to find discussions of change as it arises out of interaction, conflicts, accommodations, unrests and social contagions. And in culture lag we have a direct ancestor to the structural concepts of equilibrium, integration and stress. Ogburn wrote of inventing and of relationships among parts of cultural structures, but this culturology he called social change. With the pattern of change studies so set, the rise of the structural-functional school firmly drew students of change into the science of social stability. Others of us purported to study social change, but with more accuracy we were analyzing communicating and decision-making behaviour.

The Fallacy of Linked Functional Consequences

One seductive branch of the functional approach to change has been tracing out the chain of effects as an invention is integrated into a social structure. This method is particularly evident in contributions to the journal *Human Organization* and is classically represented in Spicer's casebook, *Human Problems in Technological* Change.[7] While this business has had special appeal to cultural anthropologists, sociologists also attempt to follow out the linked chain of effects arising from the introduction of elevators, airplanes and clocks. A classic example of this type of reconstruction is Lauriston

Sharp's thrilling story of Australian aboriginals wherein he traces step by step the dissolution of a tribal society when stone axes were replaced by steel ones.[8] This type of analysis would seem to push functional studies beyond structural adjustment analysis and really approach the problem of long range change. But the hopes that such studies could provide an approach to scientific generalizations regarding sequence and direction, have been empty ones. An important reason for so little accomplishment, beyond the proliferation of more and more cases, is the simple fact that the cases cannot be added up. The equilibrium framework offers no basis for synthesizing the respective impacts of steel axes, steam power, airplanes, television and elevators. To observe that each situation involved what Ogburn would have called a cultural lag or what current theorists describe as structural stress does not help us comprehend the determinants of direction through which stresses are resolved. Such cases are pedagogically useful in impressing us with the integrative nature of culture.

Mechanical relationships do exist in culture and there is some limit (usually quite vague) to the range of adjustive action. But we are in trouble once we move from the immediate adjustive action operationally required by an invention and begin to speak of the further chain of consequences ramifying out through the sociocultural system. Each further link in the so-called chain actually is forged from the immediately preceding response situation. Its nature depends upon the entire complex of newly created circumstances and attitudes which now become the determining forces in further "adjustments." The mechanistic view of society is partly true but largely false. Following the immediate adjustment to invention further effects arise from its precipitating cause. The logic of chain-of-consequence studies is precisely the logic of the old nursery tale, "For want of a nail a shoe was lost, for want of a shoe a horse was lost, for want of a horse..." ad nauseam, to the destruction of the solar system itself. We cannot comprehend the processes of "becoming" simply by addressing ourselves to the problems of "being." One does not study processes of life maintenance and expect thereby to come out with an ultimate theory of evolution.

Bringing the Social Back into Social Change

The eclipse of interactional concepts by cultural ones has also been detrimental to the study of change. The reification of culture dimmed our view of people. To witness this transition in theory compare a leading introductory text of 1930, Dawson and Gettys, with one of the following decade, Sutherland and Woodward, Dawson and Gettys had 21 index lines referent to the concept of culture. The 1948 edition of Sutherland and Woodward had almost 80 index lines under "culture"—nearly a tenth of total linage. In small and Vincent's introduction published in 1894 the term "culture" does not even appear in the index, yet the problem of social change was brilliantly developed.

This transition made its mark in several ways. In the first place it has become almost axiomatic in some of our circles that social change begins with innovation in the sense of a novel configuration of cultural elements. This is, of course, invention. Our preoccupation with the roots of change in response to diffusing inventions, has all but blinded us to change arising from the interaction of people, with or without associated cultural invention. The idea that innovation arises immediately out of inter-personal interaction has not been denied so much as overlooked. Drifts in social relationships through cumulative stimulus-response series, are rather little discussed in terms of social change today. Bateson's concept of schismogenesis, brilliantly introduced in the thirties, was crowded out by culturological biases in the forties.[9] Processes of group "becoming" have been largely separated from change theory. The struggle between competitive elites is little integrated with contemporary writing which emanates from the structural, culturological viewpoint. Yet this is vital stuff in many rapidly changing nations. The *creation* of norms, esprit, and role systems is now part of so-called "group dynamics," a border area of psychology and sociology not interested very much in broader issues or concepts of social change. In Everett Rogers' recent synthesis of diffusion research, one would scarcely guess that significant diffusions have been associated with emotional contagions and social movements.[10] Generalizations built out of the spread of hybrid corn, clean hog practices, television, and miracle drugs surely would gain by comparison with generalizations from the study of the spread of Negro suffrage in Mississippi, the Ghost Dance, Luddism and the small family value system. Diffusion of innovation seems to mean now the communication and decision to adopt instrumental devices. Innovations which do not fit this view are not treated as "change" as part of some other branch of sociology, collective behaviour may be.

The Progress Phobia

More headlong than our flight from interactionism was the repudiation of evolution. Panicked by Social Darwinism, the comparative method and unilinear evolution, we threw out an excellent bath along with the spoiled babies. Progress became an ethnocentric concept at best. At worst it meant a Spencerian-Sumnerian political formula. These rejections held an almost religious fervor. Most matters evolutionary were exorcised from those theorists we saved from the burning. Durkheim's quest for evolutionary formulae was played down in making him a grandfather of functionalism. Only villains could remain associated with evolutionary thought, as we credited some of our historically minded greats with "analytical abstractions" rather than empirically based formulae and temporal dichotomies. Apart from his argument on Protestantism, Max Weber as an historical social economist is subordinate to Max Weber the expositor of structural analysis.

For analytical purposes, living groups are composed into frozen models and are compared as frozen entities to equally frozen theoretic models. Structural methods quite properly remove the time dimension from on-going sociocultural systems. While such methodologies permit the comparison of structural views at different points in time they do not guide our analyses of pathways between those points. And actually even such temporally separated contrasts as in the case of Middletown are fairly uncommon.

Out of structural orientations and concepts can never come theories of sequential, processual change nor comprehension of forces and patterns in the direction of change. Yet to allege that one is a student of social evolution or of progress is nearly as bad as being called a social philosopher. Nineteenth century evolution was dismissed rather than corrected. Spencer, if not in heaven, must then be in hell. And Ward in whom there was constructive hope when cut down to size, was tainted by high idealism and an esoteric vocabulary before esoteric vocabularies enjoyed popularity in our science. With such repudiations we largely dropped that part of the sociological birthright, the science of progress, in favour of its static sister, the science of social order. In retrospect we might wonder if the science of progress was much more valuative than is one of "order." But a social science visualizing its problems through snapshot frames or reality seems far more timely in an age of existentialism and rootlessness.

Where Social Change has Lived

Like all generalities, these are improved by qualification. The study of social, processual, directional change has lived in recesses left by dominant approaches. Social change has survived in the interactional emphasis of the British social anthropologists. It has lived among social movement analysts like Rudolf Herberle and in the historical sociological scholars like Robert Nisbet. Processual change is alive in the work of anthropologists, and a few sociologists, who identify themselves with the tradition of Lewis H. Morgan. There is still life in the Gemeinschaft-Gesellschaft, status-contract, folk-urban continuum tradition, though it too is perhaps surviving better in anthropology than in sociology. During the past decade or so, Wilbert Moore, Daniel Lerner, C.P. Loomis and

Orlando Fals-Borda, among others, have brilliantly demonstrated the senses of time and direction in inducive studies of so-called transitional societies.[11] Very recently Werner Cahnman and Alvin Boskoff have firmed up and superbly moved toward catalyzing many facets of change theory.[12] While, as they imply, this reaffirmation of change study can be viewed as "historical socilogy," it is the awakening peoples of Asia, Africa and Latin America who are forcing new breath into the study of change. Here are societies not to be comprehended in terms of equilibria—not even dynamic equilibria. Living social systems are shedding old cultures and old social relationships to build new ones before our eyes. It is more than time that we fused our historically oriented efforts into a sociology of development comparable with the economics of development. With a few exceptions like Wilbert Moore, this area of sociological theory has been more realistically faced by economists and political scientists than by sociologists. Thus Bert Hoselitz apparently found relatively little to help him from his current sociological reading but he left a lot that should help sociologists.[13] J.J. Spengler and Ralph Braibanti, economist and political scientist respectively, are working from their disciplines toward what is a developmental sociological theory.[14] Economist Everett Hagen, for better or worse, has written an avowed sociological work on the theory of developing nations.[15] Also current is the composite production of the University of Chicago's Committee for the Comparative Study of New Nations, with suggestive analyses from the vantage of several disciplines toward a sociology of evolution.[16] It seems clear that if sociologists do not produce a self-conscious sociology of change—to use the nicer word—sociological theory will be written by non-sociologists in desperation.

Toward a Sociology of Development

If "evolution," and "progress" and "social telesis" are still contaminated terms, let us then speak for a *sociology of development*. This at least serves to distinguish the area from the sociology of structural adjustments and has more a flavor of the future than does the term "historical sociology." Methodological tools await the sharpening and coalescing. They range from sociological heritage of Cooley's *tentative social process*, and Ward's *karyokinesis*, to the historic inductive model building of economic historians Marc Bloch and Arthur Spiethoff.[17] It is time we who are concerned with change ceased talking in the generalities of "secularization" or "transitional societies" or "traditional" societies or the "folk-urban continuum" or "the master trend." We have been hiding historical truths in homogenizing ideal types. We know better. To ensnare Ghana, Peru, and India in the undifferentiated construct of the "folk society" or the transitional society" is to perpetuate half and quarter truths. Sociology cannot go far toward a science of development until we build model constructs out of historic realities, confessing tha logical constructs are often confounded by events. Traditionalism in some spheres is in fact compatible with rationalism and secularity in others.[18] Compatible or at least viable, syntheses of contractual and ascriptive economic relations can be found which defy the logic of culture-bound, logical model builders. Even militant traditionalism seems a fairly common ingredient in the secularizing modernization process. Social change theory requires a kind of real model building in which economic historians have much to offer us. Nor is this to say that historic processes are unique and ungeneralizable. The suggestion is rather, that we cleave the range of real societies, which are no doubt broadly classifiable on some continuum of traditionalism-modernism, into refined classes of relatively homogeneous types—not dismissing inconsistencies but classfying on the basis of prevalent inconsistencies and on lags and leads in measurable criteria of development. Howard Becker saw this need for typological refinement more clearly than anyone else but he fulfilled it through a largely deductive and non-historicalizing theory.[19] The present argument is to further what Julian Steward has described in terms of multilineal evolution.[20] Bowman and Anderson moved toward it in their "Wirtschaftstypen" paper in 1955.[21] It is to call for a revitalized comparative method whereby evolutionary change will be assessed through approximation to truly historic models. This is a task not of deductive theory but rather in measurement of contingencies; the determination of prevalent configurations in the structural attributes of developing societies. Such a comparative method based on the configurations of infrastructures is no end in itself. At this sad stage of change theorizing, it seems the most effective means for reapproaching the processes through which valuing, interacting and partly rational human beings move partly toward and partly away from the goals they set themselves. We desperately need a reconfiguration, a new catalysis, to reincorporate interacionalism with culturology and structuralism, and these with sequential evolutionary perspectives.

REFERENCES

1. Bert F. Hoselitz, "The Scope and History of Economic Growth," in *Sociological Aspects of Economic Growth* (New York: The Free Press of Glencoe, 1960). First published in *Revista de Economia Politica*, 5 (May 1953), pp. 9-28.
2. David Bidney, *Theoretical Anthropology* (New York: Columbia University Press, 1953).
3. Wayne Hield, "The Study of Change in Social Science," *British Journal of Sociology*, 5 (March 1954), pp. 1-11.
4. Alvin L. Bertrand, "The Stress-Strain Element of Social Systems: A Micro Theory of conflict and change," Presidential address, Southern Sociological Society, 1963; *Social Forces*, 42 (October, 1963), pp. 1-9.
5. George C. Homaris, "Bringing Men Back In," *American Sociological Review*, 29 (December, 1964).
6. William F. Ogburn, *Social Change with Respect to Culture and Original Nature* (New York: B. W. Huebsh, 1922).
7. Edward H. Spicer (ed.), *Human Problems in Technological Change: A Casebook* (New York: Russell Sage Foundation, 1952).
8. Lauriston Sharp, "Steel Axes for Stone Age Australians," in Spicer, *op. cit.*, pp. 69-90.

9. Gregory Bateson, Naven: *A Survey of the Problems Suggested by a Composite Picture of the Culture of a New Guinea Tribe Drawn from Three Points of View* (1st ed., 1963, 2d ed., 1958; Stanford: Stanford Uuiversity Press).

10. Everett Rogers, *Diffusion of Innovation* (New York: The Free Press of Glencoe, 1962).

11. See particularly Wilbert E. Moore and Arnold S. Feldman (eds.), *Labour Commitment and Social Change in Developing Areas* (New York: Social Seience Research Council, 1960);, Daniel Lerner, *The Passing of Traditional Society* (Glencoe, Ill.; The Free Press. 1958); Orlando Fals-Berda, "Facts and Theory of Socio-cultural Change in a Rural Social System," *Monografias Sociologicas*, 2 (2d ed., Bogeta: Universidad Nacional de Colombia, 1962).

12. Werner Cahnman and Alvin Boskoff (eds.), *Historical Sociology* (New York: The Free Press of Glencoe, 1964); Neil J. Smelser, from a base in structural-functional theory has also moved toward a processual view of change in his "Social Change in the Industrial Revolution" (Chicago: University of Chicago Press, 1939).

13. See especially his variously published essays collected in *Sociological Aspects of Economic Growth, op. cit.*, and "Theories of Stages of Economic Growth," in *Theories of Economic Growth*, Bert F. Hoselitz *et al.*, eds., (New York: The Free Press of Glencoe, 1960).

14. Ralph Braibanti and Joseph J. Spengler, (eds.), *Tradition, Values, and Socio-Economic Development* (Durham: Duke University Press, 1961).

15. Everett E. Hagen, *On the Theory of Social Change: How Economic Growth Begins* (Homewood, Ill.: The Dorsey Press, 1962).

16. Clifford Geertz (ed.), *Old Societies and New States – The Quest for Modernity in Asia and Africa* (Glencoe, Ill.: The Free Press, 1963).

17. See particularly Marc Bloch "Toward a Comparative History of European Societies," and Arthur Spiethoff, "Pure Theory and Economic Gestalt Theory; Ideal Types and Real Types," in *Enterprise and Secular Change*, Frederic C. Lane and Jelie C. Riemersma, eds., (Homewood, Ill.; Richard D. Irwin, Inc., 1953). The entire section 3 of the latter work is very much to the point of the present argument. Cf., Bert F. Hoselitz, "Theories of Stages of Economic Growth," *op cit.*

18. See for examples David Apter, "Politieal Religion in the New Nations," in *Old Societies and New States, op. cit.*; James C. Abegglen, *The Japaness Factory* (Glencoe, Ill.: The Free Press, 1958); Sol Tax, *Penny Capitalism, A Guatemalan Indian Economy,*

No. 16 (Smithsonian Institute of Social Anthropology, 1951); Simon Marcson, "Social Change and Social Structure in Transitional Societies," *International Journal of Comparative Sociology*, 1 (September, 1960); Bryce Ryan in Collaboration with L.D. Jayasena and D. C. R. Wickremesinghe, *Sinhalese Village* (Coral Gables: University of Miami Press, 1958); S.J. Tambiah and Bryce Ryan, "Secularization of Family Values in Ceylon, *American Sociological Review*, 22 (June, 1957 , pp. 292-299; S.N. Eisenstadt, "Essays on Sociological Aspects of Political and Economic Development" (Gravenhague. Mouton, 1961).

19. See his summing up "Current Sacred—Secular Theory and its Development," in Modern Sociological Theory (New York: Dryden Press, 1957). Cf. Howard Becker, "A Sacred—Secular Evaluation Continuum of Social Change," Transactions of the Third World Congress of Sociology (Amsterdam, 1956), pp. 19-41.

20. Julian H. Steward, Theory of Culture Change: The Methodology of Multilineal Evaluation (Urban: The University of Illinois Press, 1955).

21. Mary Jean Bowman and C. Arnold Anderson, "Wirtschaftstypen," in *Schmellers Jahrbuch*, 75 (1955), pp. 513-534; mimeo in English as "Types of Economy." See also their "A Typology of Societies," *Rural Sociology*, 16 (September, 1951). pp. 255-271. Cf., J. A. Pension, *The Analysis of Social Change Reconsidered*: A *Sociological Study* (The Hague: Mouton & Co., 1962), for a general theoretical approach to the whole problem and a proposed schema, Pension also presents a fresh interactional approach to social change generally. See also George A. Hillary, Jr., "The Folk Village: A Comparative Analysis," *Rural Sociology*, 26 (December, 1961).

3

SOCIAL INTEGRATION OF SCHEDULED CASTES

I

SOCIAL MOBILITY

The issue of social integration of the scheduled castes into the manstream of Indian social system is related to the question of social stratification. It is generally accepted that caste and class are different forms of social stratification. Caste and class systems stand for different patterns of distribution of properties of individuals in hereditary groups. The two systems can co-exist in an inverse relationship and the ideal typical forms of the caste and class systems constitute the opposite poles of the caste-class continuum. This continuum refers to the rigidity-fluidity dimension of social stratification.[1] We can assume that at one pole is the type which we might call absolutely closed, based entirely on inherited inequality, and at the other pole the type which we might call absolutely open—based entirely on equality of opportunity. Obviously, neither pole has ever been realised in practice, the polar opposites being ideal types. It is impossible to eliminate all competition for status, just as it is impossible to eliminate all ascription of status. Thus the stratified systems we actually find in human society are mixed types. They have both the caste element and the open class element in them. But the system may approach one pole much, more closely than another.

It is generally accepted that traditional Indian society was based largely on the principles of caste and was to that extent a particularly closed system. To test these assertions, we may here consider the functioning of the caste system in brief. Caste is a system of social organisation found in traditional India and surviving to a large extent to the present day. Till recently, Indian social life was dominated by caste. One of the well-known Indian authorities on the subject, G. S. Ghurye, describes the caste system by drawing attention to its six main features:

1. Segmental division of society,
2. Hierarchy of groups,
3. Restrictions on feeding and social intercourse,
4. Civil and religious disabilities and privileges of different sections,
5. Lack of unrestricted choice of occupation, and
6. Restrictions on marriage.[2]

It follows that membership in caste is hereditary. This inherited membership is fixed for life, because the individual cannot alter his caste by any effort of his own. The caste in the past was united by a common traditional occupation. Any group which is called a caste will exhibit most of the features listed above. Keeping in view these features, one may say that the traditional system was a closed one and that in it no mobility was possible.

But we cannot subscribe to that view, because writers like Srinivas have tried to show that mobility was possible, though not easy, in the traditional system; and that it did actually occur occasionally.[3] There has been some mobility up and down the social ladder despite the ideal of fixity. Thus it is true that there is increasing recognition of the fact that even the traditional order was not absolutely rigid but possessed its own sources of flexibility. Certain factors enabled individual castes to move up and down with the system of castes. We may recall, however, that while the traditional system allowed individual castes to move up or down, the system itself remained unaltered. In other words, there was only positional and not structural change. This kind of movement, however, where a caste is the unit of mobility, is very different from that which is becoming increasingly common in modern India. The latter allows greater scope to the individual as the unit of mobility and tends increasingly to relegate caste to a marginal position.[4]

Thus we may broadly conceive of two different types of change in the hierarchical relationships among caste groups. The first refers to a change in the relative positions of the groups in the caste hierarchy. This type of change does not impair the caste system as a form of social stratification. The second type refers to a change in the very tendency of hereditary groups to be ranked. This leads to a transformation of the caste system itself.[5] Since the nineteenth century, the closed social systems have been undergoing a process of transformation into more open systems and further, this process has been accelerated in course of the last two decades.

As is generally known, the caste system in its entirety constitutes a status hierarchy with the Brahmins at the pin nacle and the Scheduled Castes or so-called untouchables at the base. Thus the Scheduled Castes are characterised by a low, in fact, the lowest, social or ritual status in the case hierarchy, as well as by low socio-economic conditions. These strata had, on account of their low social and ritual status, been subject to a variety of disabilities under the traditional system. All through the ages, the untouchables suffered from social injustice and exploitation so as to prevent them from rising abcve the social status fixed for them. The untouchable caste, being on the last rung of the social ladder, was denied entry into several occupations which were relatively cleaner or well-paid and the field of its activities was restricted to somewhat unclean and menial jobs which yielded low incomes. They were associated with a variety of specialized traditional occupations such as scavenging, cobbling, disposal of carcasses, basketry, etc. These castes in the past had no access to education. The road to knowledge was closed to them. As a consequence, these castes have remained socially, economically and educationally backward.

Hindu society insisted on the segregation of untouchables and would not allow them to live inside their own areas. Their social identity was highlighted by the fact that they were generally required to live at a distance from the main village settlement. Residential segregation was somewhat strictly enforced.

In traditional Hindu society there were legal and ritua sactions which prevented the lower castes from imitating the life-styles of the upper castes. Apart from this, there are certain elements in the life-style of the Harijans which are perhaps ranked even lower in the traditional Hindu scheme of values. Foremost among these are the ones which pertain to their diet. Different items of food (and drink) are graded carefully in Sanskritic Hinduism, and in any given region the social rank of a caste is closely related to the food habits of its members. In general, meat-eating is ranked rather low, Harijans not only eat meat, but particular kinds of meat which are held to be especially unclean. Those among them who eat beef (or have a tradition of beef-eating) are assigned the lowest social rank.[6]

While discussing the low position of these depressed classes, Blunt says: "At all times, the Brahmin priesthood has endeavoured to keep them segregated, not only from Hindu society, but from the Hindu religion and the Hindu ceremonial; they were not allowed to hear, much less study, the Vedas; they must not enter the temples; they must carry on all ceremonies without using the mantras and no Brahmin would carry out any domestic ceremony for them."[7]

Prabhu mentions that untouchability refers to denying even human status to a group of human beings—indeed, this group is not even allowed the consideration which may be shown to creatures like animals.[8] Thus we may say that the Harijans suffered oppression at the hands of the upper castes for centuries, their economic condition was extremely depressed, they were educationally backward and they lacked political skills to hold their own against the upper caste leadership of the country. In short, the low rank of the Harijans resulted from cumulative inequalities in the economic, political and ritual systems.

A problem which has, from time to time, engaged the attention both of social reformers and of politicians is the raising of these depressed classes with the object of improving their social status and also their civic position. Their cause was championed in Bengal by Raja Ram Mohan Roy, in North India by Swami Dayanand Saraswati and in the South by Colonel Olcott and Dr. Annie Besant. The Brahmo Samaj, the Arya Samaj and the Theosophical Society sponsored movements for the amelioration of their condition. A few legislative measures for improving the conditions of these unfortunates were adopted, but no concerted move worth the name was made on a large scale to eradicate the evil from our midst. Gandhiji was the first Indian to carry on an organised movement against the inhuman treatment meted out to this stratum of society. He appealed to our sense of honesty, justice, decency and humanity and roused the enlightened conscience of the nation to fight against this evil. To the untouchables, he gave a new name—Harijan (children of God)—and thus made us conscious of the spark of divinity that is in us all. In *Young India* of 22-9-1921, he said that the existence of untouchability must remain an impassable barrier in the path of our progress, which we must break down with supreme effort.[9]

While fighting for the rights of the coloured peoples in

South Africa, Gandhiji could not be blind to the rights of the so called untouchables in his own country. That is why from the very beginning, he insisted that the untouchables should be looked upon as Hindus with all the rights, religious and political, which the caste Hindus enjoyed. That is why he was not enamoured of the idea that the untouchables should form a separate electoral bloc, for this would perpetuate their distinction from the caste Hindus. Thus, the problem of the untouchables received special attention at the hands of the Father of the Nation, who left no stone unturned to rehabilitate this downtrodden section of the Indian population. It is not necessary to recount here any of his heroic efforts in favour of the Harijans, but by his personal efforts, both by example and by precept, he secured an unprecedented share of social mobility for the depressed classes whom he renamed Harijans. While discussing social mobility, casteism and untouchability, P.G. Shaw said that when a proper history of social mobility in India would be written, the highest credit would have to be given to Mahatma Gandhi, for it was he who secured higher social mobility for the Harijans in the economic, political, occupational and religious fields.[10]

Under Gandhiji's inspiration, an all-India body, called the Harijan Sewak Sangh, with branches throughout the country, was formed and several institutions were also established which spread his gospel of equality throughout the length and breadth of the land. Thus the stages was set for the statutory protection of the so called untouchables. The way having been paved for legislative reform, the Congress governments, in the various provinces of India under British administration, took up the task of granting statutory protection to the Harijans. Several measures were adopted, but they touched only the fringe of the problem, and it was only after the emergence of India as a sovereign independent state that phenomenal progress was achieved in this field. In the Constitution of India these sections of society have been regarded as Scheduled Castes. The term "Scheduled Castes" is an expression standardised in the Constitution of India. 'Scheduled Castes' means such castes. races or tribes, or parts of or groups within such castes, races, or tribes, as are deemed, under Article 341, to be Scheduled Castes, for purposes of this Constitution.[11] In all, the Scheduled Castes total 64,504,113 individuals, according to the 1961 census, thus accounting for about 14.64 per cent of the total population of the country.

After Independence, the Government of India has been giving high priority to efforts to ameliorate the condition of the Scheduled Castes. The Constitution of India makes ample provisions to safeguard the rights and interests of these people and to remove the social disabilities from which they had suffered in the past. The demon of untouchability is supposed to have been officially killed, as Article 17 of our Constitution solemnly declares, "Untouchability is abolished and its practice in any form is forbidden. The enforcement of any disability arising out of untouchability shall be an offence punishable in accordance with law."[12] Not only this, the Indian Constitution has a section for the abolition of untouchability and the Union as well as the State Governments have taken legislative measures to enforce this section. Apart from this, every effort has been made to promote the educational and economic interests of these sections of society. They are offered big fee concessions and stipends to help them to carry on their academic pursuits. In the occupational field, special privileges by way of reservation of seats are granted to enable them to attain respectable status in society. Thus, not only has prejudicial discrimination been constitutionally abolished, but special privileges have also been given under the Constitution to safeguard the interests of the Scheduled Caste people to enable them to bridge the gulf which in the past separated them from the advanced sections of society.

In fact, they are supposed to have all the opportunities for the full growth of their personality to enable them to walk hand in hand with various other groups in society. These castes, which for years were unable either to aspire to or expect social equality, have imbibed a sense of equality and self-respect and have attained a sense of social mobility which their members had never experienced before. These new attainments were not the goals and aspirations of these castes even about two decades ago.

Traditionally, the scheduled castes were more or less homogeneous caste groups. As already stated, they occupied a low position occupationally as well as educationally. But the recent changes have enabled them to acquire as much education as they may desire, and are provided with a variety of new choices and opportunities in the occupational field. As a result, the barriers to social mobility have been eliminated and a scope for social mobility is created for them in all walks of life.

Theoretical Implications

With all these opportunities and constitutional safeguards provided to them to achieve mobility, we expect that the members of the Scheduled Castes within the hereditary group will become heterogeneous. Their social behaviour will not be uniform and, therefore, the hereditary group as a unit of social behaviour will lose its importance. As suggested by Sorokin, "When a man remains throughout his life in the same occupational, economic and political status, his behaviour inevitably becomes very rigid and non-flexible. On this account, the behaviour of the people of the same status approaches uniformity, while that of people in different social positions becomes widely divergent. A quite different picture is given by the behaviour of the members of a mobile society. A great versatility and plasticity of human behaviour is a natural result of social mobility."[13]

The present study, therefore, is an attempt to assess the social consequences of social mobility among the Scheduled Castes. Education, occupation and income have been taken up as the dimensions of socio-economic status along which social mobility has been measured, that is, social mobility has been measured in terms of movement or change in these dimensions. The study is based on the assumption that among these variables, education is relatively an important correlate of socio-economic status. Education is a prerequisite for their mobility through both occupation and income. Educational requirements are the prerequisites for entry into higher prestige jobs and into higher-income categories, Therefore, the Government of India grants them liberal concessions in the field of education because education will play the most important role in the advancement of the Scheduled Caste people, as it will be through education alone that the other two disabilities, social and economic, will resolve themselves.

Among the many possible consequences of social mobility, the present study will be concerned with its impact on:

1. Social status
2. Pattern of interaction
3. Levels of aspirations
4. Family pattern
5. Marriage pattern
6. Employment of wives
7. Awareness of Government policies.

A large variety of social consequences can be imputed to social mobility. An adequate analysis of the consequences of social mobility requires a theory, that is a series of clearly specified and logically interrelated hypotheses. The assessment of the consequences of social mobility on the above-mentioned aspects yields a number of hypotheses which have been empirically tested. Thus, we list some of tne important hypotheses which would be discussed at appropriate places.

1. One of the many consequences of social mobility, the one, perhaps much more important from a long-range point of view, can be that social mobility determines in large measure the respondents' evaluation of their social status. That is, their self-identification with a

social class should be related to their social mobility in the sense that those who have achieved greater social mobility will identify themselves with upper or middle classes as compared to the less mobile and non-mobile ones who would regard themselves as belonging to the lower and working classes.

2. Thus, while, on the one hand, social mobility may determine an individual's evaluation of his social status, on the other, it may result in some status discrepancies among the different positions that a person may hold, in the sense that a Scheduled Caste person may rise educationally and occupationally and yet may find himself excluded from those social groups to which he feels his improved status entitles him to belong. In spite of his improved educational and occupational status, he may be unable to acquire a commensurate social status because of his lowly social origins. This hypothesis gets considerable weightage from the statement made by Lipset and Bendix where they have suggested that "In every society, social mobility may result in discrepancies among the different positions one person may hold in each of these hierarchies. As a man advances his economic fortunes, he may find himself excluded from certain social groups because of his lowly social origin or his ethnic background. Again, persons who have high social status may find that they are unable to earn a commensurate income."[14]

3. Furthermore, if we consider the fact that the social status of the individual is influenced not only by his individual properties but also by the social status of the group to which he belongs (*i.e.*, his hereditary group), it may, further, be hypothesised that as the Scheduled Castes improve their occupational and educational status, they are prone to dissociate from their own caste groups.

4. It has been widely recognised that status is achieved by

associating with those of equal or greater social attainment. Therefore, it is suggested that as a consequence of social mobility, a change is likely to occur in the interaction pattern of the Scheduled Castes in the sense that those who achieve mobility will tend to change their membership of organisations and their choice of leaders and friends and may also move to a new neighbourhood in keeping with their newly gained position. The consequences of social mobility may directly be felt in interpersonal relations between Scheduled Castes and other higher castes. It is expected that non-mobiles will be intimately bound up with their own caste groups and those who move up are more likely to be oriented towards the higher caste groups and will have little contact with their own caste groups.

5. Social mobility influences the levels of aspirations of the people in the sense that those who have achieved greater social mobility will have higher aspirations for the educational and occupational careers of their children than those with lower mobility.

6. Social mobility may produce repercussions on the family and marriage patterns of the Scheduled Castes. It is recognised that the upwardly mobile are likely to be status-oriented and to have little extended family contacts. It has been hypothesised that the extended family is negatively related to social mobility and that with a rise in social mobility, the family systems moves towards some kind of conjugal pattern. In other words, the family structure will change as a consequence of social mobility leading to the establishment of nuclear households, to a decrease in the size of the family and also a decrease in any functional or effective ties with their close relatives.

7. Not only does the family pattern undergo a change, but the institution of marriage, too, witnesses a change as a result of social mobility. The traditional norms

and values change as a consequence of social mobility. Social mobility tends to exercise pressures for a higher age at marriage for men and consequently for women. It tends to bring a change in the attitudes regarding inter-caste marriages. Social mobility may grant more freedom of choice in marriage in the sense that it gives men and women the right to choose their own mates. Social mobility may also decrease opposition to divorce and widow remarriage.

8. Social mobility may have far-reaching effects on the employment of wives. It has been considered that in the lower communities, it is customary for the women to work in gainful employment. But it has been assumed here that as the socio-economic conditions of the Scheduled Castes improve, the percentage of women from the working force declines.

   It is further expected that in the case of the working wives, the status of their occupations should be consistent with that of their husbands.

9. The Constitution of India makes ample provisions to safeguard the rights and interests of the Scheduled Castes and to remove the disabilities from which they have suffered in the past. We assume that social mobility affects the Scheduled Castes' knowledge regarding the provision of opportunities and safeguards and the extent to which they avail themselves of these opportunities, *i.e.*, the upwardly mobile Scheduled Castes are more likely to be aware of the various facilities provided to them by the Government and consequently avail themselves of these facilities to a greater extent than the non-mobile ones and hence the upwardly mobile are to a larger extent satisfied with the governmental measures for the amelioration of their lot.

II

SOCIAL STATUS

The Scheduled Castes are characterised by the lowest social

or ritual status in the caste hierarchy as well as by poor economic conditions. Before the dawn of freedom, the poor and downtrodden people now known as Scheduled Castes were shrouded in the darkness of confusion and suppression and were victims of an inferiority complex deep-rooted in poverty, illiteracy, backwardness, exploitation and social oppression. As a consequence, they had remained socially, economically and educationally more backward than any of the higher castes in the country. In pre-independence India, several measures had been adopted from time to time to improve the conditions of these strata of society but they touched only the fringe of the problem. It was only after the emergence of India as a sovereign independent Republic that visible progress had been registered in this field.

Traditionally, the Scheduled Castes were more or less homogeneous caste groups. They were at a low position educationally an well as occupationally, but the recent socio-political changes have enabled them to pursue education to the extent they desire. They are also provided with a variety of new choices and opportunities in the occupational field. As the traditional barriers to social mobility have been eliminated, there is scope for them to enter all walks of life.

With the increasing tempo of developmental activities in favour of the Scheduled Castes, they are given full opportunities for the advancement of their education, the traditional barriers to occupational mobility are rapidly breaking down and many new and more remunerative fields of employment are being thrown open to the members of these classes. By taking advantage of the newly provided opportunities, the Scheduled Castes have been improving their socio-economic status along the dimensions of education, occupation and income.

An attempt was made to find out the nature of the relationship among the three variables of socio-economic status. Our data show that the co-efficient of correlation between education and occupation, education and income, and occupation and income is quite significant. To indicate the separate effect of each of these variables on the remaining two, partial correlations were worked out and we found that education was able to predict by itself the occupational prestige and income of a person to a large extent, showing thereby that among the three factors considered, education was the most efficient index of socio-economic status. Thus, education has been treated as an index of socio-economic status along which social mobility has been measured. Therefore, in dealing with the consepuences of social mobility, we have correlated all other factors with the educational background of the respondents in order to assess the differential effects of social mobility on them.

An attempt was made to measure social mobility in three generations by comparing the educational and occupational backgrounds of the respondents with those of their fathers and grandfathers. The kind of association founds to exist between the father's and son's occupational status showed that, the higher the status of the father, the smaller the proportion of sons in the lower occupational grades, and the lower the status of the father, the smaller the proportion of sons in the higher occupational grades. This in turn showed that the occupational prestige grade of the father affected the occupational prestige grade of the son. Similarly, in measuring educational mobility, we found that the higher the education of the father, the higher was the education of the son. Our data had revealed that the chances of the sons of less educated fathers to enter college for higher education were much less than the chances of those sons whose fathers had a higher education. We may, therefore, conclude that even if theoretically it is possible for all the members of the Scheduled Castes to receive any amount of education and achieve mobility, in actual practice, advancement in this field is gradual. We find that the socio-economic status of the parents does affect the socio-economic status of the sons; that persons with higher education, and, consequently, in higher prestige jobs are the children of fathers having a comparatively higher socio-economic status. Thus, there is every reason to believe that while the expansion of facilities has opened the door to social mobility for the Scheduled Castes, a large majority of them are still not able to avail themselves of such facilities unless their family background supports them. The differences in family background have their repercussions on the sons' social mobility

While dealing with the consequences of social mobility, we found that social mobility determined in large measure the respondents' evaluation of their social status. The data had clearly indicated that the respondents' own assignment to the different status levels varied according to their level of education. Some of the highly educated respondents placed themselves in the upper and middle social classes, whereas the less educated placed themselves in the working and lower social classes. This shows that their class consciousness is directly influenced by changes in their socio-economic status.

Thus, while, on the one hand, social mobility determines an individual's evaluation of his social status, on the other, it results in some status discrepancies among the different positions that a person holds. Even if the Scheduled Castes have improved their educational and occupational status, they feel that they do not get the same social status in society as given to members of the higher castes. They are aware that their improved educational and occupational statuses have not received adequate social recognition because of their lowly social origins. Our conclusion here is similar to that obtained by Lipset and Bendix, who have pointed out that an individual may acquire a high occupational status, yet find himself socially ostracised because of his family background.[15] Similarly, our respondents feel that in spite of their improved status, they are not accorded a proper social status in keeping with their newly-gained position. In other words, they feel that they are unable to achieve a commensurate social status because of their lowly social origins. Our findings here also receive some support from Bailey's study of the Boad outcastes of a village in Orissa, where he found that in spite of the considerable economic progress made by those outcastes, they had not risen correspondingly in the social estimation of the villagers.[16] It is an irony of fate that even after occupying a higher status, the Scheduled Castes are not accepted at par with the people of the same status from other communities. It is more or less taken for granted that a member of the Scheduled Caste community suffers from certain inherited handicaps. The higher castes generally have the impression that a Scheduled Caste person is backward, inefficient, incapable and gets a job only because he belongs to a Scheduled Caste.

The reason for the relatively lower status of the Scheduled Castes is evident if we consider the fact that the social status of an individual is influenced not merely by his individual possessions, but also by the social status of the group to which he belongs. Thus, even if the Scheduled Castes have improved their socio-ecnomic conditions, they feel that they are not treated on an equal level with other sections of society because of the low sacial status of their hereditary group. In practice, we find that the socio-economically advanced sections of the Scheduled Castes try to dissociate from their own caste groups, because while, on the one hand, they improve their socio-economic conditions through their own achievements, on the other, the status of the group to which they belong remains the same, which fact lowers their own social standing and as a result they hesitate to declare their respective caste names. They express an ardent desire to be freed of the stigma of being untouchables and not to be connected any longer in any way with the rejected past. They want new identities for themselves that would be accepted in society.

In order to raise their status in the caste hierarchy, the Scheduled Castes are making various efforts. They are doing their utmost to give their children education, so as to raise their social status. They feel that with education, they will move away from the low traditional caste-based occupations and thereby attain a higher status. Thus, they value education as an important determinant of social status. The Scheduled

Castes are also endeavouring to forsake all those occupations which are considered degrading. They do not want their children to follow any of those occupations which degrade their social status. Further. they are also making attempts to improve their economic status and standard of living, so as to raise their social status. Then, again, in order to raise their social status, the Scheduled Castes are adopting the way of life of the higher castes. This involves giving up eating of the forbidden variety of meat, changing their gods in favour of those of the higher castes, a tendency to abandon widow remarriage and divorce and to replace bride price by dowry. We find that the less-educated rerpondents have mostly tried to acquire the traditional symbols of high status, namely, the customs, rituals, ideas, beliefs and way of living of the higher castes to raise their social status. In the words of Srinivas, we may say that they are becoming Sanskritized. Modernization is more operative among the educated and upwardly mobile, *i.e.*, they are trying to improve their status by improving their economic status and standard of living and by acquiring education.

As a consequence of social mobility the interaction pattern of the Scheduled Castes has undergone a change. As regards their membership in voluntarily organisations, we found that a majority among the illiterates and less-educated persons were members of such organisations as compared to the highly educated persons. A large percentage of illiterates and less-educated individuals were members of their own Scheduled Caste organisations, whereas a greater percentage of the educated respondents belonged to non-Scheduled Caste organisations. Moreover, the uneducated and less-educated members were found more in the capacity of executive members, whereas a majority of the educated respondents were ordinary members.

In the case of the leadership pattern of the community, we found that it was related to the factor of social mobility in the sense that the less-educated respondents named leaders mostly from the Scheduled Caste community, while the educated went beyond their own community in identifying them. Perhaps this is more a status-saving device than anything else.

Social mobility also affects to some extent the choice of the respondents regarding their friends. A majority of the less-educated respondents counted among their best friends persons from their own caste groups, while the majority of the educated respondents did not specify their friends from any group. This may be due to the fact that these respondents could identify themselves neither with their own caste groups nor with the non-Scheduled Caste groups because of their social relationships being disturbed. They were alienated from their own caste group and at the same time were not integrated with the higher caste groups. The educated among this community not only pulled long faces but also felt perplexed and disturbed when questioned about the choice of their friends. Thus, there is no natural satisfaction of friendly feelings and generally this is a disturbing factor in life. But of the small percentage among them who specified their friends, a majority mentioned names from the non-Scheduled Caste community.

The residential pattern of the Scheduled Castes undergoes a change as a consequence of social mobility. The uneducated and less educated among the Scheduled Castes in Ambala are still clustered in some of their own caste-based colonies secluded from the localities of the higher castes. But the educated and upwardly mobile members of these groups leave their selected colonies and find residence in different parts of the city where the various castes are found living side by side. However, the possibility of some of the non-mobile members living in the higher caste localities cannot altogether be ruled out, because the sampling design of this study was not aimed at finding such persons.

Regarding actual inter-group participation between the Scheduled Castes and the higher castes at social functions, we found that social mobility minimized their contacts with the members of their own group which fact meant that the educated Scheduled Castes adopted a tendency to separate themselves from the members of their own community. The educated Scheduled Castes are, on the one hand, becoming alienated from their own community and, on the other, they are not being integrated fast enough into the higher castes. Thus, we find that in the social sphere they are left like wanderers, segregated from their own fold and unaccepted by the higher groups. As a result, they neither feel comfortable at social functions of their own community nor are they happy while participating in the social functions of the higher castes because they fully realise that invitations extended to them by the higher castes to attend their functions are merely formal. Thus, we find that the upwardly mobile. Scheduled Castes are becoming alienated from their own community, and would like to be integrated with the higher castes, but they seem to be thwarted in their efforts.

It may be mentioned that in their own class the tragedy of socio-economic uplift and social mobility is two fold in nature. For example, if a family of this community goes a step higher in attaining better social status, it does not show much concern for its less fortunate members and begins to look down upon them. But when this better-placed family knocks at the door of other socially higher communities, it is not warmly welcomed. This tragic state of affairs can best be described by the common Indian saying, "Dhobi ka Kutta na Ghar ka na Ghat ka", which, when translated, means such persons are like aimless wanderers.

Social mobility also accounts for differential levels of aspirations of respondents in respect of themselves and their children. A majority of the educated respondents were found satisfied with their present occupations. They seemed to be engaged in jobs in accordance with their merits. A great majority of the less educated respondents, however, expressed their dissatisfaction. They felt that the work they were doing was not what they deserved. Thus, merit was found to be a basis for satisfaction with present work inasmuch as those who felt that the work they were doing was in accordance with their merits also seemed to be satisfied with their present jobs. Practically all the respondents realised the importance of education because it enabled them to achieve a higher status and led to the abandonment of their low traditional occupations. Thus, almost all of them wanted to glve the best education possible to their children; they wanted them to have respectable jobs and ardently desired to do away with traditional occupations.

Social mobility has repercussions on the family and marriage patterns of the Scheduled Castes. The hypothesis that an extended family is negatively related to social mobility is substantiated by our data—we found an appreciable difference between families of the higher educated, on the one hand, and the families of the less-educated and uneducated, on the other. With a rise in social mobility, the family pattern undergoes a change in the direction of decrease in the size of the family. A larger number of members of the family live out, having decreasing functional or effective ties with the other members of the family and there is a tendency towards the establishment of nuclear households. This may be taken to mean that social mobility encourages family dissociation in the sense that as soon as the Scheduled Castes acquire education, they separate themselves from the uneducated members of the family, who are still engaged in their lowly traditional occupations, because they want to be different from them.

The institution of marriage, too, witnesses a change as a result of social mobility. Education tends to exercise pressures for a higher age at marriage for men and, consequently, for women too. Furthermore, the educated respondents preferred a higher age at marriage for sons and daughters, as compared to the illiterates and less-educated respondents. Our data have also shown some variation in the opinion of the respondents towards inter-caste marriages. The higher the social mobility, the lower was the proportion of respondents opposed to intercaste marriages. Further, it was observed that the traditional authority of parents in respect of the marriage of their children was passing gradually into the hands of the children themselves as a consequence of social mobility. Social mobility grants more freedom of choice in marriage in the sense that it gives men and women some right to choose their mates. The differential effect of social mobility has been found to be true in respect of widow remarriage and divorce. The higher-educated were found to be more in favour of divorce and widow remarriage than the less-educated individuals. Social mobility is replacing bride price by dowry.

Social mobility also affects the employment of wives among the Scheduled Castes. We found that the participation of wives in the working force was to a large extent dependent on the socio-economic status of the husband. The hypothesis that with an increase in social mobility, the women workers gradually drop out of the working force is supported by our data. In the case of working wives, as expected, we observed the status of their occupations to be consistent with that of their husbands, *i.e.*, the higher the education and occupation of the husband, the higher was the prestige of the job of the wife. While analysing the relationship between the educational levels of husbands and wives, we found a positive relationship existing between the educational backgrounds of husbands and working wives. There was, however, a greater gulf between the educational backgrounds of husbands and non-working wives. This appears to be the main reason for the wives not joining the working force because of their difficulty in securing jobs consistent with their husbands' prestige, since they lack proper education and training to fit them for jobs consistent with their family stutus.

Social mobility affects the respondents' awareness of the various governmental policies concerning the uplift of the Scheduled Castes. After 20 years of governmental concern to ameliorate the conditions of the Scheduled Castes, we find that only a part of this community is benefited by these concessions and privileges. The others could obtain scarcely any advantage from these privileges. It was only the better-educated people of this community who were aware of the facilities provided and were taking advantage of them. They were satisfied with the Government's policies.

In theory, the awareness and practical utilization of new opportunities and openings appear concrcte and real on the surface, but if we probe deeper, we find that most of the less-educated people are still unaware of them. Some of them who are aware of the new privileges complain that for them the entire concept of privileges is a big hoax. They hear of various grants provided for them by the Government and various loan facilities offered to them, but when they wish to avail themselves of these, they are completely frustrated. The much-talked-of reservations of seats for them for various posts is considered by them a mockery of the factual position. Thus, the opportunities and channels for social mobility that the Government provides to the Scheduled Castes will have little meaning unless they are taken advantage of by them in actual practice.

Having read about ail the good things which the Government is endeavouring to do for these people and then seeing the deplorable conditions in which they live, one wonders if anything at all has been done for them and whether the Government is sincere in its pledges and promises. Except for the thin upper crust that has risen, the picture is rather gloomy.

The small minority of the upwardly mobile who have attained higher standards of education and are occupying high posts are now in a class by themselves. They are becoming modernised and are following the pattern of living of the higher classes in all respects. Having secured higher posts, they have become members of another class. They have become different from their fathers and forefathers. They want to plot out their past completely. They do not mix with members of the other Scheduled Castes. Yet unfortunately they find themselves landed in a situation where too little is changing too slowly. A society still governed by the caste system does not allow them to shake off their past or completely to forget it. In this new circle, they are not accepted as equals but are looked down upon. Thus, they are neither here nor there and have become victims of the caste system in a peculiar way.

REFERENCES

1. V.S. D'Souza, "Caste and Class: A Reinterpretation", in *Journal of Asian and African Studies*, Vol. II, No. 3-4, July and October, 1967, p. 196.

2. G.S. Ghurye, *Caste & Class in India*, Bombay: The Popular Book Depot, 1950, pp. 2-17,

3. M.N. Srinivas, *Social Change in Modern India*, Bombayt Allied Publishers, 1966, p. 93.

4. Andre Bateille, *Casts: Old and New*, Bombay: Asia Publishing House, 1960, p. 58.

5. D'Souza, *op. cit.*, p. 195.

6. Bateille, *op. cit.*, p. 91.

7. E.A.H. Blunt, *Caste System of Northern India*, Delhi: S, Chand and Co., 1969, p. 336.

8. P. N. Prabhu, *Report of the Seminar on Casteism and Remaval of Untouchability*, Bombay: Published by the Indian Conference of Social Work, 1955, p. 104.

9. M.K. Candhi, *The Removal of Untouchability*, Ahmedabad: Navajivan Publishing House, 1959, p. 10.

10. P.G. Shaw, *Report of the Seminar on Casteism and Removal of Untouchability*, Bombay: Published by the Indian Conferenee of Social Work, 1955, p. 71.

11. *The Constitution of India*, Article 366(24).

12. *The Constitution of Indta*, Article 17.

13. P.A. Sorokin, *Social and Cultural Mobility*, Illinois: Free Press of Glencoe, 1959, p. 502.

14. S.M. Lipset & R. Bendix, *Social Mobility of Industrial Society*, Berkeley: University of California Press, 1959, p. 266.

15. S.M. Lipset and R. Bendix, *Social Mobility in Industrial Society*, Berkeley, University of California Press, 1959, p. 6.

16. F.G. Bariley, *Caste and the Economic Frontier*, Bombay: Oxford University Press, 1958, pp. 217-14.

4

CAUSES AND CONSEQUENCES OF INDIVIDUAL CHANGE IN SIX DEVELOPING COUNTRIES

A. INKELES

Since 1962 a group of my colleagues and I at Harvard University have been working to understand the impact on the individual of his participation in the pracess of modernization. In the pursuit of this goal we devised a complex and comprehensive questionnaire touching on a wide variety of life situations and intended to measure a substantial segment of the range of attitudes, values, and behaviours we conceive as particularly relevant to understanding the individual's participation in the roles typical for a modern industrial society.[2] This questionnaire we then administered to some 6,000 young men in six developing countries: Argentina, Chile, India, Israel, Nigeria, and East Pakistan. All three of the continents containing the overwhelming majority of developing nations are represented. The sampled countries cover the range from the newest nations which have only recently won their independence to those with a long history of self-governance; from those only now emerging from tribal life to those with ancient high cultures, and from those furthest removed from, to these most intimately linked to, the European cultural and industrial sociol order. The men interviewed were selected to represent points on a presumed continuum of exposure to modernizing influences, the main groups being the cultivator of the land still rooted in his traditional rural community; the migrant from the countryside just arrived in the city but not yet integrated into urban industrial life; the urban but non-industrial worker still pursuing a more or less traditional occupation, such as barber or carpenter, but now doing so in the urban environment even though outside the context of a modern largescale organization; and the experienced industrial worker engaged in production using inanimate power and machinery within the context of a more or less modern productive enterpeise. To these we have added sets of secondary school and university students who enjoy the presumed benefits of advanced education. Within and across these sample groups we exercised numerous controls in the selection of subjects and in the analysis of our data, both to understand the influence and to prevent the uncontrolled effects of socio-cultural and biosocial factors such as age, sex, education, social origins, ethnic membership, past life experience, and the like.

Our interview included almost 300 entries. Some 160 of these elicited attitudes, values, opinions, and reports on the behaviour of others and oneself, touching on almost every major aspect of daily life. The questionnaire included various tests of verbal ability, literacy, political information, intelligence; and psychic adjustment. In some cases it took four hours of interviewing to complete—a demanding experience for both interviewer and interviewee.

We completed our field work near the end of 1964, and since that time have been engaged in processing and then later analyzing the very substantial body of data we collected. At this time our analysis is sufficiently far advanced so that we can discern the main outlines of some of the conclusions we must draw. To present these within the rigorous limits of the time and space currently allotted for scholarly communications requires imposing a telegraphic style and forgoing the presentation of delivered evidence to support my arguments. Each of my conclusions will address itself to one of the main issues to which our research was directed. Each issue is presented in the form of a question to which I will assay an answer. The four main issues dealt with here should not be understood as being the only ones to which we addressed ourselves; neither should it be assumed that our data provide answers only to these questions.

1. How far is there an Empirically Identifiable Modern Man, and what are his Outstanding Characteristics?

Many social scientists have a conception on the modern man, but few have submitted this conception to an empirical test to ascertain whether this type really exists in nature and to determine how often he appears on the scene. Important exceptions may be found in the work of Kahl (1968), Dawson (1967), and Doob (1967).[2-a] We too have our model of the modern man, a complex one including three components which we refer to as the analytic, the topical, and the behavioural models, all of which, we assumed, might well tap one general underlying common dimension of individual modernity.[3]

We believe our evidence (presented in some detail in Smith and Inkeler 1966)[3-a] shows unmistakably that there is a set of personal qualities which reliably cohere as a syndrome and which identify a type of man who may validly be described as fitting a reasonable theoretical conception of the modern man. Central to this syndrome are:

1. openness to new experience both with people and with new ways of doing things such as attempting to control births;
2. the assertion of increasing independence from the authority of traditional figures like parents and priests and a shift of allegiance to leaders of government, public affairs, trade unions, cooperatives, and the like;

3. belief in the efficiency of science and medicine, and a general abandonment of passibity and fatalism in the face of life's difficulties; and
4. ambition for oneself and one's children to achieve high occupational and educational goals. Men who manifest these characteristics;
5. like people to be on time and show an interest in carefully planning their affairs in advance. It is also part of this syndrome to;
6. show strong interest and take an active part in civic and community affairs and local politics; and
7. to strive energetically to keep up with the news, and within this effort to prefer news of national and international import over items dealing with sports, religion, or purely local affairs.

This syndrome of modernity coheres empirically to meet the generally accepted standards for scale construction with reliabilities ranging from .754 to .873 in the six countries.[4] Looking at the range of items which enters into the scale, one can see that it has a compelling face validity. In addition, the empirical outcome accords well with our original theoretical model and indeed, with those of numerous other students of the problem. Evidently the modern man is not just a construct in the mind of sociological theorists. He exists and he can be identified with fair reliability within any population which can take our test.[5]

To discover that there are indeed men in the world who fit our model of a modern man is comforting, but perhaps not startling. After all, we can probably somewhere find an example of almost any kind of man one might care to delineate. It is important to emphasize, therefore, that men manifesting the syndrome of attitudes, values, and ways of acting we have designated "modern" are not freaks. They are not even rare. On the contrary, there are very substantial numbers of them in all six of the countries we have studied.[6]

Furthermore, we consider it to be of the utmost significance thot the qualities which serve empirically to define a modern man do not differ substantially from occupation to occupation, or more critically, from culture to culture. In constructing our standard scales of modernity we utilized a pool of 119 attitude items.[7] In each country these items were then ranked according to the size of the item-to-scale correlation, and the subset of items having the highest correlations was then selected as defining the modern man for the given country. Using this "coherence" method to construct the national modernity scales, we might have found a totally different set of items defining the syndrome of modernity in each of our six national samples. Indeed, if we used only the twenty items ranking highest in the item-to-scale correlations for each country, we could theoretically have come out with six totally different syndromes, one for each country, no one overlapping in the least with any other. The actual outcome of the analysis was totally different. The probability that even one item would come out in the top fifty in all six countries is approximately five in a thousand. We actually bad ten items which were in the top fifty in all six countries, sixteen more in the top fifty in five countries, thirteen more which were in this set in four of the six countries. The probability that the same thirty-nine item would by chance be in the top fifty in four of the six countries is so infinitesimal as to make our results notable indeed.

This means that what defines man as modern in one country also defines him as modern in another. It argues for the actual psychic unity of man-kind in a structural sense and the potential psychic unity of manking in the factual sense. In speaking of the unity of mankind in terms of psychic structure, I mean that the nature of the human personality, its inner "rules" of organization, is evidently basically similar everywhere. That is, the association of the elements or components of personality do not—and I think in substantial degree *cannot*—vary randomly or even relatively freely. There is evidently a system of inner, or what might be called structural, constraints in the organization of the human personality which increase the probability that those individuals—whatever their culture—who have certain personality traits will also more likely have others which "go with" some particular basic personality system. So far as the future is concerned, moreover, I believe that this structural unity provides the essential basis for greater factual psychic unity of mankind. Such a factual unity, not merely of structure but of *content*, can be attained insofar as the forces which tend to shape men in syndromes such as that defining the modern man become more widely and uniformly diffused throughout the world. This point requires that we consider the second issue to which our research addressed itself.

2. What are the Influences Which Make a Man Modern? Can any Significant Changes be Brought About in Men who are Already Past the Formative Early Years and have Already Reached Adulthood as Relatively Traditional Men?

Education has often been identified as perhaps the most important of the influences moving men away from traditionalism toward modernity in developing countries. Our evidence does not challenge this well-established conclusion. Both in zero-order correlations[8] and in the more complex multivariate regression analysis, the amount of formal schooling a man has had emerges as the single most powerful variable in determining his score on our measures. On the average, for every additional year a man spent in school he gains somewhere between two and three additional points on a scale of modernity scored from zero to 100.

Our modernity test is not mainly a test of what is usually learned in school, such as geography or arithmetic but is rather a test of attitudes and values touching on basic aspects of a man's orientation to nature, to time, to fate, to politics, to women, and to God. If attending school brings about such substantial changes in these fundamental personal orientations, the school must be teaching a good deal more than is apparent in its syllabus on reading, writing, arithmetic, and even geography. The school is evidently also an important training ground for inclucating values. It teaches ways of orienting oneself toward others, and of conducting oneself, which could have important bearing on the performance of one's adult roles in the structure of modern society. These effects of the school, I believe reside not maialy in its formal, explicit, self-conscious pedagogic activity, but rather are inherent in the school as an *organization.* The modernizing effects follow not from the school's curriculum, but rather from its informal, implicit, and often unconscious programme for dealing with its young charges.[9] The properties of the rational organization as a hidden pursuader—or, as I prefer to put it, as a silent and unobserved teacher—become most apparent when we consider the role of occupational experience in shaping the modern man.

We selected work in factories as the special focus of our attention in seeking to assess the effects of occupational experience in reshaping individuals according to the model of the modern man. Just as we view the school as communicating lessons beyond reading and arithmetic, so we thought of the factory as training men in more than the minimal lessons of technology and the skills necessary to industrial production. We conceived of the factory as an organization serving as a general school in attitudes, values, and ways of behaving which are more adaptive for life in a modern society. We reasoned that work in a factory should increase a man's sense of efficacy, make him less fearful of innovation, and impress on him the value of education as a general qualification for competence and advancement. Furthermore, we assumed that in subtle ways work in a factory might even deepen a man's mastery of arithmetic and broaden his knowledge of geography without the benefit of the formal lessons usually presented in the classroom. Indeed, the slogan for our project became, "The factory can be a school—a school for modernization."

Although our most sanguine hopes for the educational effects of the factory were not wholly fulfilled, the nature of a man's occupational experience does emerge as one of the strongest of the many types of variables we tested and is a quite respectable competitor to education in explaining a person's modernity. The correlation between time spent in factories and individual modernization scores is generally about 0.20.[10] With the effects of education controlled, the factory workers generally score eight to ten points higher on the modernization scale than do the cultivators.[11] There is little reason to interpret this difference as due to selection effects since separate controls show that new workers are not self—or preselected from the village on grounds of already being "modern" in personality or attitude. Nevertheless, we can apply a really stringent test by making or comparisons exclusively within the industrial labour force, pitting men with few years of industrial experience against those with many, for example, five or more. When this is done, factory experience continues to show a substantial impact on individual modernization,the gain generally being about one point per year on the overall measure of modernization (O.M.).

It is notable that even when we restrict ourselves to tests of verbal fluency and to tests of georgraphical and political information, the more experienced workers show comparable advantages over the less experienced. To choose but one of many available examples, in Chile among men of rural origin and low education (one to five years)—and therefore suffering a double disadvantage in background—the proportion who could correctly locate Moscow as being the Soviet Russian capital rose from a mere 8 per cent among the newly recruited industrial workers to 39 per cent among those with middle experience and to 52 per cent among the men who had eight years or more in the factory. Even among those with the double advantage of higher education (six to seven years) and urban origins, the proportion correctly identifying. Moscow decidedly rose along with increasing industrial experience, the percentages being 68, 81, and 92 for the three levels of industrial experience, respectively. Summary evidence from all six countries is presented in Table 4.1. It should be clear from these data that the factory is serving as a school even in those subjects generally considered the exclusive preserve of the classroom.[12]

To cite these modernizing effects of the factory is not to minimize the greater absolute impact of schooling. Using a gross occupational categorization which pits cultivators against industrial workers, we find that the classroom still leads the workshop as a school of modernization in the ratio of 3:2. Using the stricter test which utilizes factory workers only, grouped by length of industrial experience, it turns out that every additional year in school produces three times as much increment in one's modernization score as does a year in the factory, that is, the ratio goes to 3:1. The school seems clearly to be the more efficient training ground for individual modernization. Nevertheless, we should keep in mind that the school has the pupil full time, and it produces no incidental by-products other than its pupils. By contrast, the main business of the factory is to manufacture goods, and the changes it brings about in men—not insubstantial, as we have seen—are produced at virtually zero marginal cost. These personality changes in men are therefore a kind of windfall profit to a society undergoing the modernization process. Indeed, on this basis we may quite legitimately reverse the thrust of the argument, no longer asking why the school does so much better than the factory, but rather demanding to know why the school, with its full time control over the pupil's formal learning, does not perform a lot *better* than it does relative to the factory.

Our experience with the factory enables us to answer the secondary question posed for this section. Since men generally enter the factory as more or less mature adults, the effects observed to follow upon work in it clearly are later socialization effects. Our results indicate that substantial changes can be made in a man's personality or character, at least in the sense of attitudes, values, and basic orientations, long after what are usually considered the most important formative years. The experience of factory work is, of course, not the only form which this late socialization takes. It may come in

TABLE 4.1

Percentage of Industrial Workers Among Low[a] Educated Giving Correct Answers on Information Tests (By Country and Months of Factory Experience)

Question	*Country and Average Months Experience*					
	Argentina		*Chile*		*India*	
	3	90	2	96	2	72
Identify electrical apparatus[b]	37	63*	33	62***	44	76***
Identify movie camera	60	69*	6	8	29	51**
Cite 3 or more city problems	5	18	15	32***	0	1
Identify international leader[c]	26	67**	47	85***	1	31***
Identify local leader	33	51	27	81***	15	52***
Identify Moscow	36	60*	17	67***	1	16***
Name 3 or more newspapers[d]	12	21	81	92	6	28**
Approximate *N* cases	40	70	90	130	75	130

Question	Country and Average Months Experience					
	Israel		Nigeria		East Pakistan	
	3	84	3	48	1	48
Identify electrical apparatus[a]	80	88	91	91	50	70*°
Identify movie camera	84	88	68	70	9	37***
Cite 3 or more city problems	24	25	30	22	52	52*
Identify international leader[c]	80	81	11	17	2	26**
Identify local leader	67	92	70	70	52	79*
Identify Moscow	86	86	11	17	2	2
Name 3 or more newspapers[d]	75	61	81	91	20	44**
Approximate *N* cases	25	100	60	25	65	120

*t-test score significant at the .05 level.

**Significance at the .01 level.

***Significance at the .001 level or better.

°Data for high education groups on these seven questions in each country provide an additional 42 tests of which 33 were in accord with the conclusion that men with more factory experience score higher on information tests, 7 were inconclusive, and 2 contradictory.

[a]In Pakistan, India, and Nigeria a picture of a radio was shown; in Argentina, Chile, and Israel, a picture of a tape recorder was used instead.

[b]Respondents were asked to identify Lyndon Johnson in Chile, Argentina, and Israel; John F. Kennedy in Pakistan and India; Charles de Gaulle in Nigeria.

[c]In Argentina, "name books" was substituted for "name newspapers."

TABLE 4.2

Variance in Scores of Individual Modernization (OM-3) Accounted for by Early and Late Socialization Influences in Six Developing Countries

Per Cent

Variable	*Argentina*	*Chile*	*India*	*Israel*	*Nigeria*	*Pakistan*
Early Socialization	28.8	26.0	52.4	22.1	23.0	22.2
Late Socialization	31.6	34.4	31.4	22.4	28.2	28.3

the form of travel or migration, by exposure to the media of mass communication, or through later life in the city for men who grew up in the countryside.[13] We therefore combined our explanatory variables into two main sets, one representing *early* socialization experience—as in formal schooling—and the other reflecting late socialization experiences—as in one's adult occupation. We may observe (from Table 4.2) that the late socialization experiences stake out a very respectable place for themselves in the competition to account for the observed variance in individual modernization scores.[14] In five countries the set of late socialization variables explained as much or more of the variance in modernization scores as did the combined early socialization variables, each set explaining between one-fourth and one-third of the variance.

In India the early socialization variables were decidedly more powerful-accounting for 52 per cent as against 31 per cent of the variance explained by the late socialization variables. But in absolute terms, the late experiences are still doing very well.[15] All in all, we take this to be impressive evidence for the possibility of bringing about substantial and extensive changes in the postadolescent personality as a result of socialization in adult roles.

3. Are there any Behavioural Consequences Arising from the attitudinal Modernization of the Individual? Do Modern Men act Differently from the Traditional man?

Many people who hear of our research into individual modernization respond to it by acknowledging that we may have discovered what modern man *says*, but they are more interested in knowing what he *does*. This view overlooks the fact, that taking a stand on a value question is also an action, and one which is often a very significant one for the respondent.[16] Our critics' comment also tends implicitly to underestimate the importance of a climate of expressed opinion as an influence on the action of others. And it probably assumes too arbitrarily that men use speech mainly to mislead rather than to express their true intentions. Nevertheless, the question is a legitimate one, and we addressed ourselves to it in our research. Although this part of our analysis is least advanced, we can offer some tentative conclusions on the basis of preliminary analysis.

We have the definite impression that the men we delineate as modern not only *talk* differently, they act differently. To explore this relationship we constructed a scale of modernization based exclusively on attitudinal questions, rigorously excluding those dealing with action rather than belief or feeling.[17] This measure of attitudinal modernity we then related to the behavioural measures in our survey. In all six countries we found action intimately related to attitude. At any given educational level, the man who was rated as modern on the attitudinal measure was also more likely to have joined voluntary organizations, to receive news from newspapers every day, to have talked to or written to an official about some public issue, and to have discussed politics with his wife. In many cases the proportion who claimed to have taken those actions was twice and even three times greater among those at the top as compared with those at the bottom of the scale of attitudinal modernity. Table 4.3 presents the relevant evidence. We should note, furthermore, that the items included in Table 4.3 are illustrative of a larger gruop of about thirty individual questions and a dozen scales selected on theoretical grounds as appropriate tests of the relation between expressed attitudes and reported behaviour. The items used for illustration were not arbitrarily selected as the only ones supporting our assumptions.[18]

The particular behaviours we cited above are all "self-reported." The question inevitably arises as to whether then we are not merely testing attitudinaly consistency – or merely consistency in response—rather than any strict correspondence between modernity of *attitude* and modernity of *behaviour*. The answer is partly given by considering the relation of attitudinal modernity to our several tests of information. These questions did not deal with "mere" attitudes, but obliged the respondent to prove objectively whether he really knew something. Quite consistently the men who were more modern on the attitude measures validated their status as modern men by more often correctly identifying a movie camera, naming the office held by Nehru, and locating the city of Moscow. Men with the same education but with unequal modernity scores performed very differently on these tests, with those more modern in attitude scoring high on the tests of information two or more times as often as those classified as traditional in attitude. The details are summarized in the lower part of Table 4.3, which presents summary scale results.

We conducted a further and more exact check on the extent to which self-reported behaviour is fact rather than fantasy by comparing what men claimed to do with objective tests of their actual performance. For example, we asked everyone whether or not he could read. Individuals certainly might have been tempted to exaggerate their qualifications. But later in the interview we administered a simple literacy test, asking our respondents to read a few lines from local newspaper stories we had graded for difficulty. In most settings less than 1 per cent of the men who had claimed they could read failed the literacy lest. They proved objectively to have been accurately and honestly reporting their reading ability. Similarly, men who claimed to use the nass media regularly were—as they should have been—better able to correctly identify individuals and places figuring prominently in world news. In Nigeria, for example, among experienced workers of low education, the proportion who could correctly identify de Gaulle as the president of the French Republic was 57 per cent among those who claimed to pay only modest attention to the mass media, 83 per cent among those who asserted they listened or read more often, and 93 per cent among those who claimed to read a newspaper or listen to the radio almost every day. Many additional examples which test the internal consistency of attitude and behaviour are summarized in Table 4.4.[19] Clearly, the men who claim to have the attributes we score as modern give a better account of themselves on objective tests of performance. We may conclude not only that

TABLE 4.3

Percentage of High Educated Engaging in Various Forms of Modern Behaviour (by Country and Modernity Score)

Form or Behaviour	*Country and Modernity Score*[b]					
	Argentina		*Chile*		*India*	
	Low	*High*	*Low*	*High*	*Low*	*High*
Joined 2 or more organizations	26	48	50	61	32	31
Voted often	54	54	44	57	60	65
Talked politics with wife	40	57*	29	61***	74	80
Contacted official adout public issue	2	9	4	17**	20	26
Read newspapers daily	40	77***	31	53**	32	61**
High on geographic information scale	44	78***	23	60***	20	51***
High on political information scale	22	56***	18	37***	22	65***
High on consumer information scale	10	21**	7	39***	67	94*
High on opposites test	50	76	36	63***	59	86***
Approximate N cases.+	50	150	60	160	55	115

From or Behavior	Country and Modernity Score[b]					
	Israel		Nigeria		East Pakistan	
	Low	*High*	*Low*	*High*	*Low*	*High*
Joined 2 or more organizarions	2	6	86	97	0	6
Voted often	76	86				
Talked politics with wife	46	72**	50	65	65	83*
Contacted official about public issue	17	27	11	21	5	15
Read newspapers daily	36	81	63	84***	35	42
High on geographic information scale	29	75***	7	48***	9	53*
High of political information scale	36	72***	20	48***	7	39**
High on consumer information scale	29	53**	84	89	23	52***
High on opposites test	31	57***	59	71	47	78***
Approvimate N cases.+	40	110	60	120	45	125

*t-test based on the extremes of the continuum on each from of behaviour singnificant at the .05 level.

**Significance at the .01 level.

***Significance at the .001 level or better. All other t-tests of the relation were below the .01 level.

+In each country the total sample was divided at the median into a "high" and "low" educated group. The average number of years of education for the high group was: Argentina: 7.6; Chile: 6.6; India: 10.2; Lsrael: 8.6; and Pakistan: 4.8.

[b]The range of Overall Modernity Scores was split in to "low"—aottom 25 per cent "middle"—middle 50 per cent, and "high" —top 25 per cent for each country's *entire* sample. Modernity scores are highly correlated with education. Since in this table only the high educated are respresented, more men fall into the category of those with high as against low modernity scores.

[c]Ns are approximate due to the disqualification of part of the sample on certain questions, *e.g.*, those legally under age could not be expected to "vote often."

TABLE 4.4

Per cent[a] Among Low Educated[b] Whose Performance on a Test of Behaviour Accords With Their Oral Claim (By Claim and Country)

Objective Behaviour (%) and Claim	*Country*					
	Argentina	*Chile*	*India*	*Israel*	*Nigeria*	*East Pakistan*
Naming 3 newspapers among those who claim to real papers:						
Rarely/Never	*	73[d] (356)	13 (582)	68 (28)	59 (71)	38
		***	***		***	
Daily		98 (85)	60 (63)	90 (119)	85 (152)	45
Correctly identifying international leader among those claiming mainly interested in:						
Other news	43 (299)	59 (414)	8 (668)	79 (216)	7 (276)	4 (459)
	**					
World news	73 (30)	76 (29)	12 (26)	84 (68)	8 (73)	10 (10)

Correctly identifying international leader who claim on total information media exposure they are:												
Low	14 (51)	***	45 (196)	***	1 (71)	***	73 (45)		4 (78)	*	0 (85)	**
High	79 (29)		79 (76)		18 (11)		84 (38)		17 (18)		10 (40)	

* .50 level of significance reached In t-tests of the difference in the proportion manifesting a given behaviour in the case of those falling at the extremes of the continuum on each "claim."

** .01 level of significance.

*** .001 level of significance.

[a] Percentages are a proportion of the cells' base N who manifested a given behaviour. These cell Ns represent all those of low education who made the indicated behavioural claim, *e.g.*, claimed to read a newspaper daily.

[b] The average number of years of education by country was Argentina: Chile: 3.7: India: 1.0; Israel: 5.1; Nigeria: 6.2; and Pakistan: 2.

[c] Data unavailable for country.

[d] Includes "a few times a week" in "rarely or never"category.

modern is as modern does, but also that modern does as modern *speaks*.

4. Is the Consequence of the Individual Modernization Inevitably Personal Disorganization and Psychic Strain; or Can Men Go Through This Process of Rapid Sociocultural Change Without Deleterious Consequences

Few ideas have been more popular among the social philosophers of the nineteenth and twentieth centuries than the belief that industrialization is a kind of plague which disrupts social organization. destroys cultural cohesion, and uniformly produces personal demoralization and even disintegration. Much the same idea has been expressed by many anthropologists who fear—and often have witnessed—the destruction of indigenous cultures under the massive impact of their contact with the colossus represented by the European-based colonial empires. But neither the establishment of European industry in the nineteenth century, nor the culture crisis of small preliterate peoples over-whelmed by the tidal wave of colonial expansion may be adequate models for understanding the personal effects of industrialization and urbanization in developing nations.

To test the impact on personal adjustment resulting from contact with modernizing influences in our six developing countries, we administered the Psychosomatic Symptoms Test as part of our regular questionnaire. This test is widely acknowledged to be the best available instrument for cross-cultural assessment of psychic stress.[20] Using groups carefully matched on all other variables, we successively tested the effect of education, migration from the country-side to the city, factory employment, urban residence, and contact with the mass media as these modernizing experiences might affect scores on the Psychosomatic Symptoms Test. No one of these presumably deleterious influences consistently produced statistically significant evidence of psychic stress as judged by the test. Those who moved to the city as against those who continued in the village, those with many years as compared to those with few years of experience in the factory, those with much contact with the mass media as against those with little exposure to radio, newspaper, and movies, show about the same number of psychosomatic symptoms.

In each of six countries, we tested fourteen different matched groups, comparing those who migrated with those who did not; men with more years in the factory with those with fewer, etc. Because some of these matches did not apply in certain countries, we were left with seventy-four more or less independent tests of the proposition that being more exposed to the experiences identified with the process of modernization produces more psychosomatic symptoms. Disregarding the size of the difference and considering only the sign of the difference and considering only the correlation between exposure to modernization and psychosomatic symptoms as (+) or (—), it turns out that in thirty-four instances the results are in accord with the theory that modernization is psychologically upsetting, but in forty other matches the results are opposed to the theory. Very few of the differences in either direction, furthermore, were statistically significant. Indeed, the frequency of such statistically significant correlations was about what you would expect by chance. Of these significant differences, furthermore, only two supported the hypothesis while two contradicted it. This again suggests that only chance is at work here. We must conclude, therefore, that the theory which identifies contact with modernizing institutions and geographical and social mobility was certainly deleterious to psychic adjustment is not supported by the evidence. Indeed, it is cast in serious doubt. Whatever is producing the symptoms—and the test does everywhere yield a wide range of scores—it is something other than differential contact with the sources of modernization which is responsible.

Life does exact its toll. Those who have been long in the city and in industry but who have failed to rise in skill and earnings are somewhat more distressed. But this outcome can hardly be charged to the deleterious effects of contact with the modern world. Perhaps if we had studied the unemployed who came to the city with high hopes but failed to find work, we might have found them to have more psychosomatic symptoms. If we were faced with this finding, however, it would still be questionable whether the observed condition should be attributed to the effects of modernization. The fault would seem to lie equally in the inability of traditional agriculture to provide men with economic sustenance sufficient to hold them on the land.

We conclude, then, that modernizing institutions, *per se*, do not lead to greater psychic stress. We leave open the question whether the process of societal modernization in general increases social disorganization and then increases psychic tension for those experiencing such disorganization. But we are quite ready to affirm that extensive contact with the institutions introduced by modernization—such as the school, the city, the factory, and the mass media--is not in itself conducive to greater psychic stress.

Men change their societies. But the new social structures they have devised may in turn shape the men who live within the new social order. The idea that social structures influence the personal qualities of those who participate in them is, of course, as old as social science and may be found in the writings of the earliest social philosophers. Its most dramatic expression, relevant to us, was in the work of Marx, who enunciated the principle that men's consciousness is merely a reflection of their relation to the system of ownership of the means of production. The rigidity of Marx's determinism, and the counterdetermination of many people to preserve an image of man's spiritual independence and of the personal autonomy and integrity of the individual, generated profound resistance to these ideas. The idea that ownership or nonownerships of the means of production determines consciousness is today not very compelling. To focus on ownership, however, is to concentrate on the impact of macrostructural forces in shaping men's attitudes and values at the expense of studying the significance of microstructural factors. Yet it may be that these microstructural features, such as are embedded in the locale and the nature of work, are prime sources of influences on men's attitudes and behaviour.

In reviewing the results of our research on modernization, one must be struck by the exceptional stability with which variables such as education, factory experience, and urbanism maintain the absolute and relative strength of their impact on individual modernization despite the great variation in the culture of the men undergoing the experience and in the levels of development characterizing the countries in which they live.[21] This is not to deny the ability of the macrostructural elements of the social order to exert a determining influence on men's life condition and their response to it. But such macrostructural forces can account for only one part of the variance in individual social behaviour, a part, whose relative weight we have not yet measured with the required precision. When we attain that precision we may find some confirmation of popular theories, but we are also certain to discover some of them to be contradicted by the data—just as we have in our study of microstructural factors. The resolution of the competition between these two theoretical perspectives cannot be attained by rhetoric. It requires systematic measurement and the confrontation of facts however far they are marshalled in the service of ideas. The facts *we* have gathered leave *us* in no doubt that microstructural forces have great power to shape attitudes, values, and behaviour in regular ways at standard or constant rates within a wide variety of macro-structural settings.

REFERENCES

1. This paper was presented at the Dallas meeting of the American Association for the Advancement of Science in the section on "Comparative Sociology and Contemporary Social Issues," December 29, 1968. My chief collaborators from the early days of the project were Howard Schuman and Edward Ryan, who served,

respectively, as field directors for Pakistan and Nigeria, and David H. Smith, who was my assistant in Chile and later was assistant director of the project in Cambridge. The field work and later analysis were greatly facilitated by the work of our local collaborators in all six of the countries. We owe particular debt to Juan Cesar and Carlotta Garcia, Perla Gibaja, and Amar Singh who were field directors for Chile, Argentina, and India, respectively, and to Olatude Oloko who was assistant field director in Nigeria. In its different aspects, stages, and settings, the research has been supported by the Rockefeller Foundation, the Ford Foundation, the National Science Foundation, and the National Institute of Mental Health. The Cultural Affairs Division of the Department of State provided local currencies to support our field work in India, Isreal, and Pakistan, and the Office of Scientific Research of the U.S. Air Force supported technical exploration in problems of translation and computer analysis undertaken in Cambridge. All these organizations gave their support through the Center for International Affairs of Harvard University, which is the sponsor and institutional home of our project on the social and cultural aspects of economic development.

2. Some sixty-eight of the questions are listed, in abbreviated form, in Table 4.1 of Smith and Inkeles 1966. A complete copy of the questionnaire may be obtained by ordering Document 9133 from the Chief, Auxiliary Publication Project, Photoduplication Service, Library of Congress, Washington, D.C. remitting $13.50 for microoim or $117.50 for photocopies.

2-a J.A. Kahl. *The Measurement of Modernization, A Study of Values in Brazil and Mexico*, Austin and London: University of Texas Press; 1968; J.L.M. Dawson, "Traditional versus Western Attitudes in Africa: The Construction, Validation and Application of a Measuring Device", *British Journal of Social and Clinical Psychology*, 6, 2 (1967), pp. 81-96; L.W. Doob, "Scales for Assaying Psychological Modernization in Africa", *Public Opinion Quarterly*, 31 (1967), pp. 414-21.

3. This model has been sketched in a preliminary way in Alex Inkeles, "The Modernization of Man", in *Modernization*, edited by M. Weiner, New York: Basic Books, 1966. A fuller account is presented in Alex Inkeles, "A Model of the Modern Man", in *Cross-Cultural Research in Developing Areas*, edited by William A. Faunce and Herbert Garfinkel, East Lansing, Mich.: Social Science Research Bureau and New York: Free Press, Forthcoming.

3-a David H. Smith and Alex Inkeles, "The OM Scale: A Comparative Socio-Psychological Measure of Individual Modernity", *Sociometry*, 29 (1966), pp. 353-77.

4. Reference is to the reliabilities of the long form of the scale (OM-2) containing 159 items. Reliabilities for some of the various short forms were sometimes lower but were generally in the same range. *Ibid.*, 367.

5. On the basis of our experience with the longer versions of the questionnaire, we have been able to devise several short forms which permit rapid identification of the more modern and more traditional men in any population. Details on the construction aud content of these short forms are given in *Ibid.* One of these short forms (OM-12) which has proved a highly reliable instrument is currently being used in more than twenty pure—and applied-research programmes in over a dozen developing countries.

6. Of course, when you use a scale score to designate a "type" of man, the number of men who fit your typology depends entirely on your decision as to a cutting point on both the items and on the scale as a whole. For example, in one form of our modernity scale (IM-6) a representative subset of thirty-three items is scored so that only by affirming the most decidedly modern position at the end of the theoretical continuum of alternative answers does a man get a point toward his modernity score. On this strict test, getting as many as half the answers "right" would qualify 37 per cent of our Nigerian sample as "modern". If we set a higher standard, and reserve the term modern for men who get two-thirds or more of the answers "right", then only 6 per cent qualify. Raising the standard still higher to require that a man get three-fourths or more of the answers "correct" reduces the pool of modern men to 2 per cent of the sample. The comparable proportions qualifying as modern by this standard in our Pakistani sample are much lower, being 14 per cent, 2 per cent, and 0 per cent respectively. Changing the scoring standard for the individual questions would, obviously, also affect the proportions classified as modern.

7. These included all questions which in our opinion measured attitudes and could be unambiguously scored as having a "modern" and a "traditional" answer. Queries which did not meet these criteria were excluded from consideration. This meant mainly background questions, information-testing items, behavioral Measures, adjustment measures, and the like. For details see *ibid.*

8. The correlation (Pearsonian) between education and the overall measure of modernization ranges from 0.34 in Pakistan to 0.65 in India. The size of these coefficients is substantially affected by the educational "spread" in each sample. That spread is largest in India, with the cases rather evenly distributed from zero to thirteen years of education.

9. In much of the current discussion of the effectiveness and ineffectiveness of our schools, this aspect of the school's impact has been generally neglected. For an important exception see R. Dreeben, *On what is Learned in School*, Reading, Mass.: Addison—Wesley, 1968.
10. However, in India it was only 0.08. We believe this to be not a condition peculiar to India, but to our industrial sample there. Everywhere else we sampled from fifty to more than 100 factories, including all types and sizes of industry, but in India our sample was limited to eleven factories, mostly large, and two of these were not truly industrial; they processed minerals.
11. Keep in mind that the test has a theoretical range from zero to 100, and an observed ronge in our samples almost as great. With samples of our size, differences so large are significant at well above he .01 level. This test of significant and many of the other statistics percented in this report require that one meet certain conditions, such as random sampling, which our data do not meet. Nevertheless, we present such statistics in order to provide a rough guide or standard of judgement, in the belief that to do so is preferable to leaving to reader without any criterion by which to evaluate one figure as against another. The reader must be cautioned, however, not to interpret any single statistic too literally. Conclusions should be drawn not from singe fiures but from the whole array of evidence across the six countries.
12. It will be noted that the pattern manifested in the other five countries is not show in Israel. There new workers are as well informed as the experienced. We attribute this not so much to the qualities of Israeli industry as to the nature of Israeli society. In that small, mobile, and urbanized environment, information tends to be rapidly and more or less evenly diffused throughout the nation and to all classes.
13. The distinctive effectiveness of each of these potentially modernizing experiences, and others, will be assessed in the general report of our project in preparation under the authorship of Alex Inkeles and David H. Smith, to be *titled Becoming Modern*.
14. In this regression analysis we utilized as the dependent variable a long form of the modernity scale OM—3, not as describe in Smith and Inkeles, *op. cit.* Using seven principal predictor variables selected on theoretical and empirical grounds, we obtained multiple correlation coefficients of from about .57 to .76 in our six countrics. We could thus account for between 32.5 per cent and 59.0 per cent of variance in the modernity scals scores. We than grouped the predictor variables in two sets. The set of early socialization variables included ethnicity, father's education, and own formal education. Late socialization variables included occupational type, consumer goods possessed (as a measure of standard of living),

a measure of mass media exposure, and age. Each set was then used alone to ascertain what portion of the variance it could explain, as indicated in Table 4.2. A discussion of the rationale for selecting these particular variables and grouping them so, as well as details of the linear multiple regression analysis, will be presented in a later publication by David H. Smith and Alex Inkeles.

15. An alternative approach to estimating the relative contribution of the two sets of variables is to consider the decrement in the total variance explained when either set is withdrawn from the total pool of predictors. When this was done, the late socialization variables again emerged as morepowerful everywhere except in India. The following set of figures presents first, the decrement in the total variance explained resulting from withdrawal of the late socialization variables from the total predictor pool: Argentina .127/.155; Chile .100/.184; India .276/.066; Israel .101/104; Nigeria .068/.120; East Pakistan .070/.131. The fact that these decrements are so much smaller than the proportion of variance explained by each set alone indicates that to some extent the sets overlap, and when one set is dropped the other "takes over" for it in explaining some part of the variance.

16. For example, it is an act of substantial civic courage for a young man in a traditional village to tell our interviewer he would be more inclined to follow the local coop leader than the village elders, or that he considers himself more a Nigerian that an Ife, or whatever is the local tribal basis of solidarity.

17. In the project identification system this scale is designated OM-1. It includes only seventy-nine items selected from the larger pool by a panel of expert judges on the grounds that (a) they dealt only with attitudes, not information, political orientation, or action, and (b) they clearly were appropriate to test the original theoretical conception of modernity as more or less "officially" defined by the project staff.

18. This assertion is supported by consideration of the relevant gamma statistics on the relationship of attitudinal modernity (OM scores) and information tests. For this purpose low- and high-education groups were tested separately (except in Pakistan), hence the number of gamma statistics obtained is twice the number of items used. The average gamma statistics shown below are based on three-part tables which included middle as well as low and high OM. Separate results are given for items and for scales, since the scales show the combined effects of groups of items and hence are not truly "independent" additional tests of the hypothesis under scrutiny.

Tests	*Country*					
	Argentina	*Chile*	*India*	*Israel*	*Nigeria*	*Pakistan*
Based on items:						
Average gamma	201	232	342	244	205	303
Number of tests	60	62	58	52	46	29
Average gamma	305	296	449	313	276	339
Number of tests	24	24	24	28	24	10

19. For lack of space, Table 4.4 shows the percentage whose behaviour validated their oral "claim" only in the case of those falling at the extremes of the continuum on each "claim," and the t-tests are based on these same extremes. To leave no doubt that this outeome was not a fortuitous result of considering only the extremes, we note the gamma statistics for the full cross-tabulations including all steps in both the oral claim and the behavioural test. The five tests of the relation between claim and behaviour applied in six countries yield a potential thirty tests, but some were inapplicable in certain instances. The procedure was repeated separately for the "low" and "high" educated, divided at the median in each country. For the low educated, where twenty-seven of the tests were applicable, the association of claim and behaviour was in the expected direction in all cases, and the gammas ranged from 0.011 to 0.877, with a mean of 0.351 and a median of 0.334. For the high educated, the hppothesis could be tested in twenty-three full cross-tabulations. All but two of the associations were in the expected direction, the gammas ranging from —0.123 to 0.690, and over this range the mean gamma was 0,309 and the median 0.276.

20. Variants of the test were used with the Yorubaas reported by Alexander H. Leightton, T.A. Lambo, C.G, Hughes, D.C. Leighton, J.M. Murphy, and D.B. Macklon, *Psychiatric Disorder among the Yoruba*, Ithaca, N.Y.: Cornell University Press, 1963, and the Zulu as reported by Norman A. Scotch and A.J. Geiger "An Index Symptom and Disease in Zulu Culture," *Human Organization*, 22, 4 (1963-64), pp. 301-77. Details on the form of the test as we used it and the results of our investigation were presented by Alex Inkeles and David Smith to the Eighth Congress of the International Anthropological Association at Tokyo-Kyoto in September 1968 under the title "The Fate of Personal Adjustment in the Process of Modernization," and will appear in the *International Journal of Comparative Sociology*, 1970.

21. This idea is more fully elaborated in Alex Inkeles, "Industrial Man: The Relation of Status, Experience and Value," *American Journal of Sociology*, 66 (1960), pp. 1-31.

5

SOCIAL REFORM THROUGH EDUCATION

I

STATUS OF HARIJANS

The word "Harijan" means 'a man of God'. God is a friend of the friendless, help of the helpless, saviour of the doomed and strength of the despised. Truly, this has been the perception, of the vast multitude of the 'Untouchables' whom Gandhiji started calling as *Harijans* out of sympathy for their poor lot. Earlier, these people were identified as *antyajas*, *panchmas*, *depressed classes* and *exterior castes*. They were kept outside the pale of the Hindu social order for thousands of years and were, therefore, considered outcastes. Presently, they are recognised as Scheduled Castes.

More than ninety million human beings toiling in a society, tilling fields, cleaning spoils, stitching shoes, weaving cloth. disposing carcasses, constructing houses, washing linen, catching fish, doing whatever requires the sweat of the brow, and earning the denial of placement in the social order as the reward. The men, who generated wealth were kept penniless; who constructed places were not allowed a place to live anywhere; who cleaned for hygienic living were defiled; who created arts were denied education. At the top of it, the deprivation was justified by socio-religious sanctions. The abhorrence was for them and not for their labour. Such a duality in the Hindu society was an accepted practice of social justice. Discrimination was dominant in the social structure. The hierarchy of status, power and prestige determined by birth in a particular caste was an accepted social norm for thousands of years as late as the middle of the nineteenth century.

The beginning of the process of modernisation in India, sometimes in the middle of the nineteenth century, shook the ageold social structure to its very foundation. The conservative traditions started dwindling. There were thrusts for social change. The reform movements brought some consciousness for ameliorating the lot of Harijans. Educating them came to be considered as a means of raising their status, both social and economic. Efforts were initiated to create opportunities for their education and employment.

It is over hundred years now since when planners and policy framers have been endeavouring to cause educational progress among the Harijan communities. The success throughout this period, however, has been partial. These people have been recognised as weaker sections in all matters concerning social and economic living. They also remain to be the hard core amongst the illiterates. Their educational achievements are considered less than satisfactory. There is a growing dissatisfaction amongst the planners, economists, political leadership and educationists about their poor pace of educational development. At times, tensions seem to grow as hopes are belied. Sometimes, provisions for their education and employment are created without much faith that these would really benefit the needy amongst them. Why should it be like that? Do these people still suffer from the social syndrome of caste apathies? If so, at what levels? In what respects? Are the schemes for their development irrelevant in the context of their social and occupational placement? What are the past experiences of working for their educational progress and how can these be utilised? What policies, strategies and models have been tried out earlier and to what success? Which of them still hold relevance? Can educational progress be caused without simultaneous social and economic progress? Such questions call for a study in retrospect with a view to planning for the prospective programmes. A search needs to be made into the ways in which education can be instrumental in creating social equalities, and if educational progress really matters in social elevation, whnt can be the modus operandi for achieving this? The search for answers to these questions forms the theme of the present work. The effort turns out to be highly rewarding.

The data presented here have largely been collected from the primary sources: the educational records of the Government of India, proceedings of the department of Home and Education, reports on the progress of education popularly known as quinquinnial reviews, reports of the different committees and commissions on education appointed by the central and provincial governments from time to time. Contemporary journals like 'The Harijan' carrying news of the voluntary efforts of the nationalists for the uplift of Harijans during the British period also constitute valuable treasurehouse of information for this purpose. The effort in educating the Harijans was almost a crusade for many a social reformers like Jotirao Phooley, Gandhi and Ambedkar. Studies into the biographies of such eminent personalities were considered indispensable to study their thinking and the way it influenced the educational developments. The approach to writing this book has been research based. Titles on historical research and doctoral theses having a bearing on Harijans, directly or indirectly, have been studied and quoted to augment information from the primary sources. The study has adopted a unique approach. Instead of chronological account, thematic analysis on various aspects of educating Harijans has been presented. This approach, sometimes, lands the presentation into some unavoidable repititions, but the quality of thematic analysis compensates the repitition adequately.

The book runs into nine chapters. The next two chapters contain a brief description of the *painful legacy* leading to social segregation of a sizable population in the country and how gradually untouchability showed its teeth during the course of time. How did social superiority-inferiority based on birth resulted in the abhorrence of a sizable population who were the same blood as others; how did the religious sanctions perpetuate orthodoxy, tyranny and victimisation; and what precipitated realisation by pricking the social conscience?

The advent of the British brought on the Indian soil a new living style. This was devoid of caste, less characterised with custom but imbued with materialistic pursuits as the life aspirations. New jobs and careers were created. Conversion of religion could now save the Harijans from subhuman treatment. Education could provide capability to get new type of jobs with security of service and ample leisure. New legislations aimed at dispossessing the caste panchayats of their rights to penalise on caste differentiation. Low meant justice. Equality meant equal consideration for all. The new developments were a welcome augury, Further two chapters describe the status, role and shape of education as an ameliorating agent. The political change was complemented by a social reform movement. Under that current of thought even religious practices were reviewed. There was an attempt to develop scientific rationalism as a basis of religious reform. The reform movement emerged precipitating social change. Education gained currency. It came to be considered as an instrument of social change, as a fulcrum to cross over from medieval to modernity, as a key to economic advancement, as a tool of developing enlightened citizenry, and as a process generating force for ushering in social equalities. There were attempts at educating Harijans. In a way, programme for their *redemption through education* was launched. In some situations, there were counter attempts for sabotaging the effort. There were legislations for overcoming these attempts. Demands for education were combined with generating social and political consciousness in the Harijans and about the Harijans. This paved way towards equality through education. But any education could not be a wholesome thing in their case. Education to be productive must be meaningful.

The educational scene was beset with a difficulty. The Harijans through interspersed with general population lived more in primitive style. Not only that these were poor, their lot was worse than even that of wild tribes. The wild ones could afford to look to the horizons, live like free birds, eat any way, do any way, and therefore, they had tremendous capacity to learn of their own from the environment, but in the case of the Harijans, learning had been made extinct by subjecting them to subhuman humiliations over generations. To vitalise it different models of education suited to their specific conditions and vocational needs were conceived. These attempts resulted in several innovations which have their own significance today. Some of these have even been instrumental in contributing to the national system of Basic education. *Meaningful education* outlines these efforts.

The social resistences having been weakened, poverty was a major impediment for formal education of Harijan children. Parental illiteracy, role of the child in the economic activities of the family and social customs like early marriage impeded fermentation of education in these people. Incentives were visualised to counter impediments. Ancilliary services were created to reduce educational costs on the parents and motivational strategies were planned for facilitating their education. In the first place, the attempt was to seek equal participation of Harijans. Further, the attempt was directed towards accelerating the pace of progress to bridge the educational gap between Harijan communities and general population. The chapter on *impediments and incentive* describes how did the society march towards the new goal by countering impediments and creating incentives.

The chapter on *quantitative trends* is the story of the progress of education of Harijans. It highlights the enrolments and achievements for a century beginning from a scratch.

There is an attempt to review educational progress at different levels after short intervals so as to find out what caused the ebb and tide in the exponsion of education among Harijans.

The Harijans are in focus today. They ought to be the first beneficiaries of the developmental schemes. They have been provided safeguards for educational and economic progress. Still they have miles to go. The educational effort for them is a continuing task. There have been a number of researches and investigations to assess the development of education in these people. Researches have also yielded data on the weak and strong points regarding educating Harijans. The present scene, though it clearly connotes that the task is unfinished, is quite promising. The past and present together point to one of the greatest characteristics of Harijans. Whatever gains accrued to them once in matters of educational progress were always consolidated for further education and progress. This alone kindles hope. The *vision for tomorrow* appears bright. They only need a helping hand and a sympathetic socioeconomic order.

II

QUEST FOR EQUALITY

Equality has for sometime past been a subject of great interest to the freedom loving world due to the growing popularity of concepts like nationalism, democracy, secularism, socialism and the French trio of *Liberty, Equality and Fraternity*. In most of the nations, the attempt is to undo social inequalities of various forms and degrees caused on the traditional grounds of sex, slavery, colour, and caste is discernible. The idea is to minimise discrimination between man and man in legal, political and socioeconomic spheres with a view to ushering in a humanistic era. Strangely, religion is being overlooked while planning for social change. But social inequalities in India have their roots in the caste basis of the Hindu society primarily and caste itself is the product of socioreligious developments. The caste structure has a psycho-philosophical character. It is transmitted through mythological fables and somehow holds fast on to the people. This process of communication leading to the continuance of an oral institution like the caste system in India has become older by three thousand years. There is no use ignoring it. It would be interesting to know it and then work out how to save the people hard hit by this painful social legacy.

Several theories have been propounded on the origin and evolution of caste. One such popular theory is that the institution of caste developed through the inner social changes and outer influences on the Indian society. In ancient period, *dravidians* were the inhabitants. There also lived the primitive tribes, nomads and forest dwellers. The advent of *aryans* raised problems—social and political, resulting into conflicts between the inland dwellers and the Aryans. Their appearances as the different racial stocks led to identifying people by their colour. This distinction was called *varnabheda* (colour difference). The *aryans* were considered as the civilized lot and the *dasyus* as the savage.

With the passage of time, four distinct classes, namely, the *brahmins*, the *kshtriyas*, the *vaishyas* and the *sudras* emerged as the social strata. The *brahmins* devoted themselves to learning, acquiring wisdom and following the liberal arts and sciences, the *kshtriyas* devoted themselves to the theory and practice of war and to whom the executive government of the people was entrusted. The *vaishyas* took to trade and other professions and the *shudras* were to serve and help the other three classes. Further, hierarchy in these groups was established.

When they made Man how did they divide it? What was its mouth, what its arms, what thighs and what feet? In the God politic *Brahmin* was like the head, *kshtriya* was like arms, *vaishya* was like thighs and *shudra* was considered as the feet. Instead of its social division horizontally, the grouping was made vertically stratified with the higher strata assuming a higher place.

The placement of an individual on the continuum was originally proposed in relation to talent rather than birth. According to the *Shankar Digvijay*, by birth all are *shudras*, by action men become *dvija* (twice born), by reading the *vedas* one becomes *vipra* and by gaining the knowledge of God one becomes *brahmana*.

Such a social practice might have continued for a long time since there are references to mobility across the social strata. In the *aitareya brahmana* (11-3-19), it is described that Kevasha Aitusha was a *shudra* and the son of a low woman but was greatly respected for his literary attainments and admitted to the class of the *rishis* (sages). The *chandoyapanished* mentions Jabola had no family name but came to be called as *satyathma* due to his learnings. Valmiki, the author of *ramayana*, was also a *shudra* by birth but earned the eminence of a *rishi*. Shankaracharya supports this view when he maintains that neither through colour nor through ancestors can the spirit worthy of a *brakmin* be generated.[1]

With the growing complexity of the Indian society, there must have arisen a need for the division of labour into many more areas. Consequent degeneration of the society might have brought in rigidities in vertical social mobility and fixed heredity as the basis of social placement. Watters[2] account of *Yuan Chwang's Travels* in India during the ancient period describes the prevalence of heredity as a basis of social stratification and also the presence of caste system in the country. Sharma,[3] analysing the principal factors interplaying in the social life in Northern India between the period 600 A.D. to 1000 A.D., has identified the factors leading to the heredity based social stratification. The factors refer to the stress on purity of blood in a society where the contacts between Aryan and Non-Aryan races were becoming frequent leading to intermarriages between the members of different castes and resistance to the acceptance of their progeny in the same castes, influx of foreign tribes and their attempts for absorption in the native culture, and also increase in the number of occupations.

The Indian society had agriculture as its main stay. As such, the social mobility had always been quite low. The permanent settlements might have further encouraged factors leading to social segregation in the interest of internal security of the settlers. Rigid adherence to the prevailing practices ultimately created traditions and taboos, of which, the practice of untouchability was an offshoot.

In the process of work, both the head and the hands are involved. When the work demands obtaining and processing of raw materials including disposal of waste, it naturally leads to involvement in the so-called unclean situations. In primitive occupations, most of the work was done manually. It is but natural that the pursuance of occupations connected with the processing of leather or metals or even working with clay would result in soiling of hands. Even though soiling is different to defiling, it was not to be so. The general class of *shudras* took to various occupations some of which were more unclean than others. The *sikandapurana* contains an account of the different occupations that were followed by the *shudras*, The occupations, namely, *nartaka*, *kasthakara*, *prajapati*, *vardhika*, *citraka*, *sutraka*, *rajaka*, *gacchaka*, *tantukaru*, *caknika*, *carmakara*, *sunika*, *shavanika*, *kaulkika*, *hatsyachataka*, *annamika* and *chandala* were termed as *prakrtis*, implied talent or disposition for undertaking a particular art, craft or the type of labour. These were further subdivided into three categories as *uttama*, *adhama* and *antyaja*, their numbers being six, five and seven respectively. The *antyaja* were the occupations followed by *washermen*, *leather workers*, *natas*, *varadas*, *kaivaitas*, *medas* and *bhillas*.[4] Initially, the *antyaja* castes came to be regarded as belonging to the lowest order. In course of time, they were separated from the first two categories of *shudras* and identified as *untouchables*. Atri and Yama have identified *antyajas* as: *washermen*, *shoe-makers*, *dancers*, *varadas*, *fishermen*, *medas*, *and bhilas*.[5]

Some indigenous groups of Indian natives, like the *seshayas*, *kirtas*, *pulindas*, who had for long lived in forestries but now came to stay with the heredity-based caste dwellings for their work also came to be regarded as the one belonging to lowly people. In their forest recesses, these people had plenty of freedom. But in the caste based social settlements, they were given the lowest status. During the course of time, they were also classed with *antyajas*.

Another group of people who came close to the heels of *antyajas*, and ultimately mingled were the *sankrin jatis*. According to the *smritis*, new castes came to be created due to *anuloma* and *pratiloma* marriages. *Anuloma* and *pratiloma* marriages were the then intercaste marriages. In an *anuloma* marriage, the husband belonged to a caste higher than that of his wife but in *pratiloma* marriage, the wife hailed from a caste higher than that of her husband. The offsprings of the intercaste married couples were outcasted from both the castes as a social resentment. Facing social isolation, they and their progeny added to the folds of untouchables.[6] For example, the *vyassmriti* describes three types of *chandalas* as the issues of unmarried girls: the children born of the parents of the same *gotra*, and the offsprings of a *shudra* father and a *brahmin* mother.

Yet another theory on the *antyajas* is that in ancient times the *brahmins* and *kshtriyas* in the North cooperated with each other treating the vast mass of *vaishyas* and *shudras* as inferior. But the *brahmins* and *kshtriyas* whose chief occupation used to be agriculture could not form a self-sufficient economic unit by themselves. The *vaishyas* gradually picked up wealth and a fair amount of culture and joined them.[7] The *trivarnic* society, thus formed, constituted the upper starta leaving the *shudras* outside the ambit. Amongst them the people who would cling to their own native culture and continued to resist, were condemned socially and isolated. These were driven out to live on the fringes of the settlements. The isolation led to their degraded position.

Al'Beruni in his account of travelling in India gives a description of the Harijan castes, then known as *antyajas*.[8] These people were regarded outside the pale of the caste order and were only recognised by their occupations. These people lived near the villages and towns inhabited by the upper strata but outside the settlements.

In ancient and medieval periods, there were guilds governing the occupations. Since there has been a proximity between caste and occupations, the guilds mattered for castes too. There is an account of guilds[9] of cultivators, traders, herdsmen, honey dealers, workers in wood, workers in metal, leather workers, workers fabricating hydraulic engines, bamboo workers, braziers, weavers, potters, oil millers, painters, corn dealers, garland and flower sellers, mariners, robbers, forest police, stone workers, ivory workers, jewellers, basket makers, dyers and painters, fishers, butchers. The different guilds prescribed the rules and regulations for their own occupational groups. The *antyajas* who constituted some of these guilds had their own rules and regulations within the frame work of the general order prescribed in the *dhramsutras*. These guilds were rendered nonfunctional in the latter part of the ninteenth century. The British administration dispossessed them of the powers to penalise their members.

Presently, things have changed beyond shape. All restrictions on modes and manners, occupations and segregation have been done away with legally. The once called *antyajas* are recognised as the weaker sections requiring special attention and deserving special opportunities. But in regard to pursuance of occupations, a majority of them still pursue traditional occupations most of which are the offshoots of the seven *prakrties* desceibed above. As Al'Beruni had rightly caught it, no doubt these people were identified as castes but they were more identifiable as occupational groups. It is easier to identify them by their economic activities even now.

India, being a multilingual country, the connotations for different occupations are different in different languages. If the popular connotations are considered for Harijans and grouped together, the existing position with regard to different occupations pursued by the populous Harijan castes in different states and union territories would be as summarised in the following table.

The table does not include the landless labour, a large number of whom come from these castes. It would be seen from the table that most of the Harijan castes still pursue traditional occupations which are, by and large, unskilled and semiskilled. Most of these have not come under the impact of modernisation and the yield from these is quite low. The processing of raw materials is primitive and many a times unhygienic, with the result that members of the society who have to follow them for survival suffer from the stigma of uncleanliness with miserably low returns. This has been the prime reason for the unfortunate continuance of the painful legacy.

III

GOVERNMENT INTERVENTION

The plight of the Harijans would seem to be as old as the history of Hindu society, and has not undergone any striking change for their betterment, even with the impact of modernisation. It still persists, though the caste prejudices are practised in milder intensity as compared to the past. Untouchability has legally been abolished but there are time and again reports of atrocities on the Harijans. In fact, the residential pattern of the Harijans is still on the outskirts of the habitations; their vocational pursuits are still considered inferior; the food they eat is unsuited for proper growth; their educational progress is still slow. The sociocultural disabilities imposed upon them earlier have legally been removed but their traces are still perceptible in day to day living of the people, particularly in the rutal areas and more so in informal social situations.

The unfinished story of the suffering of Harijans is not old. They were forced to live a subhuman life till recently. They were debarred from drawing water from public wells, disallowed to stay in public inns, prohibited temple entry and denied

Harijan Castes and Occupations

Occupations	*Name of Castes*	*State/Union Territory where they live*
1	*2*	*3*
Leather workers	Baisaw, Bambhai, Bala, Chakkilayam, Chamar, Chandal, Dhor, Dehar, Holdar, Valhar, Mang, Pagodal, Samgar, Ramagar, Sarki.	Rajasthan, Gujarat, Karnataka, Maharashtra, Uttar Pradesh, Delhi, West Bengal, Tamilnadu, Pandicherry, Andhra Pradesh, Bihar, Orissa, Punjab, Haryana, Himachal Pradesh, Tripura, Jammu & Kashmir.
Weavers	Baiti, Balahi, Balchi, Bhuviar, Bind, Chaupal, Coidar, Ganda, Gands, Julaha, Kabirpanthi, Koli, Kori, Kuli, Loliyan, Mahara, Mahayavanshi, Malasale, Megh, Meghwal, Pan, Pane, Pankha, Pantanti, Pantratanti, Salvi, Venkar.	West Bengal, Madhya Pradesh, Maharashtra, Rajasthan, Uttar Pradesh, Delhi, Tamilnadu, Bihar, Orissa, Himachal Pradesh, Punjab, Andhra Pradesh, Gujrat, Karnataka, Dadar and Nagar Haveli Kerala, Jammu & Kashmir.
Fisheries	Bagapa, Begheti, Baghuti, Bewar, Kanda, Kandara, Kailbratha, Kest, Kayet, Mallah, Paravan, Patni, Pod. Poundra, Tiyar, Kaukani, Tier, Jalkeet.	West Bengal, Madhya Pradesh, Manipur, Tripura, Orissa, Delhi, Tamilnadu, Karnataka, Kerala, Assam.

Toddy tapping making and pig rearing etc.	Dhankia, Chuserei, Handi, Jogi, Pasi, Siyal.	Rajasthan, Orissa, Karnataka, Bihar, Gujarat, Maharashtra, Madhya Pradesh, Punjab, Uttar Pradesh, West Bengal, Himachal Pradesh, Delhi.
Basket, Mat and rope-making.	Bansaphod, Banspher, Bantar, Barahar, Barar Barwaha, Basod, Basor, Bind, Dome, Dom, Karenga, Koochband, Malayan, Mang Garaneha, Godagali, Mavilan, Mavakayana, Patiar, Beihar, Semman, Shenava, Sirkhiband, Godru, Kalradi.	Assam, Rajasthan, Madhya Pradesh, West Bengal, Bihar, Punjab, Himachal Pradesh, Jammu & Kashmir, Andhra Pradesh, Tamilnadu, Maharashtra, Karnataka, Orissa, Delhi, Kerala, Gujarat.
Weaving of cloth, Dyers and Printers.	Chimbe, Dhobi, Dheba, Mannam, Puthiraj, Vennan.	Himachal Pradesh, Assam, Bihar, Madhya Pradesh, Nagaland, Orissa, Rajasthan, Uttar Pradesh, West Bengal, Delhi, Manipur, Kerala, Tamilnadu.
Scavengers and Sweepers	Bhangi, Mehtar, Chandal, Chambher, Chehm, Chura, Doom, Looma, Damne, Halalkher, Hela, Majhabi.	Andhra Pradesh, Assam, Bihar, Gujarat, Jammu & Kashmir, Madhya Pradesh, Kerala, Tamilnadu, Maharashtra, Orissa, Punjab, Uttar Pradesh, Rajasthan, West Bengal, Himachal Pradesh, Karnataka, Tripura, Haryana.
Metal workers, Artisans and Ornament and Lack bangle makers.	Ghantar, Ghada, Ghantra, Laheri, Shilpkans, Sidhria, Sikligar.	Orissa, Uttar Pradesh, Punjab, Delhi, Himachal Pradesh.

(*Contd.*)

1	2	3
Fruit and Vegetable sellers and dealers of milk products	Gour, Khatik	Tripura, Madhya Pradesh, Maharashtra, Punjab, Rajasthan, Uttar Pradesh, West Bengal, Himachal Pradesh, Delhi.
Bone Collection and shoe-making.	Gavaria, Hapi, Nadia, Mochii, Munchi.	Rajasthan, Bihar, Gujarat, Orissa, Maharashtra, West Bengal, Uttar Pradesh, Karnataka.
Others (Manufacturers of liquors, gold washers, floating of timbers, spinners, catachumakers and masonary work etc.)	Dahole, Dula, Katia, Kharwar, Sunri, Silawant.	Himachal Pradesh, Madhya Pradesh, Maharashtra, Uttar Pradesh, West Bengal, Orissa.
Drummers, pottery, Preparing of quilt and vessel making.	Babgar, Dholi, Hira, Khumkhar, Laban.	Bihar, Rajasthan, Uttar Pradesh, West Bengal, Madhya Pradesh, Assam, Orissa.
Lime and Seashell.	Asgar, Mukri, Maniya, Velan.	Maharashtra, Gujarat, Karnataka, West Bengal, Kerala.
Carpenters, Ironsmiths, etc.	Sutrudhar, Agariya, Badhi, Nagalu, Dhogni, Sipi.	Assam, West Bengal, Uttar Pradesh, Madhya Pradesh, Tripura, Punjab.

educational facilities. In some places even their shadows were supposed to be polluting, let alone their touch. The imposition of the disabilities was due to the practice of observing ceremonial purity which was generally supported by some scriptures.

The parable of the birth of four *varnas* from the four different parts of God politic created the notion that since *shudras* were born from the feet of God, they were inferior beings. This apparently led to the imposition of certain social disabilities in the matter of company, food, marriage, educaton and other social get-togethers. These discriminations were prescribed in the form of salutations and greeting in the *dharamsutras*.

The idea that food touched by a *shudras* is defiled and cannot be taken by a *brahmin* was first expressed in the *dharamsutras*.[10] According to Apastamba, food touched by an impure *brahmin* belonging to higher caste becomes impure but not unfit for eating. But if it is brought by a *shudra*, it cannot be taken. It was viewed by Vashishta that if a *brahmin* did eat the food of a *shudra* he would be born either as a village pig or in the family of that *shudra*.

Differentiation was also created with regard to the political rights and privileges. It was prescribed that for slaying a *kshtriya*, the offender should be penalised to give one thousand cows, for slaying a *vaishya* to give one hundred cows, but for slaying a *shudra*, only ten cows were to be given. According to the law of Gautama, if a *brahmin* abused a *kshatriya* or a *vaishya*, he would have to pay a fine but if he abused a *shudra*, no fine had to be paid.[11] Apastamba provided that if a *shudra* abused a law-abiding Aryan, his tongue should be perforated. Both Apastamba and Gautama lay down that if in any maaner, say conversation, sitting, walking, a *shudra* assumes the position of a twice born *i.e.* he tries to imitate or equalise himself to a *brahmin*, *kshatriya*, or a *vaishya*, he should be flogged.

On the economic front, restrictions were imposed to impede the economic upliftment of the Harijans. The phrase that a person lived a hard life on a workman's wages commonly occurs in the *Jatakas*.[12] At one place, a workman bewails his lot in the words 'I get a masaka or half for my wages and can hardly support my mother'. Regarding the relationship that existed between the employer and the employee, it is laid down by Apastamba that if the servant in village gives up his work, he shall be given physical punishment. The same provision applied to the herdsmen who abandoned tending the cattle. There are references to the imposition of compulsory service by the artisans for day in a month by the king. The laws of inheritence also provided differential treatment and an inferior position to the issues of *shudras*. Accordingly, the issues of a *shudra* wife could inherit only one share while the issues of a *brahmin* wife could get four times as much. According to Baudhayana, a *shudra's* son could be regarded as a member of the family but not an heir.[13]

The *dharamsutras* also prescribed the way of living for the *shudras*.[14] Gautama provides that a *shudra* should use the shoes, umbrellas, garments and mats which are thrown away by the people of the higher *varnas*. He further adds that the leavings in food are meant for the *shudra* servant. Both Fahien and Heunsiang had noted that during their visits to India, the *chandalas* were required to strike a piece of wood as a warning of their approach while entering a city or bazaar so that the people might not be polluted by contact with them.[15] In some parts of the country, they were disallowed to enter a city or a common place after some hours of the afternoon lest their long shadows coming out of a westward sun pollute the higher castes. The socioeconomic prejudices reduced the suffering lot toa nonentity.

The prejudices against the Harijans were not merely confined to their socioeconomic life. They were extended to their education as well. As is well known, the tradition of education is very old in India. In the initial stages, education meant handing over the hymns, rituals and lores from father to son or some relatives within the same family. Each experienced priest, probably, taught his sons or nephews the ritual lore and hymns by word of mouth till it was committed to memory, and probably each family guarded the secrecy of its own sacred rituals. With the growth of setlements, the family system of education was broadened to include in its scope the clans and gradually the clans widened into caste groups. The institutions opened by the different caste groups tended to prepare for their own vocations. The *shudras* were not supposed to specialise in the knowledge and skills of the higher castes. And if some of them would attempt to do so, they were penalised. The story of Ekalavaya in *Mahabharta* reveals the fact that the educational competence in some of the talented individuals amongst the *shudras* only brought victimisation.[16] The Ekalavaya incident speaks of how the talent was first ignored and then destroyed, the implication being that if one was able to develop expertise on one's own merit, his skill would be destroyed due to prejudice.

Ritualistic as the Hindu society was, important events in the life of an individual were usually celebrated by the performance of ceremonies. An important ceremony for initiating an individual in education was the *upanayana sanskara*[17] (sacred thread ceremony). This ceremony marked the beginning not of literacy but of admission to the sacred and secret knowledge. The first step to education was taken by the performance of the *vidhyarambha sanskara* when the child was to worship the image of lord Ganesh in the presence of a teacher and the relatives before initiation into the alphabets. The *shudras* were not eligible for any such *sanskara*. They were not allowed to perform the *upanayana* ceremony which was the prerequisite for admission to education. They could only learn their hereditary occupations through the guilds of their family occupations.

The guilds, in fact, provided the main training for occupations in earlier days. Apart from some educational institutions providing formal education, the guilds provided for training to the respective caste groups in their vocations. In most of the cases, the system of guild education was domestic one.[18] The children had practically no choice in the matter and were brought up in the same trade as their parents. In the majority of occupations, knowledge of reading and writing would not be required for the purpose of mastering the craft, and therefore, literacy was not emphasised. In some occupations, certain Sanskrit verses were to be memorised. These verses signified traditional rules for a particular craft.

The worst hit were the Harijans who had always to do the left over. Gradually, occupational isolation led to social restrictions. Then social disabilities were generated. In some parts of the country, prejudice for them had grown so intense that even their shadows were to be avoided. In the matter of the use of wells, tanks and even rivers, the concept of pollution was created. Their entry into the temples was forbidden.[19] The Harijan sufferings continued unabated. The discrimination still persists. In many a place, they are sometimes subjected to atrocities. A slight provocation puts them in trouble. The atrocities are quite serious like criminal intimidation, arson, murder, rape, segregation and untouchability. Very often newepapers report like: 'Harijan youth axed to death'; 'Harijan woman raped and killed; 'Fire ball raid on Harijan huts'; 'Harijan girl molested'; 'Ears chopped off a Harijan youth'. Sometimes, even pathetic photographs carrying Harijan ladies with their young ones wailing near their gutted huts are flashed. The atrocities reach a climax when victims' relations are threatened even for the identification of theii dead ones. What a state of helplessness?

The complaints of harassment to Harijans can be classified broadly in seven categories, namely, those relating to service matters; untouchability and harassment; land and agriculture; education; housing; financial assistance and moral crimes. The incidents in different places could have their own local causes but a general factor permeating all through is the traditional prejudice that these communities have to remain dispossessed of material gains and confined to the lowest position.

The Commissioner for Scheduled Castes and Scheduled Tribes, Government of India, is empowered to enquire into atrocities on these sections and take necessary steps to safeguard them. The Commisioner's annual report is placed before the Parliament for a discussion and review of policies. In reports for lhe years 1975-79 and 1976-77, an analysis of atrocities is presented. It is found that policies like the distribution of land to the landless, revision of minimum wages, distribution of house sites, abolition of bonded labour lead to the creation of social tensions, particularly in the rural areas. The well-to-do upper strata from which the landlords generally come do not accept these measures easily. But instead of reacting to the Government, they retaliate on the beneficiaries. In their opinion such measures affect them in the ultimate, and therefore, they prefer to assert the existing state of affairs as feudal customs resulting in the harassment of and atrocities on the weaker sections, parsicularly the Harijans.

In addition to the atrocities, the Harijans suffer from the stigma of untouchability in some places. A constitutional safeguard created under Article 17 was the abolition of untouchability. Later on, various actions amounting to untouchability were made cognizable offence under the Untouchability (Offences) Act, 1955. But with all the legality, the social apathies continue. There appears to be a difference between the constitutional aims and the responsive behaviour of the people. Assuming that only an insignificant proportion of Harijan population, and that too where the hit is hard, would take a recourse to social justice, the number of complaints regarding untouchability have been mounting higher.[20] The figures in the following table indicate the trend.

From the above data for 22 years, it would be seen that out of 22,470 cases registered, 19,893 (90%) were taken to courts but only in 6,178 cases (31% of the challaned ones) offenders were convicted. The low number of convictions is due to the reason that a large number of case were either dismissed due to nonavailability of witnesses by the Harijans or compounded due to social pressures where threat coule be implicit.

Untouchability Cases Registered Under the Untouchability (Offences) Act

Year	*No. Reported*	*No. Challaned*	*Percentage*	*No. Convicted*	*Percentage*
1955	180	180	(100)	80	(44)
1956	693	599	(86)	149	(24)
1957	492	415	(84)	87	(21)
1958	550	477	(86)	127	(26)
1959	481	401	(83)	105	(26)
1960	509	438	(86)	89	(20)
1961	489	438	(89)	107	(24)
1962	389	338	(86)	17	(05)
1963	397	316	(80)	78	(25)
1964	484	425	(88)	196	(46)
1965	366	321	(88)	136	(42)
1966	488	447	(92)	199	(45)
1967	353	313	(89)	136	(43)
1968	214	184	(86)	35	(19)
1969	329	272	(83)	48	(18)
1970	364	291	(80)	50	(17)
1971	526	439	(83)	91	(21)
1972	1515	1416	(93)	631	(45)
1973	2649	2306	(87)	1207	(52)
1974	1908	1588	(83)	601	(38)
1975	3523	2588	(73)	936	(36)
1976*	7047	4530	(64)	1188	(26)

*(provisional)

Looking to the magnitude of the incidence of untouchability, the Untouchability (Offences) Act, 1955, was amended in 1976 as the Protection of Civil Rights Act, 1955. Presently, the amended Act makes untouchability offences both cognizable and noncompoundable. It prescribes higher punishments for such offences with a provision for a minimum punishment of both imprisonment and fine. Many types of actions have been brought within the purview of the law. These include direct or indirect preaching of untouchability or its justification on historical, philosophical, religious or traditional grounds, and compelling any person to do unclean jobs due to his ancestoral background. There is also a provision for summary trial in cases where the term of punishment does not exceed imprisonment for three months. Further, the state governments have been empowered to impose collective fines on the residents of any area who are involved in the commission or abetting of untouchability. An important feature of the present Act is that it is now imperative on the state governments to ensure that the rights accruing from the abolition of untouchability are available to and are availed of by the persons subjected to the disabilities arising out of untouchability. Provision of measures for implementing the law have been made and the central government have to lay report before the Parliament on the pursuance of the provisions of the new Act annually. It is hoped that this Act would be deterrent for those suffering from social prejudices and lead people to practise the principle of social equality.

With all the legal safeguards such as those described above, the pernicious effects of caste are still foisted at the individual level by the gospel of *karma* in the Hindu religion. *Karma* means the principle of cause and effect. In substance, the law of *karma* states that our good actions will have a good result and the bad ones would bring evil. But the common man generally takes it that the power in the hands of a bad man is due to his good actions in the previous birth and his present cruelities will be punished by God in his future birth. The theory of *karma* provides a psychological solace to the sufferer who is consoled to accept injustice as it is the result of his own acts of the past birth. This has created fatalistic attitudes. Even today a vast majority of the people including the Harijans have superstitious beliefs, though these are not the

Distribution of Harijan Population in Different States and Union Territories

Sr. No.	State/Union Territory	Total Population	Harijan Population	Percentage of Harijans to Total Population	Ranks in terms of Concentration of Harijan Population
1.	Andhra Pradesh	43,502,708	5,774,548	13.27	IV
2.	Assam	14,957,542	912,639	6.10	XV
3.	Bihar	56,353,369	7,950,632	14.28	II
4.	Gujarat	25,697,475	1,825,432	6.84	XIII
5.	Haryana	10,036,808	1,895,933	18.85	XII
6.	Himachal Pradesh	3,460,434	769,572	22.23	XVI
7.	Kerala	21,347,375	1,772,168	8.30	XIV
8.	Madhya Pradesh	41,654,119	4,453,690	10.09	V
9.	Maharashtra	50.412,225	3,025,261	6.00	X
10.	Manipur	1,072,753	16,376	15.27	XXII
11.	Meghalaya	1,011,699	3,887	0.38	XXIII
12.	Karnataka	29,299,014	3,850,034	13.14	VII
13.	Nagaland	516,449	—	—	—
14.	Orissa	21,944,615	3,310,854	15.09	IX
15.	Punjab	13,551,060	3,348,217	24.71	VIII

16. Raiasthan	25,765,806	4,075,580	15.82	VI
17. Tamil Nadu	11,199,168	7,315,595	17.75	III
18. Tripura	1,556,342	192,860	12.39	XVIII
19. Uttar Pradesh	88,341,144	18,548,916	21.00	I
20. West Bengal	44,312,011	1,816,028	19.90	XI
21. A & N Island	115,133	—	—	—
22. Arunachal Pradesh	467,511	339	0.07	XXV
23. Chandigarh	257,251	29,073	11.30	XX
24. Dadra & Nagar Haveli	74,170	1,332	1.79	XXIV
25. Delhi	4,065,698	635,598	15.63	XVII
26. Goa, Diu & Daman	857,771	16,514	1.92	XXI
27. Lakshdweep	31,810	—	—	—
28. Pondicherry	471,707	72,921	15.45	XIX
India	547,949,809	79,995,896	14.60	

Source: Figures from Census 1971. Ranking done by the author.

correct interpretations of the religious code. The injurious effects of such dogmas haunt the poor and the hardworking. Such a belief would be of strength to the haves and could be a solace to the havenots.

What is further required is a comprehensive action on the part of socio-religious organisations. The spirit of scientific rationalism has again to imbue the interpretations of religious verses. Social reformers like Vivekananda, Dayananda, and Gandhi have already paved the way for it. The need of the hour is to support the law of the land by regenerating life in the cultural, social and religious domains.

REFERENCES

1. *Ibid.*
2. Watter Thomas, *Yuan Chwang's Travels in India*, Vol. I, London, 1904, p. 168.
3. Sharma, B.N. *Social Life in Northern India (A.D. 600-1000)*, Delhi, Munshi Lal Manohar Lal, 1966, p. 36.
4. *Ibid.*
5. *Ibid.*
6. *Ibid.*
7. Report, Backward Class Commission, 1955, Government of India, Delhi, Manager of Publications, 1956, p. 16.
8. Sharma, *op. cit.* 7, p. 61.
9. Mitra, *op. cit.* 1, p. 25
10. Sharma R. S., *Shudra in Ancient India*, Delhi, Moti Lal Banarsi as, 1958, p. 113.
11. *Ibid.*, p. 107.
12. *Ibid.*
13. *Ibid.*
14. *Ibid.*, p. 94.
15. Sharama, B. N., *Social life in Northern India* (A. D. 600-1000), Delhi, Munshi Ram Manoharlal, 1966, p. 61.

16. Subramanium, Kambla, *Mahabharta*, Bombay-7, Bhartiya Vidya Bhawan, 1965, pp. 42.

17. Keay, F. E., *Ancient Indian Education*, London, Oxford University Press, 1918, p. 80

18. Mitra Ved, *Education in Ancient India*, New Delhi, Arya Book Depot, 1967, p. 25.

19. Tara Chand, *History of the Freedom Movement in India, Vol. I*, Delhi, Publications Division, Govt. of India, 1965, p. 76-77.

20. Compiled from the Reports (for the period 1974-78) of the Commissioner for Scheduled Castes and Scheduled Tribes, New Delhi.

6

DR. AMBEDKAR ON CASTE SYSTEM

Abstract

The caste problem is a vast one, both theoretically and practically. Practically, it is an institution that portends tremendous consequences. It is a local problem, but one capable of much wider mischief, for "as long as caste in India does exist, Hindus will hardly intermarry or have any social intercourse with outsiders; and if Hindus migrate to other regions on earth, Indian caste would become a world prolem".[1] Theoretically, it has defied a great many scholars who have taken upon themselves, as a labour of love, to dig into its origin. Such being the case, I cannot treat the problem in its entirety. Time, space and acumen, I am afriad, would all fail me, if I attempted to do otherwise than limit myself to a phase of it, namely, the genesis, mechanism and spread of the caste system. I will strictly observe this rule, and will dwell on extraneous matters only when it is necessary to clarify or support a point in my thesis. . . .

According to well-known ethnologists, the population of India is a mixture of Aryans, Dravidians, Mongolians and

S. Ketkar *History of Caste in India*, (1909), p. 4.

Scythians. All these stocks of people came into India from various directions and with various cultures, centuries ago, when they where in a tribal state. They all in turn elbowed their entry into the country by fighting with their predecessors, and after a stomachful of it settled down as peaceful neighbours. Through constant contact and mutual intercourse they evolved a common culture that superseded their distinctive cultures. It may be granted that there has not been a thorough amalgamation of the various stocks that make up the peoples of India, and to a traveller from within the boundaries of India the East presents a marked contrast in physique and even in colour to the West, as does the South the North. But amalgamation can never be the sole criterion of homogeneity as predicated of any people. Ethnically all people are heterogeneous. It is the unity of culture that is the basis of homogeneity. Taking this for granted, I venture to say that there is no country that can rival the Indian Peninsula with respect to the unity of its culture. It has not only a geographic unity, but it has over and above all a deeper and a much more fundamental unity—the indubiable cultural unity that covers the land from end to end. But it is because of this homogeneity that Caste becomes a problem so difficult to be explained. If the Hindus Society were a mere federation of mutually exclusive units, the matter would be simple enough. But Caste is a parcelling of an already homogenous unit, and the explanation of the genesis of Caste is the explanation of this process of parcess of parcelling.

Before launching into our field of enquiry, it is better to advise ourselves regarding the nature of a caste. It will therefore drawn upon a few of the best students of caste for their definitions of it:

1. Mr. Senart, a French authority, defines a caste as "a close corporation, in theory at any rate rigorously hereditary: equipped with a certain traditional and independent organisation, including a chief and a council, meeting on occasion in assemblies of more or less plenary authority and joining together at certain

festivals: bound together by common occupations, which relate more particularly to marriage and to food and to questions of ceremonial pollution, and ruling its members by the exercise of jurisdiction, the extent of which varies, but which succeeds in making the authority of the community more felt by the sanction of certain penalties and, above all, by final irrevocable exclusion from the group".

2. Mr. Nesfield defines a caste "a class of the community which disowns any connection with any other class and can neither intermarry nor eat nor drink with any but persons of their own community".

3. According to Sir Herbert Risely, "a caste many be defined as a collection of families or groups of families bearing a common name which usually denotes or is associated with specific occupation, claiming common descent from a mythical ancestor, human or divine, professing to follow the same professional callings and are regarded by those who are competent to give an opinion as forming a single homogenous community".

4. Dr. Ketkar defines caste as "a social group having two characteristics:

   (i) membership is confined to those who are born of members and includes all persons so born;

   (ii) the members are forbidden by an inexorable social law to marry outside the group".

To review these definitions is of great importance for our purpose. It will be noticed that taken individually the definitions of three of the writers include too much or too little: none is complete or correct by itself and all have missed the central point in the mechanism of the Caste system. Their mistake lies in trying to define caste as an isolated unit by itself, and not as a group within, and with definite relations to, the system of caste as a whole. Yet collectively all of them are complementary to one another, each one emphasising what has been obscured in the other. By way of criticism, therefore, I will take only those points common to all Castes in each of the above definitions which are regarded as peculiaricies of Caste and evaluate them as such.

To start with Mr. Senart. He draws attention to the "idea of pollution" as a characteristic of Caste. With regard to this point in may be safely said that it is by no means a peculiarity of Caste as such. It usually originates in priestly ceremonialism and is a particular case of the general belief in purity. Consequently its necesary connection with Caste may be completely denied without damaging the working of Caste. The "idea of pollution" has been attached to the institution of Caste, only because the Caste that enjoys the highest rank is the priestly Caste: while we know that priest and purity are old associates. We may therefore conclude that the "idea of pollution" is a characteristic of Caste only in so far as Caste has a religious flavour. Mr. Nesfield in his way dwells on the absence of messing with those outside the Caste as one its characteristics. In spite of the newness of the point we must say that Mr. Nesfield has mistaken the effect for the cause. Caste, being a self-enclosed unit naturally limits social intercourse, including messing etc. to members within it. Consequently this absence of messing with outsiders is not due to positive prohibition, but is a natural result of Caste, *.i.e*, exclusiveness. No doubt this absence of messing originally due to exclusiveness, acquired the prohibitory character of a religious injunction, but it may be regarded as a later growth. Sir Herbert Risley, markes no new point deserving of special attention.

We now pass on to the definition of Dr. Ketkar who has done much for the clucidation of the subject. Not only is he a native, but he has also brought a critical acumen and an open mind to bear on has study of Caste. His definition merits consideration. for he has defined Caste in its relation to a system of Castes, and has concentrated his attention only on those characteristics which are absolutely necessary for the existence of a Caste within a system, rightly excuding all others as being secondary or derivative in character. With respect to his definition it must, however, be said that in it there is a slight confusion of thought, lucid and clear otherwise it is. He speaks of Prohibition of Intermarriage and Membership by Autogeny as the two characteristics of Caste. I submit that these are but two aspects of one and the same thing, and not two different things as Dr. Ketkar supposes them to be. If you prohibit intermarriage the result is that you limit membership to those born within the group. Thus the two are the obverse and the reverse sides of the same medal.

This critical evaluation of the various characteristics of Caste leave no doubt that prohibition, or rather the absence of intermarriage—endogamy, to be concise—is the only one that can be called the essence of Caste when rightly understood. But some may deny this on abstract anthropological grounds, for there exist endogamous groups without giving rise to the problem of Caste. In a general way this may be true, as endogamous societies, culturally different, making their abode in localities more or less removed, and having little to do with each other are a physical reality. The Negroes and the Whites and the various tribal groups that go by name of American Indians in the Uniied States may be cited as more or less appropriate illustrations in support of this view. But we must not confuse matters, for in India the situation is different. As pointed out before, the peoples of India from a homogeneous whole. The various races of India occupying definite territories have more or less fused into one another and do possess cultural unity, which is the only criterion of a homogeneous population. Given this homogeneity as a basis, Caste becomes a problem altogether new in character and wholly absent in the situation constituted by the mere propinquity of endogamous social or tribal groups. Caste in India means an artificial chopping off of the population into fixed and definite units, each one prevented from fusing into another through the custom of endogamy. Thus the conclusion is inevitable that Endogamy is the only charocteristic that is peculiar to caste, and if we succeed in showing how endogamy is maintained, we shall practically have proved the genesis and also the mechanism of Caste.

It may not be quite easy for you to anticipate why I regard endogamy as a key to the mystery of the Caste system. Not to strain your imagination too much, I will proceed to give you my reasons for it.

It may not also be out of place to emphasize at this moment that no civilized society of today presents more survivals of primitive times than does the Indian society. Its religion is essentially primitive and its tribal code, in spite of the advance of time and civilization, operates in all its pristine vigour even today. One of these primitive survivals, to which I wish particularly to draw your attention is the custom of exogamy. The prevalence of exogamy in the primitive worlds is a fact too wellknown to need any explanation. With the growth of history, however, exogamy has lost its efficacy, and excepting the nearest blood-kins, there is usually no social bar restricting the field of marriage. But regarding the peoples of India the law of exogamy is a positive injunction even today. Indian society still savours of the clan system, even though there are no clans; and this can be easily seen from the law of matrimony which centres round the principle of exogamy, for it is not that Sapindas (blood-kins) cannot marry, but a marriage even between Sagotras (of the same class) is regarded as a sacrilege.

Nothing is therefore more important for you to remember than the fact that endogamy is foreign to the people of India. The various Gotras of India are and have been exogamous: so are the other groups with totemic organization. It is no exaggeration to say that with the people of India exogamy is a creed and none dare infringe it, so much so that, in spite of the endogamy of the Castes within them, exogamy is strictly observed and that there more rigorous penalties for violating exogamy than there are for violating endogamy. You will, therefore, readily see that with exogamy as the rule there could be no Caste, for exogamy means fusion. But be have castes; consequently in the final analysis creation of Castes, so far as India is concerned, means the superposition of endogamy on exogamy. However, in an originally exogamous population an easy working out of endogarny (which is equivalent to the creation of Caste), is a grave problem, and it is in the consideration of the means utilized for the preservation of endogamy against exogamy that we may hope to find the solution of our problem.

Thus the Superposition of Endogamy on Exogamy Means the Creation of Caste. But this is not an easy affair. Let us take an imaginary group that disires to make itself into a Caste and analyse what means it will have to adopt to make itself endogamous. If a group desires to make itself endogamous a formal injunction against intermarriage with outside groups will be of no avail, especially if prior to the introduction of endogamy, exogamy had been the rule in all matrimonial relations. Again, there is a tendency in all groups lying in close contact with one another to assimilate and amalgamate, and thus consolidate into a homogeneous society. If this tendency is to be strongly counteracted in the interest of Caste formation, it is absolutely necessary to circumscribe a circle outside which people should not contract marriages.

Nevertheless, this encircling to prevent marriages from without creates problems from within which are not very easy of solution. Roughly speaking, in a normal group the two sexes are more or less evenly distributed, and generally speaking there is an equality between those of the same age. The quality is, however, never quite realized in actual societies. At the same time to the group that is desirous of making itself into a caste the maintenance of equality between the sexes becomes the ultimate goal, for without it endogamy can no longer subsist. In other words, if endogamy is to be preserved conjugal rights from within have to be provided for, otherwise members of the group will be driven out of the circle to take care of themselves in any way they can. But in order that the conjugal rights be provided for from within, it is absolutely necessary to maintain a numerical equality between the marriageable units of the two sexes within the group desirous of making itself into a Caste, it is only through the maintenance of such an equality that the necessary endogamy of the group can be kept intact, and a very large disparity is sure to break it.

The problem of Caste, then, ultimately resolves itself into one of repairing the disparity between the marriageable units of the two sexes within it. Left to nature, the much needed parity between the units can be realized only when a couple dies simultaneously. But this is a rare contingency. The husband may die before the wife and create a surplus woman, who must be disposed of, else through intermarriage she will violate the endogamy of the groop. In like manner the husband may survive his wife and be surplus man whom the group, while it many sympathise with him for the sad bereavement, has to dispose of, else he will marry outside the Caste and will break the endogamy. Thus both the surplus man and the surplus woman constitute a menace to the Caste if not taken care of, for not finding suitable partners inside their prescribed circle (and left to themselves they cannot find any, for if the matter be not regulated there can only be just enough pairs to go round) very likely they will transgress the boundary, marry outside and import offspring that is foreign to the Caste.

Let us see what our imaginary group is likely to do with this surplus man and surplus woman. We will first take up the case of the surplus woman. She can be disposed of in two different ways so as to preseve the endogamy of the Caste.

First: burn her on the funeral pyre of her deceased husband and get rid of her. This, however, is rather an impracticable way of solving the problem of sex disparity. In some cases it may work, in others it may not. Consequently every surplus woman cannot thus be disposed of, because it is an easy solution but a hard realization. And so of the surplus woman (=widow), if not disposed of, remains in the group: but in her very existence lies a double danger. She may marry outside the Caste and violate endogamy, or she may marry within the Caste and through competition encroach upon the chances of marriage that must be reserved for the potential brides in the Caste. She is therefore a menance in any case, and something must be done to her if she cannot be burned along with her deceased husband.

The second remedy is to enfore widowhood on her for the rest of her life. So far as the objective results are concerned, burning is a better solution than enforcing widowhood. Burning the widow eliminates all the three evils that a surplus woman is fraught with. Being dead and gone she creates no problem of remarriage either inside or outside the Caste. But compulsory widowhood is superior to burning because it is more practicable. Besides being comparatively humane it also guards against the evils of remarriage as does burning; but it fails to guard the morals of the group. No doubt under compulsory widowhood the woman remains, and just because she is deprived of her natural right of being a legitimate wife in future, the incentive to immoral conduct is increased. But this is by no means an insuperable difficulty. She can be degraded to a condition in which she is no longer a source of allurement.

The problem of surplus man (=widower) is much more important and much more difficult than that of the surplus woman in a group that desires to make itself into a Caste. From time immemorial man as compared with woman has had the upper hand. He is a dominant figure in every group and of the two sexes has greater prestige. With this traditional superiority of man over woman his wishes have always been consulted. Woman, on the other hand, has been an easy prey to all kinds of iniquitous injunctions, religious, social or economic. But man as a maker of injunctions is most often above them all. Such being the case, you cannot accord the same kind of treatment to a surplus man as you can to a surplus woman in a Caste.

The project of burning him with his deceased wife is

hazardous in two ways: first of all it cannot be done, simply because he is a man. Secondly, if done, a sturdy soul is lost to the Cast. There remain then only two solutions which can conveniently of him. I say conventiently, because he is an asset to the group.

Important as he is to the group, endogamy is still more important, and the solution must assure both these ends. Under these circumstances he may be forced or I should say induced, after the manner of the widow, to remain a widower for the rest of his life. This solution is not altogether difficult, for without any compulsion some are so disposed as to enjoy self-imposed celibacy, or even to take a further step of their own accord and renounce the world and its joys. But, given human nature as it is, this solution can hardly be expected to be realized. On the other hand, as is very likely to be the case, if the surplus man remains in the group as an active participator in group activities, he is a danger to the morals of the group. Looked at from a different point of view celibacy, though easy in cases where it succeeds, is not so advantageous even then to the material prospects of the Caste. If he observes genuine celibacy and renounces the world, he would not be a menace to the preservation of Caste endogamy or Caste morals as he undoubtedly would be if he remained a secular person. But as an ascetic celibate he is as good as burned, so far as the material well-being of his Caste is concerned. A Caste, in order that it may be large enough to afford a vigorous communal life, must be maintained at a certain numerical strength. But to hope for this and to proclaim celibacy is the same as trying to cure atrophy by bleeding.

Imposing celibacy on the surplus man in the group, therefore, fails both theoretically and practically. It is in the interest of the Caste to keep him as a *Grahastha* (one who raises a family), to use a Sanskrit technical term. But the problem is to provide him with a wife from within the Caste. At the outset this is not possible, for the ruling ratio in a caste has to be one man to one woman and none can have two chances of marriage, for in a Caste thoroughly self-enclosed there are always just enough marriageable women to go round for the marriageable men. Under these circumstances the surplus man can be provided with a wife only by recruiting a bride from the ranks of those not yet marriageable in order to tie him down to the group. This is certainly the best of the possible solutions in the case of the surplus man. By this, he is kept within the Caste. By this means numerical depletion through constant outflow is guarded against, and by this endogamy and morals are preserved.

It will now be seen that the four means by which numerical disparity between the two sexes is conveniently maintained are:

1. burning the widow with her deceased husband;
2. compulsory widowhood—a milder from of burning;
3. imposing celibacy on the widower; and
4. wedding him to a girl not yet marriageable.

Though, as I said a bove, burning the widow and imposing celibacy on the widower are of doubtful service to the group in its endeavour to preserve its endogamy, all of them operate as *means*. But means, as forces, when liberated or set in motion create an end. What then is the end that these means create? They create and perpetuate endogamy, while caste and endogamy, according to our analysis of the various definitions of caste, are one and the same thing. Thus the existence of these means is identical with caste and caste involves these means.

This, in my opinion, is the general mechanism of a caste in a system of castes. Let us now turn from these high generalities to the castes in Hindu Society and inquire into their mechanism. I need hardly premise that there are a great many pitfalls in the path of those who try to unfold the past, and caste in India to be sure is a very ancient institution. This is especially true where there exist no authentic or written records or where the people, like the Hindus, are so constituted that to them writing history is a folly, for the world is an illusion. But institutions do live, though for a long time they may remain unrecorded and as often as not customs and morals are like fossils that tell their own history. If this is true, our task will be amply rewarded if we scrutinize the solution the Hindus arrived at to meet the problems of the surplus man and surplus woman.

Complex though it be in its general working the Hindu Society, even to a superficial observe, presents three singular uxorial customs, namely:

(i) *Sati* or the burning of the widow on the funeral pyre of her deceased husband.

(ii) Enforced widowhood by which a widow is not allowed to remarry.

(iii) Girl marriage.

In addition, one also notes a great hankering after *Sannyasa* (renunciation) on the part of the widower, but this may in some cases be due purely to pyschic disposition.

So far as I know, no scientific explanation of the origin of these customs is forthcoming even today. We have plenty of philosophy to tell us why these customs were honoured, but nothing to tell us the causes of their origin and existence. *Sati* has been honoured (Cf. A.K. Coomaraswamy, *Sati*: A Defence of the Eastern Woman in the British Sociological Review, Vol. VI, 1913) because it is a "proof of the perfect unity of body and soul" between husband and wife and of "devotion beyond the grave", because it embodied the ideal of wifehood, which is well expressed by Uma when she said, "Devotion to her Lord is woman's honour, it is her eternal heaven: and O Maheshvra", she adds with a most touching human cry, "I desire not paradise itself if thou are not satisfied with me!" Why cumpulsory widowhood is honoured I know not, nor have I yet met with any one who sang in praise of it, though there are a great many who adhere to it. The eulogy in honour of girl marriage is reported by Dr. Ketkar to be as follows:

> "A really faithful man or woman ought not to feel affection for a woman or a man other than the one with whom he or she is united. Such purity is compulsory not only after marriage, but even before marriage, for that is the only corrrct ideal of chastity. No maiden could be considered pure if she feels love for a man other than the one to whom she might be married. As she does not know to whom she is going to be married, she must not feel affection for any man at all before marriage. If she does so, it is a sin. So it is better for a girl to know whom she has to love before any sexual consciousness has been awakened in her,"[2] Hence girl marriage.

This high-flown and ingenious sophistry indicates why these institutions were honoured, but does not tell us why they were practiced. My own interpretation is that they were honoured because they were practised. Any one slightly acquainted with rise of individualism in the 18th century will appreciate my remark. At all times, it is the movement that is most important and the philosophies grow around it long afterwards to justify it and give it a moral support. In like manner I urge that the very fact that these custom were so highly eulogized prove that they needed eulogy for their prevalence. Regarding the question as to why they arose, I submit that they were needed to create the structure of caste and the philosophies in honour of them were intended to popularize them, or to gild the pill, as we might say, for they must have been so abominable and shocking to the moral sense of she unsophisticated that they needed a great deal of sweetening. These customs are essentially of the nature of *means*, though they are represented as ideals. But this should not blind us from understanding the *results* that flow from them. One might safely say that idealization of means is necessary and in this particular case was perhaps motivated to endow them with greater efficacy. Calling a means an end does no harm, except that it disguises its real character; but it does not deprive it of its real nature, that of a means. You may pass a law that all cats are dogs, just as you can call a means an end. But you can no more change the nature of means thereby than you can turn cats into dogs; consequently I am justified in holding that, whether regarded as ends or as means, *sati, enforced widowhood* and *girl marriage* are customs that were primarily intended to solve the problem of the surplus man and surplus woman in a caste and to maintain its endogamy. Strict endogamy could not be preserved without these customs, while caste without endogamy is a fake.

Having explained the mechanism of the creation and preservation of Caste in India; the further question as to its genesis naturally arises. The question of origin is always an annoying question and in the study of Caste it is sadly neglected; some have connived at it, while others have dodged it. Some are puzzled as to whether there could be such a thing as the origin of caste and suggest that "if we can not control our fondness for the word 'origin', we should better use the plural from *viz*. 'origins of caste' ". As for myself I do not feel puzzled by the Origin of Caste in India for, as I have established before, endogamy is the only characteristic of Caste and when I say Origin of Caste I mean The Origin of Mechanism for Endogamy.

The atomistic conception of individual in a Society so greatly popularised—I was about to say vulgarized—in political orations is the greatest humbug. To say that individuals make up society is trivial; society is always composed of classes. It may be an exaggeration to assert the theory of class-conflict, but the existence of definite classes in a society is a fact. Their basis may differ. They may be economic or intellectual or social, but an individual in a society is always a member of a class. This is a universal fact and early Hindu society could not have been an exception to this rule, and, as a matter of fact, we know it was not. If we bear this generalization in mind, our study of the genesis of caste would be very much facilitated, for we have only to determine what was the class that first made itself into a caste, for class and caste, so to say, are next door neighbours, and it is only a span that separates the two. *A Caste is an Enclosed Class.*

The study of the origin of caste must furnish us with an answer to the question—what is the class that raised this "enclosure" around itself? The question may seem too inquisitorial, but it is pertinent, and an answer to this will serve us to elucidate the mystery of the growth and development of castes all over India. Unfortunately a direct answer to this question is not within my power. I can answer it only indirectly. I said just above that the customs in question were current in the Hindu society. To be true to facts it is necessary to qualify the statement, as it connotes universality of their prevalence. These customs in all their strictness are obtainable only in one caste, namely the Brahmins, who occupy the highest place in the social hierarchy of the Hindu society; and as their prevalence in non-Brahmin castes is derivative of their observance is neither strict nor complete. This important fact can serve as a basis of an important observation. If the prevalence of these customs in the non-Brahmin Castes is derivative, as can be shown very easily then it needs no argument to prove what class is the father of the institution of caste. Why the Brahmin class should have enclosed itself into a caste is a different question, which may be left as an employment for another occasion. But the strict observance of these customs and the social superiority arrogated by the priestly class in all ancient civilizations are sufficiently to prove that they the originators of this "unnatural institution" founded ond maintained through these in natural means.

I now come to the third part of my paper regarding the question of the growth and spread of the caste system all over India. The question I have to answer is: How did the institution of caste spread among the rest of the non-Brahmin population of the country? The question of the spread of the castes all over India has suffered a worse fate than the question of genesis. And the main cause, as it seems to me, is that the two questions of spread and of origin are not separated. This is because of the common belief among scholars that the caste system has either been imposed upon the docile population of India by a law-given as a divine dispensation, or that it has grown according to some law of social growth peculiar to the Indian people.

I first propose to handle the law-giver of India. Every country has its law-giver, who arises as an incarnation (*avatar*) in times of emergency to set right a sinning humanity and give it the laws of justice and morality. Manu, the law-giver of India, if he did exist, was certainly an audacious person. If the story that he gave the law of caste be credited, then Manu must have been a daredevil fellow and the humanity that accepted has dispensation must be a humanity quite different from the one we are acquainted with. It is unimaginable that the law of caste was *given*. It is hardly an exaggeration to say that Manu could not have outlived his law, for what is that class that can submit to be degraded to the status of brutes by the pen of a man, and suffer him to raise another class to the pinnacle? Unless he was a tyrant who held all the population in subjection it cannot be imagined that he could have been allowed to dispense his patronage in the grossly unjust meanner, as may be easily seen by a mere glance at his "Institutes". I mav seem hard on Manu, but I am sure my force is not strong enough to kill his ghost. He lives, like a disembodied spirit and is appealed to, and I am afraid will yet live long. One thing I want to impress upon you is that Manu did not give the law of Caste and that he could not do so. Caste existed long before Manu. He was an upholder of it and therefore philosophised about it, but certainly he did not and could not ordain the present order of Hindu Society. His work ended with the condification of existing caste rules and the preaching of Caste *Dharma*. The spread and growth of the Caste system is too gigantic a task to be achieved by the power or cunning of an individual or of a class. Similar in argument is the theory that the Brahmins created the Caste. After what I have said regarding Manu, I need hardly say anything more, except to point out that it is incorrect in thought and malicious in intent. The Brahmins may have been guilty of many things, and I dare say they were, but the imposing of the caste system on the non-Brahmin population was beyond their mettle. They may have helped the process by their glib philosophy, but they certainly could not have pushed their scheme beyond their own confines. To fashion society after one's own pattern! How hard! One can take pleasure and eulogize its furtherance, but cannot further it very far. The vehemence of my attack may seem to be unnecessary; but I can assure you that it is not uncalled for. There is a strong belief in the mind of orthodox Hindus that the Hindu Society was somehow moulded into the framework of the Caste System and that it is an organization consciously created by the shastras. Not only does this belief exist, but it is being justified on the ground that it can not but be good because it is ordained by the shastras and the shastras cannot be wrong. I have urged so much on the adverse side of this attitude, not because the religious sanctity is grounded on scientific basis, nor to help those reformers who are preaching against it. Preaching did not make the caste system neither will it unmake it. My aim is to show the falsity of the attitude that has exalted religious sanction to the position of a scientific explanation.

Thus the "great man" theory does not help us very far in solving the spread of castes in India. Western scholars, probably not much 'given to hero-worship, have attempted other explanations. The nuclei, round which have "formed" the various castes in India, are, according to them:

1. occupation;
2. survivals of tribal organizations etc.;
3. the rise of new belief;
4. cross-breeding; and
5. migration.

The question may be asked whether these nuclei do not exist in other societies and whether they are peculiar to India.

If they are not peculiar to India, but are common to the world, why is it that they did not "form" caste on other parts of this planet? Is it because those parts are holier than the land of the Vedas, or that the professors are mistaken? I am afraid that the latter is the truth.

In spite of the high theoretic value claimed by the several authors for their respective theories based on one or other of the above nuclei, one regrets to say that on close examination they are nothing more than filling illustrations—what Mattew Arnold means by "the grand name without the grand thing in it". Such are the various theories of caste advanced by Sir Denzil Ibbetson, Mr. Nesfield, Mr. Senart and Sir H. Risley. To criticise them in a lump would be to say that they are a disguised from of the *Petitio Principii* of formal logic. To illustrate: Mr. Nesfield says that "function and fuction only was the foundation upon which the whole system of Castes in India was built up". But the may rightly be reminded that he does not very much advance our thought by making the above statement, which practically amounts to saying that castes in India are functional, occupational which is very poor discovery! We have yet to know from Mr. Nesfield why is it that an occupational group turned into an occupational caste? I would very cheerfully have undertaken the task of dwelling on the theories of other ethnologists, had it not been for the fact that Mr. Nesfield's is a typical one.

Without stopping to criticize those thories that explain the caste system as a natural phenomenon occurring in obedience to the law of disintegration, as explained by Herbert Spencer in his formula of evolution, or as natural as the structural differentiation within an organism"—to employ the phraseology of orthodox apologists—, or as an early attempt to test the laws of eugencies—as all belonging to the same class of fallacy which regards the caste system as inevitable, or as being consciously imposed in anticipation of these laws on a helpless and humble population, I will now lay before you my own view on the subject.

We shall be well advised to recall at the outset that the Hindu society, in common with other societies, was composed of classes and the earliest known are the:

1. Brahmins or the priestly class;
2. the Kshatriya, or the military class;
3. the Vaishya, or the merchant class; and
4. the Shudra; or the artisans and mental class.

Particular attention has to be paid to the fact that this was essentially a class system, in which individuals, when qualified, could change their class, and therefore classes did change their personnel. At same time in the history of the Hindus, the priestly class socially detached itself from the rest of the body of people and through a closed-door policy became a caste by itself. The other classes being subject to the law of social division of labour underwent differentiation, some into large, others into very minute groups. The Vaishya and Shudra classes were the original inchoate plasm, which formed the sources of the numerous castes of today. As the military occupation does not very easily lend itself to very minute sub-division, the Kshatriya class could have differentiated into soldiers and administrators.

This sub-division of a society is quite natural. But the unnatural thing about these sub-divisions is that they have lost the open-door character of the class system and have become self-enclosed units called castes. The question is: were they compelled to close their doors and become endogamous, or did they close them of their own accord? I submit that there is a double line of answer: *Some closed the door: Others found it closed against them.* The one of a psychological interpretation and the other is mechanistic, but they are complementary and both are necessary to explain the phenomena of caste-formation in its entirety.

I will first take up the psychological interpretation. The question we have to answer in this connection is: Why did these sub-division or classes, if you please, industrial, religious or otherwise, become self-enclosed or endogamous? My answer is because the Brahmins were so. Endogamy or the closed-door system, was a fashion in the Hindu society, and as it had originated from the Brahmin caste it was whole-heartedly imitated by all the non-Brahmin sub-divisions or classes, who, in their turn, became endogamous castes. It is "the infection of imitation" that caught all these sub-divisions on their onward march of differentiation and has turned them into castes. The propensity to imitate is a deep-seated one in the human mind and need not be deemed an inadequate explanation for the formation of the various castes in India. It is so deep-seated that Walter Bagehot argues that, "We must not think of...imitation as voluntary, or even conscious. On the contrary it has its seat mainly in very obscure parts of the mind, whose notions, so far from being consciously produced, are hardly felt to exist; so far from being conceived before-hand, are not even felt at the time. The main seat of the imitative part of our nature is our belief, and the causes predisposing us to believe this or disinclining us to believe that are among the obscurest parts of our nature. But as to the imitative nature of credulity there can be no doubt,"[3] This propensity to imitate has been made the subject of a scientific study by Gabriel Trade, who lays down three laws of imitation. One of his three laws is that imitation flows from the higher to the lower or, to quote his own words, "Given the opportunity, a nobility will always and everywhere imitate its leaders, its kings or sovereigns and the people likewise, given the opportunity, its nobility."[4] Another of Tarde's laws of imitation is: that the extent or intensity of imitation varies inversely in proportion to distance, or in his own words "The thing that is most imitated is the most superior one of those that are nearest." In fact, the influence of the model's example is efficacious inversely to its distance as well as directly to its superiority. Distance is understood here in its sociological meaning. However distant in space a stranger may be, he is close by, from this point of view, if we have numerous and daily relations with him and if we have every facility to satisfy our desire to imitate him. This law of the imitation of the nearest, of the least distant, explains the gradual and consecutive character of the spread of an example that has been set by the higher social ranks."[5]

In order to prove my thesis—which really needs no proof that some castes were formed by imitation, the best way, it seems to me, is to find out whether or not the vital conditions for the formation of castes by imitation exist in the Hindu Society. The conditions for imitation, according to this standard authority are:

1. that the source of imitation must enjoy prestige in the group; and
2. that there must be "numerous and daily relations" among members of a group.

That these conditions were present in India there is little reason to doubt. The Brahmin is a semi-god and very nearly a demi-god. He sets up a mode and moulds the rest. His prestige is unquestionable and is the fountain-head of bliss and good. Can such a being, idolised by scriptures and venerated by the priest-ridden multitude, fail to project his personality on the suppliant humanity? Why, if the story be true, he is believed to be the very end of creation. Such a creature is worthy of more than mere imitation, but at least of imitation; and if he lives in an endogamous enclosure, should not the rest follow his example? Frail humanity! Be it embodied in a grave philosopher or a frivolous housemaid, it succumbs. It cannot be otherwise. Imitation is easy and invention is difficult.

Yet another way of demonstrating the play of imitation in the formation of castes is to understand the attitude of non-Brahmin classes towards those customs which supported the structure of caste in its nascent days until, in the course of history, it became embedded in the Hindu mind and hangs there to this day without any support—for now it needs no prop but belief—like a weed on the surface of a pond. In a way, but only in a way, the status of a caste in the Hindu Society varies directly with the extent of the observance of the customs of *Sati*, enforced widowhood, and girl marriage. But observance of the customs varies directly with the distance (I am using the word in the Tardian sense) that separates the caste. Those castes that are nearest to the Brahmins have imitated all the three customs and insist on the strict observance thereof. Those that are less near have imitated enforced widowhood and girl marriage; others, a little further off, have only girl marriage and those furthest off have imitated only the belief in the caste principle. This imperfect imitation, I dare say, is due partly to what Tarde calls "distance" and partly to the barbarous character of these customs. This phenomenon is a complete illustration of Tarde's law and leaves no doubt that the whole process of caste-formation in India is a process of imitation of the higher by the lower. At this juncture I will turn back to support a former conclusion of mine, which might have appeared to you as too sudden or unsupported. I said that the Brahmin class first raised the structure of caste by the help of those three customs in question. My reason for that conclusion was that their existence in other classes was derivative. After what I have said regarding the role of imitation in the spread of these customs among the non-Brahmin castes, as means or as ideals, thought the imitators have not been aware of it, they exist among them as derivatives; and, if they are derived, there must have been prevalent one original caste that was high enough to have served as a pattern for the rest. But in a theocratic society, who could be the pattern but the servant of God?

This completes the story of those that were weak enough to close their doors. Let us now see how others were closed in as a result of being closed out. This I call the mechanistic process of the formation of caste. It is mechanistic because it is inevitable. That this line of approach as well as the psychological one, to the explanation of the subject has escaped my predessors is entirely due to the fact that they have conceived caste as a unit by itself and not as one within a System of Caste. The result of this oversight or lack of sight has been very detrimental to the proper understanding of the subject matter and therefore its correct explanation. I will proceed to offer my own explanation by making one remark which I will urge you to bear constantly in mind. It is this: that *caste in the singular number is an unreality. Castes exist only in the plural number*. There is no such thing as a caste; there are always castes. To illustrate my meaning: while making themselves into a caste, the Brhmins, by virtue of this, created non-Brahmin caste; or; to express it in my own way, while closing themselves in they closed others out. I will clear my point by taking another illustration. Take India as a whole with its various communities designated by the various creeds to which they owe allegiance, to wit, the Hindus, Mohammedans, Jews, Christians and Parsis. Now, barring the Hindus, the rest within themselves are non-caste communities. But with respect to each other they are castes. Again, if the first four enclose themselves, the Parsis are directly closed out, but are indirectly closed in. Symbolically, if Group a wants to be endogamous, Group B has to be so by sheer force of circumstances.

Now apply the same logic to the Hindu society and you have another explanation of the "fissiparous" character of caste, as a consequence of the virtue of self-deplication that is inherent in it. Any innovation that seriously antagonises the ethical, religious and social code of the Castes is not likely to bc tolerated by the Caste, and the recalcitrant members of a Caste are in danger of being thrown out of the Caste, and left to their own fate without having the alternative of being admitted into or absorbed by other Castes. Caste rules are inexorable and they do not wait to make nice distinctions between kinds of offence. Innovation may be of any kind, but all kinds will suffer the same penalty. A novel way of thinking will create a new Caste for the old ones will not tolerate it. The noxious thinker respectfully called Guru (Prophet) suffers the same fate as the sinners in illegitimate love. The former creates a caste of the nature of a religious sect and the latter a type of mixed caste. Castes have no mercy for a sinner who has the courage to violate the code. The penalty is excommunication and the result is a new caste. It is not peculiar Hindu psychology that induces the excommunicated to form themselves into a caste; far from it. On the contrary, very often they have been quite willing to be humble members of some caste (higher by preference) if they could be admitted within its fold. But castes are enclosed units and it is their conspiracy with clear conscience that compels the excommunicated to make themselves into a caste. The logic of this opdurate circumstance is merciless, and it is in obedience to its force that some unfortunate groups find themselves enclosed, because others in enclosing, themselves have closed them out, with the result that new group (formed on any basis obnoxious to the caste rules) by a mechanical law are constantly being converted into castes to a bewildering multiplicity. Thus is told the second tale in the process of a Caste formation in India.

Now to summarise the main points of my thesis. In my opinion there have been several mistakes committed by the students of Caste, which have misled them in their investigations. European students of Caste have unduly emphasised the role of colour in the Caste system. Themselves impregnated by colour prejudices, they very readily imagined it to be the chief factor in the Caste problem. But nothing can be further from the truth, and Dr. Ketkar is correct when he insists that "All the princes whether they belonged to the so-called Aryan race, or the so-called Dravidian race, were Aryas. Whether a tribe or a family was racially Aryan or Dravidian was a question which never troubled the people of India, until foreign scholars came in and began to draw the line. The colour of the skin had long ceased to be a matter of importance."[6] Again, they have mistaken mere descriptions for explanation and fought over them as though they were theories of origin. There are occupational, religious etc., castes, it is true, but it by is no means an explanation of the origin of Caste. We have yet to find out why occupational groups are castes; but this question has never been raised. Lastly they have taken Caste very lightly as though a breath had made it. On the contrary, Caste, as I have explained it, is almost impossible to be sustained: for the difficulties that it involves are tremendous. It is true that Caste rests on belief, but before belief comes to be the foundation of an institution, the institution itself needs to be the perpetuated and fortified. My study of the Caste problem involves four main points:

1. that in spite of the composite make-up of the Hindu population, there is a deep cultural unity;
2. that caste, is a parcelling into bits of a larger cultural unit;
3. that there was one caste to start with; and
4. that classes have become Castes through imitation and excommunication.

Peculiar interest attaches to the problem of Caste in India today; as persistent attempts are being made to do away with this unnatural institution. Such attempts at reform, however, have aroused a great deal of controversy regarding its origin, as to whether it is due to the conscious command of a Supreme Authority, or is an unconscious growth in the life of a human society under peculiar circumstances. Those who hold the latter view will, I hope, find some food for thought in the standpoint adopted in this paper. Apart from its practical importance, the subject of Caste as an all-absorbing problem and the interest aroused in me regarding its theoretic foundations has moved me to put before you some of the conclusions, which seem to me well founded, and the grounds upon which they may be supported. I am not, however, so presumptuous us to think them in any way final, or anything more than a contribution to a discussion of the subject. It seems to me that the car has been shunted on wrong lines, and the primary object of the paper is to indicate what I regard to be the right path of investigation, with a view to arrive at a serviceable truth. We must, however, guard against approaching the subject with a bias sentiment must be outlawed from the domain of science and things should be judged from an objective standpoint. For myself I shall find as much pleasure in a positive destruction of my own ideology, as in a rational disagreement on a topic, which, notwithstanding many learned disquisitions, is likely to remain controversial forever. To conclude, while I am ambitious to advance a Theory of Caste, if it can be shown to be untenable I shall be equally willing to give it up.

REFERENCES

1. S. Ketkar *History of India in Caste*, (1909), p. 4.
2. *Ibid.*, pp. 2-33.
3. *Physics and Politics*, 1915. p. 60.
4. *Laws of Imitation*, Tr. by E.C. Parsons, 2nd edition, p. 217.
5. *Ibid.*, p. 224.
6. Ketkar, *op. cit.*, p. 8

Appendix I

UNPUBLISHED SPEECH OF DR. B.R. AMBEDKAR

I

The path of social reform like the path to heaven at any rate in India, is strewn with many difficulties. Social reform in India has few friends any many crities. The critics fall into two distinct classes. One class consists of political reformers and the other of the socialists.

It was at one time recognized that without social efficiency no permanent progress in the other fields of activity was possible, that owing to mischief wrought by the evil customs, Hindu Society was not in a state of efficiency and that ceaseless effort must be made to eradicate these evils. It was due to the recognition of this fact that the birth of the National Congress was accompanied by the foundation of the Social Conference. While the Congress was concerned with defining the weak points in the political organisation of the country, the Social Conference was engaged in removing the weak points in the social organisation of the Hindu Society. For some time the Congress and the Conference worked as two wings of one common activity and they held their annual sessions in the same pandal. But soon the two wings developed into two parties, a Political Reform Party and a Social Reform Party, between whom there raged a fierce controversy. The Political Reform Party supported the National Congress and Social Reform Party supported the Social Conference. The two bodies thus became two hostile camps. The point ot issue was whether social reform should precede political reform. For a decade the forces were evenly balanced and the battle was fought without victory to either side. It was howcver evident that the fortunes of the Social Conference were ebbing fast. The gentlemen who presided over the sessions of the Social Conference lamented that the majority of the educated Hindus were for political advancement and indifferent to social reform and that while the number of those who attended the Congress was very large and the number who did not attend but who sympathized with it even larger, the number of those who attended the Social Conference was very much smaller. This indifference, this thinning of its ranks was soon followed by active hostility from the politicians. Under the leadership of the late Mr. Tilak, the courtesy with which the Congress allowed the Social Conference the use of its pandal was withdrawn and the spirit of enmity went to such a pitch that when the Social Conference desired to erect its own pandal a threat to burn the pandal was held out by its opponents. Thus in course of time the party in favour of political reform won and the Social Conference vanished and was forgotten. The speech, delivered by Mr. W.C. Bonnerji in 1892 at Allahabad as President of the eight session of the Congress, sounds like a funeral oration at the death of the Social Conference and is so typical of the Congress attitude that I venture to quote from it the following extract. Mr. Bonnerji said:

"I for one have no patience with those who say we shall not be fit for political reform until we reform our social system. I fail to see any connection between the two......Are we not fit (for political reform) because our widows remain unmarried and our girls are given in marriage earlier than in other countries? Because our wives and daughters do not drive about with us visiting our friends? because we do not send our daughters to Oxford and Cambridge?" (Cheers)

I have stated the case for political reform as put by Mr. Bonnerji. There were many who are happy that the victory went to the Congress. But those who believe in the importance of social reform may ask, is the argument such as that of Mr. Bonnerji final? Does it prove that the victory went to those who were in the right? Does it prove conclusively that social reform has no bearing on political reform? It will help us to understand the matter if I state the other side of the case. I will draw upon the treatment of the untouchables for my facts.

Under the rule of the Peshwas in the Maratha country the untouchable was not allowed to use the public streets if a Hindu was coming along lest he should pollute the Hindu by his shadow. The untouchable was required to have a black thread either on his wrist or in his neck as a sign or a mark to prevent the Hindus from getting themselves polluted by his touch through mistake. In Poona, the capital of the Peshwa, the untouchable was required to carry, strung from his waist, a broom to sweep away from behind the dust he treaded on lest a Hindu walking on the same should be polluted. In Poona, the untoucbable was required to carry an earthen pot, hung in his neck wherever he went, for holding his spit lest his spit falling on earth should pollute a Hindu who might unknowingly happen to tread on it. Let me take more recent facts. The tyranny practised by the Hindus upon the Balais, an untouchable community in Central India, will serve my purpose. You will find areport of this in the Times of India of 4th January, 1928. The correspondent of the Times of India reported that high caste Hindus, *viz.* Calotas, Rajputs and Brahmins including the Patels and Patwaris of villages of Kanaria, Bicholi-Habsi-Mardana and of about 15 other villages in the Indore district (of the Indore State) informed the Balais of their respective village that if they wished to live among them they must conform to the following rules:

1. Balais must not wear gold-lace-bordered pugrees.
2. They must not wear dhotis with coloured or fancy borders.

3. They must convey intimation of the death of any Hindu to relatives of the decreased—no matter how far away these relatives may be living.
4. In all Hindu marriages, Balais must play music before the processions and during the marriage.
5. Balai women must not wear gold or silver ornaments; they must not wear fancy gowns or jackets.
6. Balai women must attend all cases of confinement of Hindu women.
7. Balais must render services without demanding remuneration and must accept whatever a Hindu is pleased to give.
8. If the Balais do not agree to abide by these terms they must clear out of the villages. The Balais refused to comply; and the Hindu element proceeded against them. Balais were not allowed to get water from the village wells; they were not allowed to let go their cattle to graze. Balais were prohibited from passing through land owned by a Hindu, so that if the field of a Balai was surrounded by fields owned by Hindu, the Balai could have no access to his own field. The Hindus also let their catte graze down the fields of Balais. The Balias submitted petitions to the Darbar against these persecutions: but as they could get no timely relief, and the oppression continued, hundreds of Balais with their wives and children were obliged to abandon their homes in which their ancestors lived for generations and to migrate to adjoining States, *viz.*, to villages in Dhar, Dewas, Bagli, Bhopal, Gwalior and other States. What happened to them in their new homes may for the present be left out of our consideration. The incident at Kavitha in Gujarat happened only last year. The Hindus of Kavitha ordered the untouchables not to insist upon sending their children to the common village school maintained by Government. What sufferings the untouchables of Kavitha had to

undergo for daring to exercise a civic right against the wishes of the Hindus is too well known to need detailed description. Another instance occurred in the village of Zanu in the Ahmedabad district of Gujarat. In November, 1935 some untouchable women of well-to-do families started fetching water in metal pots. The Hindus looked upon the use of metal pots by untouchables as an affront to their dignity and assaulted the untouchable women for their impudence. A most recent event is reported from the village Chakwara in Jaipur State. It seems from the reports that have appeared in the newspapers that an untouchable of Chakwara who had returned from a pilgrimage had arranged to give a dinner to his fellow untouchables of the village as an act of religious piety. The host desired to treat the guests to a sumptuous meal and the items served included ghee (butter) also. But while the assembly of untouchables was engaged in partaking of the food, the Hindus in their hundreds, armed with lathis, rushed to the scene, depoiled the food and belaboured the untouchtables who left the food they were served with and ran away for their lives. And why was this murderous assault committed on defenceless untouchables? The reason given is that the untouchable host was impudent enough to serve ghee and his untouchable guests were foolish enough to taste it. Ghee is undoubtedly a luxury for the rich. But no one would think that consumption of ghee was a mark of high social status. The Hindus of Chakwara thought otherwise and in righteous indignation avenged themselves for the wrong done to them by the untouchables, who insulted them by treating ghee as an item of their food which they ought to have known could not be theirs, consistently with the dignity of the Hindus. This means that an untouchable must not use ghee even if he can afford to buy it, since it is an act of arrogance towards the Hindus. This happened on or about the 1st of April, 1936!

Having stated the facts, let me now state the case for social reform. In doing this, I will follw, Mr. Bonnerji, as nearly as I can ask the political-minded Hindus "Are you fit for political power even through you do not allow a large class of your own countrymen like the untouchables to use public schools? Are you fit for political power even though you do not allow them the use of public wells? Are you fit for political power even though you do not allow them the use of public streets? Are you fit for political power even though you do not allow them to wear what apparel or ornaments they like? Are you fit for political power even though you do not allow them to eat any food they like?" I can ask a string of such questions. But these will suffice. I wonder what would have been the reply of Mr. Bonnerji. I am sure no sensible man will have the courage to give an affirmative answer. Every Congressman who repeats the dogma of Mili that one country is not fit to rule another country must admit that one class is not fit to rule another class.

How is it then that the Social Reform Party lost the battle? To understand this correctly it is necessary, to take note of the kind of social reform which the reformers were agitating for. In this connection it is necessary to make a distinction between social reform in the sense of the reform of the Hindu Family and social reform in the sense of the reorganization and reconstruction of the Hindu Society. The former has relation to window remarriage, child marriage etc., while the latter relates to the aboilition of the Caste System. The Social Conference was a body which mainly concerned itself with the reform of the high caste Hindu Family· It consisted mostly of enlightened high caste Hindus who did not feel the necessity for agitating for the abolition of caste or had not the courage to agitate for it. They felt quite naturally a greater urge to remove such evils as enforced widowhood, child marriage etc., evils which prevailed among them and which were personally felt by them. They did not stand up for the reform the Hindu society. The battle that was fought centered round the question of the reform of the family. It did not relate to the social reform in the sense of the break-up of the caste system. It was never put in issue by the reformers. That is the reason why the Social Reform Party lost.

I am aware that this argument cannot alter the fact that political reform did in fact gain precedence over social reform. But the argument has this much value if not more. It explains why social reformers lost the battle. It also helps us to understand how limited was the victory which the Political Reform. Party obtained over the Social Reform Party and that the view that social reform need not precede political reform is a view which may stand only when by social reform is meant the reform of the family. That political reform cannot with impunity take precedence over social reform in the sense of reconstruction of society is a thesis which. I am sure, cannot be controverted. That the makers of political constitutions must take account of social forces is a fact which is recognized by no less a person than Ferdinand Lassalle, the friend and co-worker of Karl Marx. In addressing a Prussian audience in 1862 Lassalle said:

> "The constitutional questions are in the first instance not questions of right but questions of might. The actual constitution of a country has its existenee only in the actual condition of force which exists in the country: hence political constitutions have value and premanence only when they accurately express those conditions of forces which exist in practice within a society."

But it is not necessary to go to Prussia. There is evidence at home. What is the significance of the Communal Award with its allocation of political power in defined proportions to diverse classes and communities? In my view, its significance lies in this that political constitution must take note of social organisation. It shows that the politicians who denied that the social problem in India had any bearing on the political problem were forced to reckon with the social problem in devising the constitution. The Communal Award is so to say the nemesis following upon the indifference and neglect of social reform. It is a victory for the Social Reform Party which shows that though defeated they were in the right in insisting upon the importance of social reform. Many, I know, will not accept this finding. The view is current, and it is pleasant to believe in it, that the Communal Award is unnatural and that it is the result of an unholy alliance between the minorities and the bureaucracy. I do not wish to rely on the Communal Award as a piece of evidence to support my contention if it is said that it is not good evidence. Let us turn to Ireland. What does the history of Irish Home Rule show? It is well-known that in the course of the negotiations between the representatives of Ulster and Southern Ireland, Mr. Redmond, the representative of Southern Ireland, in order to bring Ulster in a Home Rule Constitution common to the whole of Ireland said to the representatives of Ulster: "Ask any political safeguards you like and you shall have them." What was the reply that Ulstermen gave? Their reply was "Damn your safeguards, we don't want to be ruled by you on any terms." People who blame the minorities in India ought to consider what would have happened to the political aspirations of the majority if the minorities had taken the attitude which Ulster took. Judged by the attitude of Ulster to Irish Home Rules, is it nothing that the minorities agreed to be ruled by the majority which has not shown much sense of statesmanship, provided some safeguards were devised for them? But this is only incidental. The main question is why did Ulster take this attitude? The only answer I can give is that there was a social problem between Ulster and Southern Ireland the problem between Catholics and Protestants, essentially a problem of Caste. That Home Rule in Ireland would be Rome Rule was the way in which the Ulstermen had framed their answer. But that is only another way of stating that it was the social problem of Caste between the Catholics and Protestants, which prevented the solution of the political problem. This evidence again is sure to be challenged. It will be urged that here too the hand of the Imperialist was at work. But my resources are not exhausted. I will give evidence from the History of Rome. Here no one can say the any evil genus was at work. Any one who has studied the History of Rome will know that the Republican Constitution of Rome bore marks having strong resemblance to the Communal Award. When the kingship in Rome was abolished, the kingly power or the Imperium was divided between the Consuls and the Pontifex Maximus. In the Consuls was vested the secular authority of the King, while the latter took over the religious authority of King. This Republican Constitution had provided that, of the two Consuls one was to be Patrician and the other Plebian. The same constitution had also provided that, of the Priests under the Pontifex Maximums, half were to be Plebians and the other half Patricians. Why is it that the Republican Constitution of Rome had these provisions which, as I said, resemble so strongly the provisions of the Communal Award? The only answer one can get is that the Constitution of Republican Rome had to take account of the social division between the Patricians and the Plebians, who formed two distinct castes. To sum up, let political reformers turn to any direction they like, they will find that in the making of a constitution, they cannot ignore the problem arising out of prevailing social order.

The illustrations which I have taken in support of the proposition that social and religious problems have a bearing on political constitutions seem to be too particular. Perhaps they are. But it should not be supposed that the bearing of the one on the other is limited. On the other hand one can say that generally speaking History bears out the proposition that political revolutions have always been preceded by social and religious revolutions. The religious Reformation started by Luther was the precursor of the political emancipation of the European people. In England Puritanism led to the establishment of political liberty. Puritanism founded the new world. It was Puritanism which won the war of American Independence and Puritanism was a religious movement. The same is true of the Muslim Empire. Before the Arabs became a political power they had undergone a thorough religious revolution started by the Prophet Mohammad. Even India

History supports the same conclusion. The political revolution led by Chandragupta was preceded by the religious and social revolution of Buddha. The political revolution led by Shivaji was preceded by the religious and social reform brought about by the saints of Maharashtra. The political revolution of the Sikhs was preceded by the religious and social revolution led by Guru Nanak. It is unnecessary to add more illustrations. These will suffice to show that the emancipation of the mind and the soul is a necessary preliminary for the political expansion of the people.

II

Let me now turn to the Socialists. Can the Socialists ignore the problem arising out of the social order? The Socialists of India following their fellows in Europe are seeking to apply the economic interpretations of history to the facts of India. They propound that man is an economic creature, that his activities and aspirations are bound by economic facts, that property is the only source of power. They, therefore, preach that political and social reforms are but gigantic illusions and that economic reform by equalization of property must have precedence over every other kind of reform. One may join issue on every one of these premises on which rests the Socialists' case for economic reform having priority over every other kind of reform. One may contend that economic motive is not the only motive by which man is actuated. That economic power is the only kind of power no student of human society can accept. That the social status of an individual by itself often becomes a source of power and authority is made clear by the sway which the Mahatmas have held over the common man. Why do millionaires in India obey penniless Sadhus and Fakirs? Why do millions of paupers in India sell their trifling trinckets which constitute their only wealth and go to Benares and Mecca? That religion is the source of power is illustrated by the history of India where the priest holds a sway over the common man often greater than the magistrate and where everything, even such things as strikes and elections, so easily take a religious turn and can so easily be given a religious twist. Take the case of the Plebians of Rome as a further illustration of the power of religion over man. It throws great light on this point. The Plebs had fought for a share in the supreme executive under the Roman Republic and had sccured the appointment of a Plebian Consul elected by a separate electorate constituted by the Commitia Centuriata, which was an assembly of Plebians. They wanted a Consul of their own because they felt that the Patrician Consule used to discriminate against the Plebians in carrying on the administration. They had apparently obtained a great gain because under the Republican Constitution of Rome one Consul had the power of vetoing an act of the other Consul. But did they in fact gain anything? The answer to this question must be in the negative. The Plebians never could get a Plebian Consul who could be said to be a strong man and who could act independently of the Patrician Consul. In the ordinary course of things the Plebians should have got a strong Plebian Consul in view of the fact that his election was to be by a separate electorate of Plebians. The question is why did they fail in getting a strong Plebian to officiate as their Consul? The answer to this question reveals the dominion which religion exercises over the minds of men. It was an accepted creed of the whole Roman populus that no official could enter upon the duties of his office unless the Oracle of Delphi declared that he was acceptable to the Goddess. The priests who were in charge of the temple of the Goddess of Delphi were all Patricians. Whenever therefore the Plebians elected a Consul who was known to be a strong party man opposed to the Patricians or "communal" to use the term that is current in India, the Oracle invariably declared that he was not acceptable to the Goddess. This is how the Plebians were cheated out of their rights. But what is worthy of note is that the Plebians the permitted themselves to be thus cheated because they too like Patricians, held firmly the belief that the approval of the Goddess was a condition precedent to the taking charge by an official of his duties and that election by the people was not enough. If the Plebians had contended that election was enough and that the approval by the Goddess was not necessary they would have derived the fullest benefit from the political right which they had obtained. But they did not. They agreed to elect another, less suitable to themselves but more suitable to the Goddess which in fact meant more amenable to the Particians. Rather than give up religion, the Plebians give up material gain for which they had fought so hard. Does this not show that religion can be a source of power as great as money if not greater? The fallacy of the Socialists lies in supposing that because in the present stage of European Society property as a source of power is predominant, that the same is true of India or that the same was true of Europe in the past. Religion, social status and property are all sources of power and authority, which on man has, to control the liberty of another. One is predominant at one stage, the other is predominant at another stage. That is the only difference. If liberty is the ideal, if liberty means the destruction of the dominion which one man holds over another then obviously it cannot be insisted upon that economic reform must be the one kind of reform worthy of pursuit. If the source of power and dominion is at any given time or in any given society social and religious then social reform and religious reform must be accepted as the necessary sort of reform.

One can thus attack the doctrine of Economic Interpretation of History adopted by the Socialists of India. But I recognize that economic interpretation of history is not necessary for the validity of the Socialist contention that equalization of property is the only real reform and that it must precede everything else. However, what I like to ask the Socialists is this: Can you have economic reform without first bringing about a reform of the social order? The Socialists of India do not seem to have considered this question. I do not wish to them an injustice. I give below a quotation from a letter which a prominent Socialist wrote a few day ago to a friend of mine in which he soid. "I do not believe that we can build up a free society in India so long as there is a trace of this ill-treatment and suppression of one class by another. Believing as I do in a socialist ideal, inevitably I believe in perfect equality in the treatment of various classes and groups. I think that Socialism offers the only true remedy for this as well as other problems." Now the question that I like to ask is: Is it enough for a Socialist to say, "I believe in perfect equality in the treatment of the various classes?" To say that such a belief is enough is to disclose a complete lack of understanding of what is involved in Socialism. If Socialism is a practical programme and is not merely an ideal, distant and far off, the question for a Socialist is not whether he believes in equality. The question for him is whether he minds one class ill-treating and suppressing another class as a matter of system, as a matter of principle and thus allow tyranny and opperession to continue to divide one class from another. Let me analyse the factors that are involved in the realization of Socialism in order to explain fully my point. Now it is obvious that the economic reform contemplated by the Socialists cannot come about unless there is a revolution resulting in the seizure of power. That seizure of power must be by a proletariat. The first question I ask is: Will the proletariat of India combine to bring about this revolution? What will move men to such an action? It seems to me that other things being equal the only thing that will move one man to take such an action is the feeling that other man with whom he is acting are actuated by feeling of equality and fraternity and above all of justice. Men will not join in a revolution for the equalization of property unless they know that after the revolution is achieved they will be treated equally and that there will be no discrimination of caste and creed. The assurance of a Socialist leading the revolution that he does not believe in caste, I am sure, will not suffice. The assurance must be the assurance proceeding from much deeper foundation, namely, the mental attitude of the compatriots towards one another in their spirit of personal equality and fraternity. Can it be said that the proletariat of India, poor as it is, recognize on distinctions except that of rich and the poor? Can it be said that the poor in India recognize no such distinctions of caste or creed, high or low? If the fact is that they do, what unity of front can be expected from such a proletariat in its action against the rich? How can there be a revolution if the proletariat cannot present a united fiont? Suppose for the sake of argument that by some freak of fortune a revolution does take place and the Socialists come in power, will they not have to deal with the problems created by the particular social order prevalent in India? I can't see how a Socialist State in India can function for a second without having to grapple with the problems created by the prejudices which make Indian people observe the distinctions of high and low, clean and unclean. if Socialists are not to be content with the mouthing of fine phrases, if the Socialists wish to make Socialism a definite reality then they must recognize that the problem of social reform is fundamental and that for them there is no escape from it. That, the sacial order prevalent in India is a matter which a Socialist must deal with, that unless he does so he cannot achieve his revolution and that if he dose achieve it as a result of good fortune he will have to grapple with it if he wishes to realize his ideal, is a proposition which in my opinion is incontrovertible. He will be compelled to take account of caste after revolution if he does not take account of it before revolution. This only another way of saying that, turn in any direction you like, caste is the monster that crosses your path. You cannot have political reform, you cannot have economic reform, unless you kill this monster.

III

It is a pity that Caste even today has its defenders. The defences are many. It is defended on the ground that the Caste System is but another name for division of labour and if division of labour is a necessary feature of every civilized society then it is argued that there is nothing wrong in the Caste System. Now the first thing is to be urged against this view is that Caste System is not merely division of labour. It is also a division of labourers. Civilized society undoubtedly needs division of labour. But in no civilized society is division of labour accompanied by this unnatural division of labourers into water-tight compartments. Caste System is not merely a division of labourers which is quite different from division of labour—it is an heirarchy in which the divisions of labourers a re graded one above the other. In no other country is the division of labour accompained by this gradation of labourers. There is also a third point of criticism against this view of the Caste System. This division of labour is not spontaneous, it is not based on natural aptitudes. Social and individual efficiency requires us to develop the capacity of an individual to the point of competency to choose and to make his own career. This principle is violated in the Caste System in so far as it involves an attempt to appoint tasks to individuals in advance, selected not on the basis of trained original capacities, but on that of the social status of the parents. Looked at from another point of view this stratification of occupations which is the result of the Caste System is positively pernicious. Industry is never static. It undergoes rapid and abrupt changes. With such changes an individual must be free to change his occupation. Without such freedom to adjust himself to changing circumstances it would be impossible for him to gain his livelihood. Now the Caste System will not allow Hindus to take to occupations where they are wanted if they do not belong them by heredity. If a Hindu is seen to starve rather than take to new occupations not assigned to his Caste, the reason is to be found in the Caste System. By not permitting readjustment of occupations caste becomes a direct cause of much of the unemployment we see in the country. As a form of division of labour the Caste System suffers from another serious defect. The division of labour brought about by the Caste System is not a division based on choice. Individual sentiment, individual preference has no phace in it. It is based on the dogma of predestination. Considerations of social efficiency would compel us to recognize that the greatest evil in the industrial system is not so much poverty and the suffering that it involves as the fact that so many persons have callings which make no appeal to those who are engaged in them. Such callings constantly provoke one to aversion, ill-will and the desire to evade. There are many occupations in India which on account of the fact that they are regarded as degarded by the Hindus provoke those who are engaged in them to aversion. There is a constant desire to evade and escape from such occupations which arises solely because of the blighting effect which they produce upon those who follow them owing to the slight and stigma cast upon them by the Hindu religion. What efficiency can there be in a system under which neither men's hearts nor their minds are in their work? As an economic organization Caste is therefore a harmful institution inasmuch as, it involves the subordination of man's natural powers and inclinations to the exigencies of social rules.

IV

Some have dug a biological trench in defence of the Caste System. It is said that the object of Caste was to preserve purity of race and purity of blood. Now ethnologists are of opinion that men of pure roce exist nowhere and that there has been a mixture of all races in all parts of the world. Especially is this the case with the people of India. Mr. D. R. Bhandarkar in this paper on Foreign Elements in the Hindu Population has stated that "There is hardly a class, or Caste in India which has not a foreign strain in it. There is an admixture of alien blood not only among the warrior classes—the Rajputs and the Marathas—but also among the Brahmins who are under the happy delusion that they are free from all foreign elements." The Caste System cannot be said to have grown as means of preventing the admixture of races or as a means of maintaining purity of blood. As a matter of fact Caste System came into being long after the different races of India had commingled in blood and culture. To hold that distinctions of Castes of really distinctions of race and to treat different Castes as though they were so many different races is a gross perversion of facts. What racial affinity is there between the Brahmin of the Punjab and the Brahmin of Madras? What racial affinity is there between the untouchable of Bengal and the untouchable of Madras? What racial difference is there between the Brahmin of the Punjab and the Chamar of the Punjab? What racial difference is there between the Brahmin of Madras and the Pariah of Madras? The Brahmin of the

Punjab is racially of the same stock as the Chamar of the Punjab and the Brahmin of Madras is of the same race as the Pariah of Madras. Caste System does not demarcate racial division. Caste System is a social division of people of the same race. Assuming it, however, to be a case of racial divisions one may ask. What harm could there be if a mixture of races and of blood was permitted to take place in India by intermarriages between different Castes? Men are no doubt divided from animals by so deep a distinction that science recognizes men and animals as two distinct species. But even scientists who believe in purity of races do not assert that the scientists who believe in purity of races do not assert that the different races constitute different species of men. They areonly varieties of one and the same species. As such they can inter-breed and produce an offspring which is capable of breeding and which is not sterile. An immenes lot of nonsense is talked about heredity and eugenics in defence of thc Caste System. Few would object to the Caste System if it was in accord with the basic principle of eugenics because few can object to the improvement of the race by judicious mating. But one fails to understand how the Caste System secures judicious mating. Caste System is a negative thing. It merely prohibits persons belonging to different Castes from intermarrying. It is not a positive method of selecting which two among a given Caste should marry. If Caste is eugenic in origin then the origin of sub-Castes must also be eugenic. But can any one seriously maintain that the origin of sub-Castes is eugenic? I think it would be absued to contend for such a proposition and for a very obvious reason. If Caste means race then differences of sub-Castes cannot mean differences of race because sub-Castes become exhypothesia sub-divisions of one and the same race. Consequently the bar against intermarrying and interdining between sub-Castes cannot be for the purpose of maintaining purity of race or of blood. If sub-Castes cannot be eugenic in origin there cannot be any substance in the contention that Caste is eugenic in origin. Again if Caste is eugenic in origin one can understand the bar against intermarriage. But what is the purpose of the interdict placed on interdining between

Castes and sub-Castes alike? Interdining cannot infect blood and therefore cannot be the cause either of the improvement or of deterioration of the race. This shows that Caste has no scientific origin and that those who are attempting to give it an eugenic basis are trying to support by science what is grossly unscientific. Even today eugenics cannot become a practical possibility unless we have definite knowledge regarding the laws of heredity. Prof. Batcson in his Mendel's Principles of Heredity says. "There is nothing in the descent of the higher mental qualities to suggest that they follow any single system of transmission. It is likely that both they and the more marked developments of physical powers result rather from the coincidence of numerous factors than from the possession of any one genetic element." To argue that the Caste System was eugenic in its conception is to attribute to the forefathers of present-day Hindus a knowledge of heredity which even the modern scientists do not possess. A tree should be judged by the fruits it yields. If caste is eugenic what sort of a race of men it should have produced? Physically speaking the Hindus are a C_3 people. They are a race of Pygmies and dwarfs stunted in stature and wanting in stamina. It is a nation 9/10ths of which is declared to be unfit for military service. This shows that the Caste System does not embody the eugenics of modern scientists. It is a social system which embodies the arrogance and selfishness of a perverse section of the Hindus who were superior enough in social status to set it in fashion and who had authority to force it on their inferiors.

V

Caste does not result in economic efficiency. Caste cannot and has not improved the race. Caste has however done one thing. It has completely disorganized and demoralized the Hindus.

The first and foremost thing that must be recognized is that Hindu Society is a myth. The name Hindus is itself a foreign name. It was given by the Mohammedans to the natives for the purpose of distinguishing themselves. It does not occur in any Sanskrit work prior to the Mohammedan invasion. They did not feel the necessity of a common name because they had no conception of their having constituted a community. Hindu society as such does not exist. It is only a collection of castes. Each caste is conscious of its existence. Its survival is the be all and end all of its existence. Castes do not even form a federation. A caste has no feeling that it is affiliated to other castes except when the is a Hindu-Muslim riot. On all other occasions each caste endeavours to segregate itself and to distinguish itself from other castes. Each caste not only dines among itself and marries among itself but each caste prescribes its own distinctive dress. What other explanation can there be of the innumerable styles of dress worn by the men and women of India which so amuse the tourists? Indeed the ideal Hindu must be like a rat living in his own hole refusing to have any contact with others. There is an utter lack among the Hindu of what the sociologists call "consciousness of kind." There is no Hindu consciousness of kind. In every Hindu the consciousness that exists is the consciousness of his caste. That is the reason why the Hindus cannot be said to form a society or a nation. There are however many Indians whose patriotism does not permit them to admit that Indians are not a nation, that they are only an amorphous mass of people. They have insisted that underlying the apparent diversity there is a fundamental unity which marks the life of the Hindus in as much as there is a similarity of habits and customs, beliefs and thoughts whlch obtain all over the continent of India. Similarity in habits and customs, beliefs and thoughts there is. But one cannot accept the conclusion that therefore, the Hindus constitute a society. To do so is to misunderstand the essentials which go to make up a society. Men do not become a society by living in physical proximity any more than a man ceases to be a member of his society by living so many miles away from other men. Secondly similarity in habits and customs, beliefs and thoughts is not enough to constitute men into society. Things may be passed physically from one to another like bricks. In the same way habits and customs, beliefs and thought of one group may be taken over by another group and there may thus appear a similarity between the two. Culture spreads by diffusion and that is why one finds similarity between various primitive tribes in the matter of their habits and customs beliefs and thoughts, although they do not live in proximity. But no one could say that because there was this similarity the primitive tribes constituted one society. This is because similarly in certain things is not enough to constitute a society. Men constitute a society because they have things which they possess in common. To have similar thing is totally different from possessing things in common. And the only way by which men can come to possess things in common with one another is by being in communication with one another. This is merely another way of saying that Society continues to exist by communication indeed in communication. To make it concrete, it is not enough if men act in a way which agrees with the acts of others. Parallel activity, even if similar, is not sufficient to bind men into a society. This is proved by the fact that the festivals observed by the different Castes amongst the Hindus are the same. Yet these parallel performances of similar festivals by the different castes have not bound them into one integral whole. For that purpose what is necessary is for a man to share and participate in a common activity so that the same emotions are aroused in him that animate the others. Making the individual a sharer or partner in the associated activity so that he feels its success as his success, its failure as his failure is the real thing that binds men and makes a society of them. The Caste System prevents common activity and by preventing common activity it has prevented the Hindus from becoming a society with a unified life and a consciousness of its own being.

VI

The Hindus often complain of the isolation and exclusiveness of a gang or a clique and blame them for anti-social spirit.

But they conveniently forget that this anti-social spirit is the worst feature of their own Caste System. One caste enjoys singing a hymn of hate against another caste as much as the Germans did in singing their hymn of hate against the English during the last war. The literature of the Hindus is full of caste genealogies in wich an attempt is made to give a noble origin to one caste and an ignoble origin to other castes. The Sahyadrikhand is a notorious instance of this class of literature. This anti-social spirit is not confined to caste alone. It has gone deeper and has poisoned the mutual relations of the sub-castes as well. In my province the Golak Brahmins, Deorukha Brahmins, Karada Brahmins and Palshe Brahmins and Chitpavan Brahmins, all claim to be sub-divisions of the Brahmin Caste. But the anti-social spirit that prevails between them is quite as marked and quite as virulent as the anti-social spirit that prevails between them and other non-Brahmin castes. There is nothing strange in this. An anti-social spirit is found wherever one group has "interests of its own" which shut it out from full interaction with other groups, so that its prevailing purpose is protection of what it has got. This anti-social spirit, this spirit of protecting its own interests is as much a marked feature of the different castes in their isolation from one another as it is of nations in their isolation. The Brahmin's primary concern is to protect "his interest" against those of the non-Brahmins and the non-Brahmin's primary concern is to protect their interests against those of the Brahmins. The Hindus, therefore, are not merely an assortment of castes but they are so many warring groups each living for itself and for its selfish ideal. There is another feature of caste which is deplorable. The ancestors of the present-day English fought on one side or the other in the wars of the Roses and the Cromwellian War. But the descendants of thoes who fought on the one side do not bear any animosity—any grudge against the descendants of those who fought on the other side. The feud is forgotten. But the present-day non-Brahmins cannot forgive the present-day Brahmins for the insult their ancestors gave to Shivaji. The present-day Kayasthas will not forgive the present-day Brahmins for the infamy cast upon their forefathers by the forefathers of the latter. To what is this difference due? Obviously to the Caste System. The existence of Caste and Caste Consciousness has served to keep the memory of past feuds between castes green and has prevented solidarity.

VII

The recent discussion about the excluded and partially included areas has served to draw attention to the position of what are called the aboriginal tribes in India. They number about 13 millions if not more. Apart from the questions whether their exclusion from the new Constitution is proper or imporper, the fact still remains that these aborigines have remained in their primitive uncivilized State in a land which boasts of a civilization thousands of years old. Not only are they not civilized but some of them follow pursuits which have led to their being classified as criminals. Thirteen millions of people living in the midst of civilization are still in a savage state and are leading the life of hereditary criminals! But the Hindus have never felt ashamed of it. This is a phenomenon which in my view is quite unparalleled. What is the cause of this shameful state of affairs? Why has no attempt been made to civilize these aborigines and to lead them to take to a more honourable way of making a living? The Hindus will probably seek to account for this savage state of the aborigines by attributing them congenital stupidity. They will probably not admit that the aborigines have remained savages because they had made no effort to civilize them, to give them medical aid, to reform them, to make them good citizens. But supposing a Hindu wished to do what the Christian missionary is doing for these aborigines, could he have done it? I sumbit not. Civilizing the aborigines means adopting them as your own, living in their midst, and cultivating fellow-feeling, in-short loving them. How is it possible for a Hindu to do this? His whole life is one anxious effort to preserve his caste. Caste is his precious possession which he must save at any cost. He cannot consent to lose it by establishing contact with the aborigines the remnants of the hateful Anaryas of the Vedic days. Not that a Hindu could not be taught the sense of duty to fallen humanity, but the trouble is that no amount of sense of duty can enable him to overcome his duty to preserve his caste. Caste is, therefore, the real explanation as to why the Hindu has let the savage remain a savage in the midst of his civilization without blushing or without feeling and sense of remorse or repentance. The Hindu has not realized that these aborigines are a source of potential danger. If these savages remain savages they may not do any harm to the Hindus. But if they are reclaimed by non-Hindus and converted to their faiths they will swell the ranks of the enemies of the Hindus. If this happens the Hiudu will have to thank himself and his Caste System.

VIII

Not only has the Hindu made no effort for the humanitarian cause of civilizing the savages but the higher-caste Hindus have deliberately prevented the lower castes who are within the pale of Hinduism from rising to the cultural level of the higher castes. I will give two instances, one of the Sonars and the other of the Pathare Prabhus. Both are communities quite well-known in Maharashtra. Like the rest of the communities desiring to raise their status these two communities were at one time endeavouring to adopt some of the ways and habits of the Brahmins. The Sonars were styling themselves Daivadnya Brahmins and were wearing their "dhotis" with folds on and using the word namaskar for salutation. Both, the folded way of wearing the "dhoti" and the namaskar were special to the Brahmins. The Brahmins did not like this imitation and this attempt by Sonars to pass off as Brahmins. Under the authority of the Peshwas the Brahmins successfully put down this attempt on the part of the Sonars to adopt the ways of the Brahmins. They even got the President of the Councils of the East India Company's settlement in Bombay to issue a prohibitory order against the Sonars residing in Bombay. At one time the Pathare Prabhus had widow—remarriage as a custom of their caste This custom of widow—remarriage was later on looked upon as a mark of social inferiority by some members of the caste especially because it was contrary to the custom prevalent among the Brahmins. With the object of raising status of their community some Pathare Prabhus sought to stop this practice of widow—remarriage that was prevalent in their caste. The community was divided into two camps, one for and the other against the innovation. The Peshwas took the side of those in favour of widow-remarriage and thus virtually prohibited the Pathare Prabhus from following the ways of the Brahmins. The Hindus criticise the Mohammedans for having spread their religion by the use of the sword. They also ridicule Christianity on the score of the inquisition. But really speaking who is better and more worthy of our respect—the Mohammedans and Christians who attempted to thrust down the throats of unwilling persons what they regarded as necessary for their salvation or the Hindu who would not spread the light, who would endeavour to keep others in darkness, who would not consent to share his intellectual and social inheritance with those who are ready and willing to make it a part of their own make-up? I have no hesitation in saying that if the Mohammedan has been cruel the Hindu has been mean and meanness is worse than cruelty.

Appendix II

EXPLANATORY NOTES TO MEMORANDUM SUBMITTED TO CONSTITUENT ASSEMBLY

Preamble

The Preamble gives constitutional shape and form to the Resolution on objectives passed by the Constituent Assembly on Wednesday the 22nd January, 1947.

ARTICLE I—Section I

Clauses 1 to 4

The admission of the six hundred and odd Indian States into the Union raises many difficulty questions. The most difficult of them is the one which relates to their admission into the Union. Every Indian State is claiming to be a Sovereign State and is demanding to be admitted into the Union in its own right. The Indian States fall into different classes from the view of size, population, revenue and resources. It is obvious that every State admitted into the Union as a State must have the capacity to bear the burden of modern administration to maintain peace within its own borders and to possess the resources necessary for the economic advancement of its people. Otherwise, the United States of India is likely to be encumbered with a large number of weak States which, instead of being a help to the Central Government, will be a burden upon it. The Union Government with such small and weak States as its units will never be able to pull its full weight in an emergency. It is therefore obvious that it would be a grave danger to the future safety to India if every Indian State were admitted into the Union without any scrutiny of its capacity to bear the burden of modern administration and maintaining internal peace. To avoid this danger, the Article proceeds to divide the Indian States into two classes:

1. Qualified Indian States, and
2. Unqualified Indian States.

It proposes that a list of Qualified Indian States should be drawn up as a first step in the procedure to be followed for the admission of the Indian States into the Union. A Qualified Indian State will be admitted into the Union on an application for admission and the fulfilment of the provisions of the Enabling Act which the Union Legislature is authorized to pass for the purpose of requiring an appropriate form of internal Government set up within the State which will be in consonance to the principles underlying the Constitution of the United States of India. The territory in the occupation of the Unqualified Indian States will be treated as the territory of the United States of India and will be reorganized into States of suitable sizes by the United States of India. In the meantime those who are rulers of the territory shall continue to administer, the territory under the supervision of the United States of India. The Act also declares that the Indian territory whether in the occupation of British Indian Provinces or of the Indian States is one and integral and will be so even though an Indian State has not entered into the Union.

Clause 4 provides that once a State is admitted into the Union, its integrity shall be maintained and it shall not be liable to subdivision except in accordance with the provisions contained in the clause.

ARTICLE I—Section II

Clauses 1 and 2

Clause 1 permits the United States of India to incorporate States which are independent but which are on the border and which desire to join the Union.

Clause 2 enables the United States of India to acquire territory and to incorporate it or to treat it as separate territory.

ARTICLE II—Section I

The inclusion of Fundamental Rights in the Constitution requires no justification. The necessity of Fundamental Rights is recognized in all Constitutions old and new. The Fundamental Rights included in the Article are borrowed from the Constitutions of various countries particularly from those wherein the conditions are more or less analogous to those existing in India.

ARTICLE II—Section II

Clause 1

Right are real only if they are accompanied by remedies. It is no use giving rights if the aggrieved person has no legal remedy to which he can resort when his rights are invaded. Consequently when the Constitution guarantees rights it also becomes necessary to make provision to prevent the Legislature and the Executive from overriding them. This function has been usually assigned to the judiciary and the Courts have been made the special guardians of the rights guaranteed by the Constitution. The clause does no more than this. The clause proposes to give protection to the citizen against Executive tyranny by investing the Judiciary with certain powers of inquisition against the abuse of authority by the Executive. This power takes the form of issue of writs. The High Courts in India possess these powers under the Government of India and under their letters parent. These powers are however subject to two limitations. In the first place the powers given by the Letters Patent are available only to the High Courts in the Presidency Towns and not to all. Secondly these powers are subject to laws made by the Indian Legislature. Thirdly the powers given by the Government of India Act, 1935 are restricted and may prove insufficient for the protection of the aggrieved person. The clause achieves two objectives:

1. to give the fullest power to the Judiciary to issue what under the English Law are called Prerogative Writs; and
2. to prevent the Legislature from curtailing these powers in any manner whatsoever.

Clause 2

It is difficult to expect that in a country like India where most persons are communally minded those in authority will give equal treatment to those who do not belong to their community. Unequal treatment has been the inescapable fate of the Untouchables in India. The following extract from the Proceedings of the Board of Revenue of the Government of Madras No. 723 dated 5th November, 1892, illustrates the sort of unequal treatment which is meted out to the Scheduled Castes by Hindu Officers. Says the report:

"134. There are forms of oppression only hitherto hinted at which must be at least cursorily mentioned. To punish disobedience of Pariahs, their masters:

(a) bring false cases in the village Court or in the criminal Courts;

(b) obtain, on application, from Government, waste lands lying all round the paracheri, so as to impound the Pariahs' cattle or obstruct the way to their temple;

(c) have mirasi names fraudulently entered in the Government account against the paracheri;

(d) pull down the huts and destroy the growth in the backyards;

(e) deny occupancy right in immemorial sub-tenancies;

(f) forcibly cut the Pariays' crops, and ôn being resisted charge them with theft and rioting;

(g) under misrepresentations, get them to execute documents by which they are afterwards ruined;

(h) cut off the flow of water from their fields;

(i) without legal notice, have the property of sub-tenants attached for the handlords' arrears of revenue."

"135. It will be said there are civil and criminal Courts for the redress of any of these injuries. There are the Courts indeed; but India does not breed village Hampdens. One must have courage to go to the Courts; money to employ legal knowledge, and meet legal expenses; and means to live during the case and the appeals Further most cases depend upon the decision of the first Court; and these Courts are presided over by officials who are sometimes corrupt and who generally for other reasons, sympathize with the wealthy and landed classes to which they belong."

"136. The influence of these classes with the official world can hardly be exaggerated. It is extreme with natives and great even with Europeans. Every office, from the highest to the lowest, is stocked with their representatives, and there is no proposal affecting their interests but they can bring a score of influence to bear upon it in its course from inception to execution."

The Punjab Land Alienation Act is another illustration of unequal treatment of the Untouchables by the Legislature.

Many other minority communities may be suffering from similar treatment at the hands of the majority community. It is therefore necessary to have such a provision to ensure that all citizens shall have equal benefit of Laws. Rules and Regulations.

The provisions of Clause 2 are borrowed from Civil Rights Protection Act, 1866, and of March 1st, 1875 passed by the Congress of the United States of America to project the Negroes against unequal treatment.

Clause 3

Discrimination is another menace which must be guarded against if the Fundamental Rights are to be real rights. In a country like India where it is possible for discrimination to be practised on a vast scale and in a relentless manner Fundamental Rights can have no meaning. The Remedy follows the lines adopted in the Bill which was recently introduced in the Congress of the U.S.A. the aim of which is to prevent discrimanation being practised against the Negroes.

Clause 4

The main purpose behind the clause is to put an obligation on the State of plan the economic life of the people on lines which would lead to highest point of productivity without closing every avenue to private enterprise, and also provide for the equitable distribution of wealth. The plan set out in the clause proposes State ownership in agriculture with a collectivised method of cultivation and a modified form of State Socialism in the field of industry. It places squarely on the shoulders of the State the obligation to supply capital necessary for agriculture as well as for industry. Without the supply of capital by the State neither land nor industry can be made to yield better results. It also proposes to nationalize insurance with a double objective. Nationalized Insurance gives the individual greater security than a private Insurance Firm does inasmuch as it pledges the resources of the State as a security for the ultimate payment of his insurance money. It also gives the State the resources necessary for financing its economic planning in the absence of which it would have to resort to borrowing from the money market at a high rate of interest. State Socialism is essential for the rapid industrialization of India. Private enterprize cannot do it and if it did it would produce those inequalities of wealth which private capitalism has produced in Europe and which should be a warning to Indians. Consolidation of Holdings and Tenancy Legislation are worse than useless. They cannot bring about prosperity in agriculture. Neither Consolidation nor Tenancy Legislation can be of any help to the 60 millions of Untouchables who are just landless labourers. Neither Consolidation nor Tenancy Legislation can solve their problem. Only collective farms on the lines set out in the proposal can help them. There is no expropriation of the interests concerned. Consequently there ought to be no objection to the proposal on that account.

The plan has two special features. One is that it proposes State Socialism in important fields of economic life. The second special feature of the plan is that it does not leave the establishment of State Socialism to the will of the Legilature. It establishes State Socialism by the Law of the Constitution and thus makes it unalterable by any act of the Legislature and the Executive.

Students of Constitutional Law will at once raise a protest. They are sure to ask. Does not the proposal go beyond the scope of the usual type of Fundamental Rights? My answer is that it does not. If it appears to go beyond it is only because the conception of Fundamental Rights on which such criticism is based is a narrow conception. One may go further and say that even from the narrow conception of the scope of the Constitutional Law as comprising no more than Fundamental Rights the proposal can find ample justification. For what is the purpose of prescribing by law the shape and form of the economic structure of society? The purpose is to protect the liberty of the individual from invasion by other individuals which is the object of enacting Fundamental Rights. The connection between individual liberty and the shape and form of the economic structure of society may not be apparent to everyone. None the less the connection between the two is real. It will be apparent if the following considerations are borne in mind.

Political Democracy rests on four premises which may be set out in the following terms:

(i) The individual is an end in himself.

(ii) That the individual has certain inalienable rights which must be guaranteed to him by the Constitution.

(iii) That the individual shall not be required to relinquish any of his constitutional rights as a condition precedent to the receipt of a privilege.

(iv) That the State shall not delegate powers to private persons to govern others.

Anyone who studies the working of the system of social economy based on private enterprise and pursuit of personal gain will realize how it undermines, if it does not actually violate, the last two premises on which Democracy rests. How many have to relinquish their constitutional rights in order to gain their living? How many have to subject themselves to be governed by private employers?

Ask those who are unemployed whether what are called Fundamental Rights are of any value to them. If a person who is unemployed is offered a choice between a job of some sort, with some sort of wages, with no fixed hours of labour and with an interdict on joining a union and the exercise of his right to freedom of speech, association, religion, etc., can there be any doubt as to what his choice will be. How can it be otherwise? The fear of starvation, the fear of losing a house, the fear of losing savings if any, the fear of being compelled to take children away from school, the fear of having to be a burden on public charity, the fear of having to be burned or buried at public cost are factors too strong to permit a man to stand out for his Fundamental Rights. The unemployed are thus compelled to relinquish their Fundamental Rights for the sake of securing the privilege ta work and to subsist.

What about those who are employed? Constitutional

Lawyers assume that the enactment of Fundamental Rights is enough to safeguard their liberty and that nothing more is called for. They argue that where the State refrains from intervention in private affairs—economic and social—the residue is liberty. What is necessary is to make the residue as large as possible and State intervention as small as possible. It is true that where the State refrains from intervention what remains is liberty. But this does not dispose of the matter. One more question remains to be answered. To whom and for whom is this liberty? Obviously this liberty is liberty to the landlords to increase rents, for capitalists to increase hours of work and reduce rate of wages. This must be so. It cannot be otherwise. For in an economic system employing armies of workers, producing goods en masse at regular intervals some one must make rules so that workers will work and the wheels of industry run on. If the State does not do it the private employer will. Life otherwise will become impossible. In other words what is called liberty from the control of the State is another name for the dictatorship of the private employer.

How to prevent such a thing happening? How to protect the unemployed as well as the employed from being cheated out of their Fundamental Rights to life, liberty and pursuit of happiness? The useful remedy adopted by Democratic countries is to limit the power of Government to impose arbitrary restraints in political domain and to invoke the ordinary power of the Legilature to restrain the more powerful individual from imposing arbitrary restraints on the less powerful in the economic field. The inadequacy may the futility of the plan has been well-established. The successful invocation by the less powerful of the authority of the Legislature is a doubtful proposition. Having regard to the fact that even under adult suffrage all Legislatures and Governments are controlled by the more powerful an appeal to the Legislature to intervene is a very precarious safeguard against the invasion of the liberty of the less powerful. The plan follows quite a different method. It seeks to limit not only the power of Government to impose arbitrary restraints but also of the more powerful individuals or to be more precise to eliminate the possibility of the more powerful having the power to impose arbitrary restraints on the less powerful by withdrawing from the control he has over the economic life of people. There cannot be slightest doubt that of the two remedies against the invasion by the more powerful of the rights and liberties of the less powerful the one contained in the proposal is undoubtedly the more effective. Considered in the light of these observations the proposal is essentially a proposal for safeguarding the liberty of the individual. No Constitutional Lawyer can therefore object to it on the ground that it goes beyond the usual scope of Constitutional Law.

So far as the plan has been considered purely as a means of safeguarding individual liberty. But there is also another aspect of the plan which is worthy of note. It is an attempt to establish State Socialism without abrogating Parliamentary Democracy and without leaving its establishment to the will of a Parliamentary Democracy. Critics of State Socialism even its friends are bound to ask why make it a part of the Constitutional Law of the land? Why not leave it to the Legislature to bring it into being by the ordinary process of Law. The reason why it cannot be left to the ordinary Law is not difficult to understand. One essential condition for the success of a planned economy is that it must not be liable to suspension or abadonment. It must be permanent. The question is how this permanence can be secured. Obviously it cannot be secured under the form of Government called Parliamentary Democracy under the system of Parliamentary Democracy, the policy of the Legislature and of the Executive is the policy of the majority for the time being. Under the system of Parliamentary Democracy the majority in one election may be in favour of State Socialism in Industry and in Agriculture. At the next election the majority may be against it. The anti-State Socialism majority will use its Law-making power to undoing the work of the pro-State Socialism majority and the pro-State Socialism majority will use its Law-making power to doing over again what has been undone by their opponents. Those who want the economic structure of society to be modelled on State Socialism must realize that they cannot leave the fulfilment of so fundamental a purpose to the exigencies of ordinary Law which simple majorities—whose political fortunes are never determined by rational causes—have a right to make and unmake. For these reasons Political Democracy seems to be unsuited for the purpose.

What is the alternative? The alternative is Dictatorship. There is no doubt that Dictatorship can give the permanence which State Socialism requires as an essential condition for its fructification. There is however one fact against Dictatorship which must be faced. Those who believe in individual freedom strongly object to Dictatorship and insists upon Parliamentary Democracy as a proper form of Government for a Free Society. For they feel that freedom of the individual is possible only under Parliamentary Democracy and not under Dictatorship. Consequently those who want freedom are not prepared to give up Parliamentary Democracy as a form of Government. However, much they may be anxious to have State Socialism they will not be ready to exchange Parliamentary Democracy for Dictatorship even though the gain by such an exchange is the achievement of State Socialism. The problem therefore is to have State Socialism without Dictatorship, to have State Socialism with Parliamentary Democracy. The way out seems to be to retain Parliamentary Democracy and to prescribe State Socialism by the Law of the Constitution so that it will be beyond the reach of a Parliamentary majority to suspend, amend or abrogate it. It is only by this that one can achieve the triple object, namely, to establish socialism, retain Parliamentary Democracy and avoid Dictatorship.

The proposal marks a departure from the existing Constitutions whose aim is merely to prescribe the form of the political structure of society leaving the economic structure untouched. The result is that the political structure is completely set at naught by the forces which emerge from the economic structure which is at variance with the political structure. Those who want socialism with Parliamentary Democracy and without Dictatorship should welcome the proposal.

The soul of Democracy is the doctrine of one man, one value. Unfortunately, Democracy has attempted to give effect to this doctrine only so far as the political structure is concerned by adopting the rule of one man, one vote which is supposed to translate into fact the doctrine of one man, one value. It has left the economic structure to take the shape given to it by those who are in a position to mould it. This has happened because Constitutional Lawyers have been dominated by the antiquated conception that all that is necessary for a perfect Constitution for Democracy was to frame a Constitutional Law which would make Government responsible to the people and to prevent tyranny of the people by the Government. Consequently, almost all Laws of Constitution which relate to countries which are called Democratic stop with Adult Suffrage and Fundamental Right. They have never advanced to the conception that the Constitutional Law of Democracy must go beyond Adult Suffrage and Fundamental Rights. In other words, old time Constitutional Lawyers believed that the scope and function of Constitutional Law was to prescribe the shape and form of the political structure of society. They never realized that it was equally essential to prescribe the shape and form of the economic structure of society, if Democracy is to live up to its principle of one man, one value. Time has come to take a bold step and define both the economic structure as well as the political structure of society by the Law of the Constitution. All countries like India which are late-comers in the field of Constitution-making should not copy the faults of other countries. They should profit by the experience of their predecessors.

ARTICLE II—Section III

Clause 1

In the Government of India Acts of 1919 and 1935 the model that was adopted for framing the structure of the Executive in the Provinces and in the Centre was of the British type or what is called by Constitutional Lawyers Parliamentary Executive as opposed to the American type of Executive which in contradistinction of the British type is called Non-Parliamentary Executive. The question is whether the pattern for the Executive adopted in the two Acts should be retained or whether it should be abandoned and if so what model should be adopted in its place. Before giving final opinion on this issue it would be desirable to set out the special features of the British type of the Executive and the consequences that are likely to follow if it was applied to India.

The following may be taken to be the special features of British or the Parliamentary Executive:

1. It gives a party which has secured a majority in the Legislature the right to form a Government.
2. It gives the majority party the right to exclude from Government persons who do not belong to the Party.
3. The Government so formed continues in office only so long as it can command a majority in the Legislature. If it ceases to command a majority it is bound to resign either in favour of another Government formed out of the existing Legislature or in favour of a new Government formed out of a newly elected Legislature.

As to the consequences that would follow if the British System was applied to India the situation can be summed up in the following proposition:

1. The British System of Government by a Cabinet of the majority party rests on the premise that majority is a political majority. In India the majority is a communal majority. No matter what social and political programme it may have the majority will retain its character of being a communal majority. Nothing can alter this fact. Given this fact it is clear that if the British System was copied it would result in perma-

nently vesting Executive power in a Communal majority.

2. The British System of Government imposes no obligation upon the Majority Party to include in its cabinet the representatives of Manority Party. If applied to India the consequence will be obvious. It wouid make the majority community a governing class and the minority community a subject race. It would mean that a communal majority will be free to run the administration according to its own ideas of what is good for the minorities. Such a state of affairs could not be called democracy. It will have to be called imperialism.

In the light of these consequences it is obvious that the introduction of British type of the Executive will be full of menace to the life, liberty and pursuit of happiness of the minorities in general and of the Untouchables in particular.

The problem of the Untouchables is a formidable one for the Untouchables to face. The Untouchables are surrounded by a vast mass of Hindu population which is hostile to them and which is not ashamed of committing any inequity or atrocity against them. For a redress of these wrongs which are matters of daily occurrence, the Untouchables have to call in the aid of the administration. What is the character and composition of this administration? To be brief, the administration in India is completely in the hand of the Hindus. It is their monopoly. From top to bottom it is controlled by them. There is no Department which is not dominated by them. They dominated the Police, the Magistracy and the Revenue Services indeed any and every branch of the administration. The next point to remembers is that the Hindus in the administration have the same positive anti-social and inimical attitude to the Untouchable which the Hindus outside the administration have. Their one aim is to discriminate against the Untouchables and to deny and deprive them not only of the benefits of Law, but also of the protection of the Law against tyranny and oppression. The result is that the Untouchables are placed between the Hindu population and the Hindu-ridden administration, the one committing wrong against them and the other protecting the wrong-dore, instead of helping the victims.

Against this background, what can Swaraj mean to the Untouchables? It con only mean one thing, namely, that while today it is only the administration that is in the hands of the Hindus, under Swaraj the Legislature and Executive will also be in the hands of the Hindus. It goes without saying that such a Swaraj would aggravate the sufferings of the Untouchables. For, in addition to an hostile administration, there will be an indifferent Legislature and a callous Executive. The result will be that the administration unbridled in venom and in harshness, uncontrolled by the Legislature and the Executive, may pursue its policy of inequity towards the Untouchables without any curb. To put it diffcreatly, under Swaraj the Untouchables will have no way of escape from the destiny of degradation which Hindus and Hinduism have fixed for them.

These are special considerations against the introduction of British System of Executive which have their origin in the interests of the minorities and the Scheduled Castes. But there is one general consideration which can be urged against the introduction of the British Cabinet System in India. The British Cabinet System has undoubtedly given the British people a very stable system of Government. Question is will it produce a stable Government in India? The chances are very slender. In view of the clashes of castes and creeds there is bound to be a plethora of parties and groups in the Legislature in India. If this happens it is possible, may certain, that under the system of Parliamentary Executive like the one that prevails in England under which the Executive is bound to resign upon an adverse vote in the Legislature. India may suffer from instability of the Executive. For it is the easiest thing for groups to align and realign themselves at frequent intervals and for petty purposes and bring about the downfall of Government. The present solidarity of what are called the Major Parties cannot be expected to continue. Indeed as soon as the Problem of the British in India is solved the cement that holds these parties together will fall away. Constant overthrow of Government is nothing short of anarchy. The present Constitution has in it Section 93 which provides a remedy against it. But Section 93 would be out of place in the Constitution of a free India. Some substitute must therefore be found for Section 93.

Taking all these consideration together there is no doubt that the British type of the Executive is entirely unsuited to India.

The form of the Executive proposed in the clause is intended to serve the following purposes:

(i) To prevent the majority from forming a Government without giving any opportunity to the minorities to have a say in the matter.

(ii) To prevent the majority from having exclusive control over administration and thereby make the tyranny of the minority by the majority possible.

(iii) To prevent the inclusion by the Majority Party in the Executive representatives of the minorities who have no confidence of the minorities.

(iv) To provide a stable Executive necessary for good and efficient administration.

The clause takes the American form of Executive as a model and adapts it to Indian conditions especially to the requirements of minorities. The form of the Executive suggested in the proposal cannot be objected to on the ground that it is against the principle of responsible government. Indians who are used to the English form of Executive forget that this is not the only form of democratic and responsible Government. The American form of Executive is an equally good type of democratic and responsible form of Government. There is also nothing objectionable in the proposal that a person should not be qualified to become a Minister merely because he is elected to the Legislature. The principle that a member of the Legislature before he is made a Minister should be chosen by his constituents was fully recognized by the British Constitution for over hundred years. A member of Parliament who was appointed a Minister had to submit himself for election before taking up his appointment. It was only lately given up. There ougnt therefore to be no objection to it on the ground that the proposals are not compatible with responsible Government. The actual proposal is an improved edition of the American form of Government, for the reason that under it members of the Executive can sit in the Legislature and have a right to speak and answer questions.

Clause 2

The proposal cannot be controversial. The best remedy against tyranny and oppression by a majority against the minority is inquiry, publicity and discussion. This is what the safeguard provides for. A similar proposal was also recommended by the Sapru Committee.

Clause 3

Social boycott is always held over the heads of the Untouchables by the Caste Hindus as a sword of Democles. Only the Untouchables know what as terrible weapon it is in the hands of the Hindus. Its effects and forms are well described in the Report made by a Committee appointed by the Government of Bombay in 1928 to investigate the grievances of the Depressed Classes and from which the following extracts are made. It illuminates the situation in a manner so simple that everybody can understand what tyranny the Hindus are able to practise upon the Untouchables. The Committee said:

> "Although we have recommended various remedies to secure to the Depressed Classes their rights to all public utilities we fear that there will be difficulties in the way of their exercising them for a long time to come. The first

difficulty is the fear of open violence against them by the orthodox classes. It must be noted that the Depressed Classes form a small minority in every village, oppose to which is a great majority of the orthodox who are bent on protecting their interests and dignity from any supposed invasion by the Depressed Classes at any cost. The danger of prosecution by the Police has put a limitation upon the use of violence by the orthodox classes and consequently such cases are rate.

The second difficulty arises from the economic position in which the Depressed Classes are found today. The Depressed Classes have no economic independence in most parts of the Presidency. Some cultivate the lands of the orthodox classes as their tenants at will. Others live on their earnings as farm labourers employed by the orthodox classes and the rest subsist on the food or grain given to them by the orthodox classes in lieu of service rendered to them as village servants. We have hard of numerous instances where the orthodox classes have used their economic power as a weapon against those Depressed Classes in their villages, when the latter have dared to exercise their rights, and have evicted them from their land, and stopped their employment and discontinued their remuneration as village servants. This boycott is often planned on such an extensive scale as to include the prevention of the Depressed Classes from using the commonly used paths and the stoppage of sale of the necessaries of life by the village Bania. According to the evidence, sometimes small causes suffice for the proclamation of a social boycott against the Depressed Classes. Frequently it follows on the exercise by the Depressed Classes of their right to use the common well, but cases have been by no mean rare where a stringent boycott has been proclaimed simply because a Depressed Class man has put on the sacred thread, has bought a piece of land, has put on good clothes or ornaments, or has carried a marriage procession with a bridegroom on the horse through the public street."

This was said in 1928. Lest it should be regarded as a phase which has now ended I reproduce below a copy of a petition by the Untouchables of the village Kheri Jessore in the Punjab addressed to the Deputy Commissioner of the Rohtak District in February, 1947 and a copy of which was sent to me. It reads as follows:

"From

The Scheduled Caste People (Chamars).
Village Kheri Jessore, Tehsil and District Rohtak.

To

The Deputy Commissioner,
Rohtok District, Rohtak.

Sir,

We, the following Scheduled Caste (Chamars) of the Village Kheri Jessore, beg to invite your kind attention to the hard plight, we are put to, due to the under pressure and merciless treatment by the Caste Hindu Jats of this village.

It was about four months back that the Jats of the village assembled in the Chopal and told us to work in the fields on a wage in kind of one bundle of crops, containing only about one seer of grains per day per man instead of food at both times and a load of crops, and annas 8 in addition which we used to get before above announcement was made. As it was too little and insufficient to meet both ends, we refused to go to work. At this they were enraged and declared a Social Boycott on us. They made a rule that our cattle would not be allowed to graze in the jungle unless we would agree to pay a tax not leviable under Government for the animals, which they call as "Poochhi." They even do not allow our cattle to drink water in the village pool and have prevented the sweepers from cleaning the streets where we live so that heaps of dust and dirt are lying there which may cause some disease if left unattend ed to. We are forced to lead a shameful life and they are always ready to beat us and to tear down our honour by behaving indecently towards our wives, sisters and daughters. We are experiencing a lot of trouble of the worst type. While going to the school, the children were even beaten severely and in a merciless manner.

We submitted an application detailing the above facts to yourself but we are sorry that no action has been taken as yet.

It is also for your kind consideration that the Inspector of Police and Tehsildar of Rohtak, whom we approached in this connection, made a careless investigation and in our opinion, no attention was paid to redress the difficulties of the poor and innocent persons.

We, therefore, request your good self to consider over the matter and make some arrangement to stop the merciless treatment and threats which the Jats give us in different ways. We have no other approach except to knock at your kind door and hope your honour will take immediate steps th enable us to lead an honourable and peaceful life which is humanity's birth-right.

We beg to remain,
Sir,
Your most obedient servants,
Scheduled Caste People (Chamars),
of Village Kheri Jessore,
Tehsil and District Rohtak,

Thumb Impressions.

× × × × ×

Copy forwarded to the Hon'ble Dr. B.R. Ambedkar,
Western Court, New Delhi.
Received on 1st February, 1947."

This shows that what was true in 1928 is true even today. What is true Bombay is true of the whole of India. For evidence of the general use of boycott by the Hindus against the Untouchables one has only to refer to the events that occurred all over India in the last elections to the Provincial Legislatures. Only when boycott is made criminal will the Untouchables be free from being the slaves of the Hindus.

The weawon of boycott is nowadays used against other communities besides the Scheduled Castes. It is therefore in the interests of all minor communities to have this protection.

The provisions relating to boycott are taken bodily from the Burma Anti-Boycott Act, 1922.

Clause 4

Such a provision already exists in Section 150 of the Government of India Act, 1935.

ARTICLE II—Section IV

PART I—CLAUSE I

There is nothing new in this clause. The right to representation in the Legislature is conceded by the Poona Pact. The only points that require to be reconsidered relate to:

1. Quantum of Representation,
2. Weightage and
3. The System of Electorates.

1. Quantum

The quantum of representation allowed to the Scheduled Castes by the Poona Pact is set out in Clause I of the Pact. The proportion set out in the Pact was fixed out of the balance of seats which remained after:

(i) the share of the other communities had been taken out;

(ii) after weightage to other communities had been allotted, and

(iii) after seats had been allocated to special interests.

This allottment of seats to the Scheduled Castes has resulted in great injustice. The loss due to seats taken out as weightage and seats given to special interests ought not to have been thrown upon the Scheduled Castes. The allotment of those seats had already been made by the Communal Award long before the Poona Pact. It was therefore not possible then to rectify this injustice.

2. Weightage

There is another injustice from which the Scheduled Castes have been suffering. It relates to their right to a share in weightage.

As one can see the right to weightage has become a matter of double controversy. One controversy is between the majority and the minorities, the other is a matter of controversy between the different minorities.

The first controversy relates to the principle of weightage. The majority insists that the minority has no right to representation in excess of the ratio of its population to the total population. Why this rule is insisted upon by the majority it is difficult to understand. Is it because the majority wants to establish its own claim to population ratio so that it may always remain as a majority and act as a majority? Or is it because of the fact that a minority no matter how much weightage was given to it must remain a minority and cannot alter the fact that the majority will always be able to impose its will upon it. The first ground leads to a complete negation of the basic conception of majority rule which if rightly understood means nothing more than a decision of the majority to which the minority has reconciled itself. This cannot be the intention of the majority. One must put a more charitable construction and assume that the argument on which the contention of the majority rests is the second and not the first. That a minority even with weightage will remain a minority has to be accepted in view of the insistence of a Communal Majority to remain a majority and to claim the privileges of a political majority which it is not. But surely there is a difference between a defeat which is a complete rout and a defeat which is almost victory though not a victory. Cricketers know what difference there is between the defeat of a team by a few runs, a defeat by a few wickets and a defeat by one whole innings. The defeat by one whole innings is complete frustration which a defeat by a few runs is not. Such a frustration when it comes about in the political life of a minority depresses and demoralizes and crushes the spirit of the minority. This must be avoided at any price. Looked at from this point of view there is no doubt that the rule of population--ratio—representation insisted upon by the majority is wrong. What a minority needs is not more representation but effective representation.

And what is effective representation? Obviously the effectiveness of representation depends upon its being large enough to give the minority the sense of not being entirely overwhelmed by the majority. Representation according to population to a minority or to the minorities combined may be effective by reason of the fact that the population of a minority where there is only one or of the combined minorities where there are many is large enough to secure effective minority representation. But there may be cases where the population of a minority or of the minorities combined is too small to secure such effective representation if the population ratio of a minority is taken as an inflexible standard to determine its quantum of representation. To insist upon such a standard is to make mockery of the protection to the minority which is the purpose behind the right to representation which is accepted as the legitimate claim of a minority. In such cases weightage which is another name for deduction from the quantum of representation which is due to the majority on the basis of its population becomes essential and the majority if it wishes to be fair and honest must concede it. There can therefore be no quarerl-

over the principle of weightage. On this footing the controversy becomes restricted to the question, how is the magnitude of weightage to be determined? This obviously is a question of adjustment and not of principle.

There can therefore be no manner of objection to the principle of weightage. The demand for weightage is however a general demand of all the minorities and the Scheduled Castes must join them in it where the majority is too big. What is however wrong with the existing weightage is unequal distribution among the various minorities. At present, some minorities have secured a lion's share and some like the Untouchables have none. This wrong must be rectified by a distribution of the weightage on some intelligible principles.

3. Electorates

1. The method of election to the seats allotted to the Scheduled Castes is set out in clauses (2) to (4) of the Poona Pact. It provides for two elections:

1. Primary election; and
2. Final election.

The Primary election is by a separate electorate of the Scheduled Castes. It is only a qualifying election and determines who is entitled to stand in the Final election on behalf of the Scheduled Castes for the seats reserved to them. The Final election is by a joint electorate in which both caste Hindus and the Scheduled Castes can vote and the final result is determined by their joint vote.

2. Clause 5 of the Poona Pact has limited the system of Primary election to ten years which means that any election taking place after 1947 will be by a system of joint electorates and reserved seats pure and simple.

3. Even if the Hindus agreed to extend the system of double election for a further period it will not satisfy the Scheduled

Castes. There are two objections to the retention of the Primary election. Firstly, it does not help the Scheduled Castes to elect a man who is their best choice. As will be seen from Appendix III, the Scheduled Caste candidate who tops the poll in the Primary election fails to succeed in the Final election and the Scheduled Caste candidate who fails in the Primary election tops the poll in the Final election. Secondly, the Primary election is for the most part a fiction and not a fact. In the last election, out of 151 seats reserved for the Scheduled Castes there were Primary elections only in 43. This is because it is impossible for the Scheduled Castes to bear the expenses of two election—Primary and Final. To retain such a system is worse than useless.

4. Things will be much worse under the system of joint electorates and reserved seats which will hereafter become operative under the terms of the Poona Pact. This is no mere speculation. The last election has conclusively proved that the Scheduled Castes can be completely disfranchised in a joint electorate. As will be seen from the figures given in Appendix III, the Scheduled Caste candidates have not only been elected by Hindu votes when the intention was that they should be elected by Scheduled Caste votes but what is more the Hindus have elected those Scheduled Caste candidates who had failed in the Primary election. This is a complete disfranchisement of the Scheduled Castes. The main reason is to be found in the enormous disparity between the voting strength of the Scheduled Castes and the caste Hindus in most of the constituencies as may be seen from figures given in Appendix III. As the Simon Commission has observed, the device of the reserved seats ceases to be workable where the protected community constitutes an exceedingly small fraction of any manageable constituency. This is exactly the case of the Scheduled Castes. This disparity cannot be ignored. It will remain even under adult suffrage. That being the case, a fool-proof and a knave-proof method must be found to ensure real representation to the Scheduled Castes. Such a method must involve the abolition of—

(i) the Primary election as a needless and heavy encumbrance, and

(ii) the substitution of separate electorates.

5. One of the issues which has embittered the relation between the Hindus and the Scheduled Castes in the political field is the issue of electorate. The Scheduled Castes are insisting upon separate electorates. The Hindus are equally insistent on opposing the demand. To arrive at a settlement on this issue—without which there can be no peace and amity between the Hindus and the Scheduled Castes—it is necessary to determine who is right and who is wrong and whether the opposition is based on rational grounds or is based on mere prejudice.

6. The grounds which are generally urged against the demand of the Scheduled Castes for separate electorates are:

(i) that the Scheduled Castes are not a minority;

(ii) that the Scheduled Castes are Hindus and therefore they cannot have separate electorates;

(iii) that separate electorates will perpetuate untouchability;

(iv) that separate electorates are anti-national; and

(v) that separate electorates enables British Imperialism to influence the communities having separate electorates to act against the interests of the country.

7. Are these arguments valid?

(i) To say that the Scheduled Castes are not a minority is to misunderstand and the meaning of the word 'minority'. Separation in religion is not the only test of a minority. Nor is it a good and efficient test. Social discrimination constitutes the real test for determining whether a social group is or is not a minority. Even Mr. Gandhi thought it logical and practical to adopt this test in preference to that of religious separation. Following this test, Mr. Gandhi in an editorial under the heading. 'The Fiction of Majority' in the Harijan dated 21st October, 1939 has given his opinion that the Scheduled Castes are the only real minority in India.

(ii) To argue that the Scheduled Castes are Hindus and therefore cannot demand separate electorates is to put the same argument in a different form. To make religious affiliation the determining factor for constitutional safeguards is to overlook tne fact that the religious affiliation may be accompanied by an intense, degree of social separation and discrimination. The belief that separate electorates go with separation in religion arises from the fact that those minorities who have been given separate electorates happen to be religious minorities. This, however, is not correct. Muslims are given separate electorates not because they are different from Hindus in point of religion. Thcy are given separate electorates because—and this is the fundamental fact—the social relations between the Hindus and the Musalmans are marked by social discrimination. To put the point in a somewhat different manner, the nature of the electorates is determined not by reference to religion but by reference to social consideration. That it is social considerations and not religious affiliation or disaffiliation which is accepted as the basis of determining the nature of the electorates is best illustrated by the arrangements made under the Government of India Act (1945) for the Christian community in India. The Christian community is divided into three sections—Europeans, Anglo-Indians and Indian Christians. In spite of the fact that they all belong to the same religion, each section has a separate electorate. This shows that what is decisive is not religious affiliation but social separation.

(iii) To urge that separate electorates prevent solidarity between the Untouchables and the Caste Hindus is the result of confused thinking. Elections take place once in five years. Assuming there were joint electorates, it is difficult to understand how social solidarity between the Hindus and the Untouchables can be promoted by their devoting one day for voting together when out of the rest of the five years they are leading severally separate lives? Similarly, assuming that there were separate electorates it difficult to understand how one day devoted to separate voting in the course of five years can make for greater separation than what already exist? Or contrarywise, how can one day in five years devoted to separate voting prevent those who wish to work for their union from carrying out heir purposes. To make is concrete, how can separate electorate for the Untouchables prevent inter-marriage or inter-dining being introduced between them and the Hindus? It is therefore futile to say that separate electorates for the Untouchables will perpetuate separation between them and the Hindus.

(iv) To insist that separate electorates create anti-national spirit is contrary to experience. The Sikh have separate electorates. But no one can say that the Sikhs are anti-national. The Muslims have had separate electorates right from 1909. Mr. Jinnah had been elected by separate electorates. Yet, Mr. Jinnah was the apostle of Indian Nationalism up to 1935. The Indian Christians have separate electorates. Nonetheless a good lot of them have shown their partiality to the Congress if they have not been actually returned on the Congress ticket. Obviously, nationalism and anti-nationalism have nothing to do with the electoral system. They are the result of extra electoral forces.

(v) This argument has no force. It is nothing but escapism. Be that as it may, with free India any objection to separate electorates on such a ground must vanish.

8. The reason why the arguments advanced by the opponents of separate electorates do not stand the scrutiny of logic

and experience is due enirely to the fact that their approach to the subjects is fundamentally wrong. It is wrong in two respects:

(i) They fail to realize that the system of electorates has nothing to do with the religious nexus or communal nexus. It is nothing but a mechanism to enable a minority to return its true representative to the Legislature. Being a mechanism for the protection of a minority it follows that whether the electorate should be joint or separate must be left to be determined by the minority.

(ii) They fail to make any distinction between the demand for separate electorates by a majority community and a similar demand made by a minority community. A majority community has no right to demand separate electorates. The reason is simple. A right by a majority community to demand separate electorates is tantamount to a right to establish the Government of the majority community over the minority community without the consent of the minority. This is contrary to the well-established doctrine of democracy that government must be with the consent of the governed. No such evil consequence follows from the opposite principle namely that a minority community is entitled to determine ths nature of the electorates suited to its interests, because there is no possibility of the minority being placed in a position to govern the majority.

9. A correct attitude towards the whole question rests on the following axioms:

(i) The system of electorates being a devise for the protection of the minority, the issue whether the electoral system should be the joint electorate or separate electorate must be left to the wishes of the minority. If it is large enough to influence the majority it will choose joint electorates. If it is too small for the purpose, it will prefer separate electorates for fear of being submerged.

(ii) The majority, being in a position to rule can have no voice in the determination of the system of electorates. If the minority wants joint electorates, the majority must submit itself to joint electorates. If the minority decides to have separate electorates for itself the majority cannot refuse to grant them. In other words, the majority must look to the decision of the minority and abide by it.

PART I—Clause 2

This demand may appear to be outside the Poona Pact in as much as the Poona Pact made no provision for it. This would not be correct. As a matter of fact, if no provision was made, it was because there was no need to make such a provision. This was due to two reasons:

1. it was due to the fact that at the time when the Poona Pact was made no community was guaranteed by Law a specific quantum of representation in Exective,
2. the representation of the communities in the Executive was left to a convention which the Governor by his instrument of instructions was required to see observed. Experience has shown that the quantum of representation of the Scheduled Castes in the Executive should now be fixed.

PART I—Clause 3

This is not a new demand. Clause 8 of the Poona Pact guarantees to the Scheduled Castes fair representation in Public Services. It does not, however, define the quantum of representation. The demand has been admitted by the Government of India as legitimate and even the quantum of representation has been defined. All that remains is to give it a statutory basis.

PART II—Clause 1

This is not a new demand. Clause 9 of Poona Pact guarantees that an adequate sum shall be earmarked for the education of the Scheduled Castes. It does not define the quantum. All that the demand does is to define the quantum of liability the State should take. In this connection reference may be made to Section 83 of the Government of India Act, 1935, which relates to the education of the Anglo-Indians and Europeans and to the grants made to Aligarh and Benaras Hindu Universities by the Central Government.

PART II—Clause 2

This a new demand but is justified by circumstances. At present, the Hindus live in the village and the Untouchables live in the Ghettoes. The object is to free the Untouchables from the thraldom of the Hindus. So long as the present arrangement continues it is impossible for the Untouchables either to free themselves from the yoke of the Hindus or to get rid of their Untouchability. It is the close knit association of the Untouchables with the Hindus living in the same villages which marks them out as Untouchables and which enables the Hindus to identify them as being Untouchables. India is admittedly a land of villages and so long as the village system provides an easy method of marking out and identifying the Untouchables, the Untouchable has no escape from Untouchability. It is the system of the Village plus the Ghetto which perpetuates Untouchability and the Untouchables therefore demand that the nexus should be broken and the Untouchables who are as a matter of fact socially separate should be made separate geographically and territorially also, and be setted into separate villages exclusively of Untouchables in which the distinction of the high and the low and of Touchable and Untouchable will find no place.

The second reason for demanding separate settlement arises out of the economic position of the Untouchables in the villages. That their condition is most pitiable no one will deny.

They are a body of landless labourers who are enirely dependent upon such employment as the Hindus may choose to give them and on such wages as the Hindus may find it profitable to pay. In the villages in which they live they cannot engage in any trade or occupation, for owing to Untouchability to Hindu will deal with them. It is therefore obvious that there is no way of earning a living which is open to the Untouchables so long as they live in a Ghetto as a dependent part of the Hindu village.

This economic dependence has also other consequences besides the condition of poverty and degradation which proceeds from it. The Hindu has a Code of life, which is part of his religion. This Code of life gives him many privileges and heaps upon the Untouchable many indignities which are incompatible with the dignity and sanctity of human life. The Untouchables all over India are fighting against the indignities and injustices whieh the Hindus in the name of their religion have heaped upon them. A perpetual war is going on every day in every village between the Hindus and the Untouchables. It does not see the light of the day. The Hindu Press is not prepared to give it publicity lest it should injure the cause of their freedom in the eyes of the world. The existence of a grim struggle between the Touchables and the Untouchables is however a fact. Under the village system the Untouchables has found himself greatly handicapped in his struggle for free and honourable life. It is a contest between the Hindus who are economically and socially strong and the Untouchables who are economically poor and numerically small. That the Hindus most often succeed in suppressing the Untouchables is due to many causes. The Hindus have the Police and the Magistracy on their side. In a quarrel between the Untouchables and the Hindus the Untouchables will never get protection from the Police and justice from the Magistrate. The Police and the Magistracy naturally love their class more than their duty. But the chief weapon in the armoury of the Hindus is economic power which they possess over the poor Untouchables living in the village. The proposal may be dubbed escapism. But the only alternative is perpetual slavery.

PART III—Clause 1

No country which has the problem of Communal majority and Communal minority is without some kind of an arrangement whereby they agree to share political power. South Africa has such an understanding. So has Canada. The arrangement for sharing political power between the English and the French in Canada is carried to the minutes office. In referring to this fact Mr. Porritt in his book on the Evolution of the Dominion of Canada says:

> "Conditions at Ottawa, partly due to race and language, and partly to long-prevailing ideas as to the distribution of all government patronage, have militated against the Westminster precedent of continuing a member in the chair for two or three parliaments, regardless of the fortunes of political parties at general elections. There is a new speaker at Ottawa for each new House of Commons; and it has long been a custom that when one political party continues in power for two or three parliaments, if the speaker in one parliament is of British extraction the next one shall be a French-Canadian.
>
> "It is a rule also that the offices of speaker and of deputy speaker can at no time be held by men of the same race. If the speaker is a French-Canadian, the deputy speaker, who is also Chairman of committees, must be an English speaking Canadian; for the rule of the House is that the member elected to serve as deputy speaker shall be required to possess the full and practical knowledge of the language which is not that of the speaker for the time being.
>
> The clerkship and the assistant clerkship of the House, and the offices of sergeant-at-arms and deputy sergeant-at-arms—all appointive as distinct from elective offices—

are, by usage, also similarly divided between the two races.

Nearly all the offices, important and unimportant, connected with parliament, with the Senate as well as with the House, are distributed in accordance with these rules or usages. A roll call of the staffs of the two Houses, including even the boys in knicker-bockers who act as pages, would contain the names of almost as many French-Canadians as Canadians of British ancestry.

The rules and usages by virtue of which this distribution of offices is made are older than Confederation. They date back to the early years of the United Provinces, when Quebec and Ontario elected exactly the same number of members to the Legislature, and when these were the only provinces in the union

Quebec today elects only 65 of the 234 members of the House of Commons. Its population is not one-fourth of the population of the Dominion. Its contribution to Dominion revenues does not exceed one-sixth. But an equal division of the offices of the House of Commons is regarded by Quebec as necessary to the preservation of its rights and privileges; and so long as each political party, when it is in power, is dependent on support from French-Canada, it will be nearly as difficult to ignore the claim of Quebec to these parliamentary honours and offices as it would be to repeal the clause in the British North America Act that safeguards the separate schools system."

Unfortunately for the minorities in India, Indian Nationalism has developed a new doctrine which may be called the Divine Right of the Majority to rule the minorities according to the wishes of the majority. Any claim for the sharing of power by the minority is called communalism while the monopolizing of the whole power by the majority is called Nationalism. Guided by such a political philosophy the majority is not prepared to allow the minorities to share political power nor is it willing to respect any convention made in that behalf as is evident from their repudiation of the obligation (to include representatives of the minorities in the cabinet) contained in the Instrument of Instructions issued to the Governors in the Government of India Act of 1935. Under these circumstances there is no way left but to have the rights of the Scheduled Castes embodied in the Constitution.

PART III—Clause 2

This is not a new demand. It replaces Clause 6 of the Poona Pact which provides that the system of representation for the Scheduled Castes by reserved seats shall continue until determined by mutual consent between the communities concerned in the settlement. Since there is no safe method of ascertaining the will of the Scheduled Castes as to how to amend and alter the safeguards provided for them it is necessary to formulate a plan which will take the place of Clause 6 of the Pact. Provisions having similar objective to those contained in the proposal exist in the Constitution of Australia, America and South Africa.

In dealing with a matter of this sort two consideration have to be borne in mind. One is that it is not desirable to rule out the possibility of a change in the safeguards being made in the future by the parties concerned. On the other hand it is by no means desirable to incessant struggle over their revision. If the new Union and State Legislatures are to address themselves successfully to their responsibilities set out in the preamble it is desirable that they should not be distracted by the acute contentions between religions and classes which questions of change in the safeguards are bound to raise. Hence a period of twenty-five years has been laid down before any change could be considered.

PART IV

The object of this provision is to see that whatever safeguards are provided for the Scheduled Castes in British India are also provided for the Scheduled Castes in the Indian States. The provision lays down that an Indian State seeking admission to the Union shall have to satisfy that its Constitution contains these safeguards.

PART V—Interpretation

Whether the Scheduled Castes are a minority or not has become a matter of controversy. The purpose of First Provision to set this controversy at rest. The Scheduled Castes are in a worst position as compared to any other minority in India. As such they required and deserve much more protection than any other minority does. The least one can do is to treat them as a minority.

The purpose of Second Provision is to remove the provincial bar. There is no reason why a person who belongs to Scheduled Castes in one Province should lose the benefit of political privileges given by the Constitution merely because he happens to change his domicile.

Appendix III

DYNAMICS OF SOCIAL STATUS

The Indian Caste System is first and foremost a system of stratification in which the status of the individual is determined by his birth and ritual purity. Traditionally both the principles have been so interlinked that for practical purposes they have been treated as one and the same principle. Historically, however, birth and ritual have always functioned as two independent and separate principles. As we shall show below in the caste society of today, both have been recognized as determinants of social status. But a man who enjoys a superior status by virtue of his high birth may not be enjoying a superior ritual status also. At any rate the traditional principles of stratification are still operative in the Indian society and the caste system, in many respects, continues to be a closed system even today. In our previous discussion of intercaste commensality, we have shown how the notion of ritual purity determines the area of commensal relations within the caste hierarchy. This notion to a large extent governs the differentiation of status also. The way people try to protect their ritual purity and the strictness with which the commensal taboos are observed creates an impression that the caste system as Hocart[1] tried to show is really a sacrificial organization in which the status of each individual and group is fixed according to its position in sacrificial operation. Hocart's theory may not be wholly correct but there is hardly any doubt about the fact that ritual plays a very significant part in determining the status of the group or the individual within the caste society. Let us then see how the concept of ritual purity functions as a basis of status differentiation in the caste system of rural Andhra. We have already referred to the restrictions on eating and drinking observed by the various castes in Andhra. The main reason why certain castes do not accept food and drink from other castes is that they consider ritual purity as a hall-mark of their superior status which can be preserved only by keeping a definite ritual distance between them and other castes. As we pointed out earlier, food prepared or cooked with water is considered *kachcha food.* On the other hand, food that is cooked with clarified butter (Ghee) is considered as *pakka food.* The food cooked by *ghee* (clarified butter) is, perhaps, considered to be pure because ghee, being the product of the sacred cow, is endowed with power to be immune to impurity. It is needless to emphasize that cow is held in the highest esteem and veneration by Hindus. *Panchagavya*, the five products of the cow, are treated as the most sacred things. The polluting capacity of a caste is further directly proportional to the habit of beef eating or dealing with the skin and hides of the dead animals, particularly cows and oxen. *Kachcha* food is restricted only to a few castes who possess of similar or equal ritual purity. On the other hand, a greater number of castes can take *Pakka* food. But this does not apply to milk and fruits. They are generally not considered ritually impure.

"The Brahman", says Dr. Ketkar, "is at the top of society because he is more pure and sacred than other castes while Mahar and Paraiyan are at the bottom because they are impure. Thus purity is the pivot on which the entire system turns. Rank, social position, economic condition have no direct effect on the gradation from the standpoint of caste."

Those who cause pollution by contact with or without proximity to the high castes are also hed to be capable of polluting temples and are therefore denied admission to them. Not only were some castes formerly denied admission into the temples, but among those who were allowed to enter into the temples, there were gradations as to the extent to which they could move inside the temples. For instance, the *Garbha Gudi* or Sanctum Sanctorum was accessible only to Brahmans (some times only to Vaidiki Brahmans who officiated as temple priests) in both the Shiva and Vishnu temples. But in some of the Shaivite temples, the *Garbha Gudi* was also accessible to Jangamas who acted as temple priests in them. Only in rare cases, did the lower middle castes like Satanis (Chattada Shri Vaishnavas) and Dasaries also act as temple priests—mostly in Hanuman temples and local Deities' temples—and as such they entered into the innermost part of those temples. But such temples were mostly avoided by the upper castes such as Brahmans, Vaishyas and so forth.

It may be noted that the Brahman group generally had access to the *Garbha Gudi* both in the Shaiva and Vaishnava temples. The Veerashaiva group in general, jangamas in particular, had access into the *Garbha Gudi* of most of the Shaiva temples whereas they were denied this privilege in the Vaishnava temples. Most of the other caste groups such as the Vaishya Group, Kshatriya group, Non-Brahman upper castes group etc. entered the temple into *Alayamu* portion only. Some of the detribalized castes and others only permitted into the *Prangamamu*. Even the Service castes in some districts were allowed upto *Prangamamu* in the temples. The Untouchables were allowed only upto the main entrance, and some times were even kept far away from the premises of the temples. Though the recent legislation clearly stands against such discrimination among the different caste groups in the temples, yet in most of the villages where the power and authority is concentrated in the hands of the upper caste people, who are still tradition bound, such differentiation between castes in the matter of temple entry still exists and it is bound to take quite a long time for the complete elimination of such social distance among castes. But the legislation has had its own impact. Among the 88 respondents of the Brahman group only 21 (23 per cent) did not claim the entrance into *Garbha Gudi* as a privilege while 67 (76.2 per cent) felt that they were entitled to enter into it. But none of the Brahmans and allied group claimed entrance beyond the precincts of the *Garbha Gudi* where they could have the *darshan* of the presiding deity. Among the 15 Kshatriya group respondents, only one (6.6 per cent) claimed entry into the *Garbha Gudi* whereas the rest 14 (93.4 per cent) were content with entrance upto the gates of *Garbha Gudi*. So also among 48 Vaishya group people, 8 (16.7 per cent) claimed entrance into the *Garbha Gudi* and others (83.3 per cent) made no such claim. Of the 356 non-Brahman upper castes group respondents, 12 (3.3 per cent) pressed for entry into the *Garbha Gudi* and 5 (1.4 per cent) were even satisfied with admission into the *Pranganamu* (or Parlour). This is so because some of the constituent castes of this group had regional variation in their social status depending upon their wealth and numerical strength in the village. Similar was the position of the Artisan castes group with regard to entry. As many as 68 (95.8 per cent) among the 71 respondents were satisfied by entry into the temples upto the entrance of the *Garbha Gudi*, though 2 (2.8 per cent) of them claimed the right to enter the Sanctum Sanctorum. Three (2.5 per cent), 107 (87.0 per cent) and 4 (3.2 per cent) of the 123 Service castes respondents were of the opinion that they were permitted respectively upto the main entrance (*Mukha Dwaramu*), into the parlour (*Pranganamu*), upto the entrance of the *Garbhagudi* and into the *Garbhagudi*. It can be seen from this that the bulk of them (87.0 per cent) staked their claims for entry upto the door of the *Garbhagudi*. Traditionally most of them might have been permitted only upto *Pranganamu* in the temple. So also, 77.1 per cent of the Detribalized castes and others were asserting their claim for entrance upto the *Garbhagudi* in a temple. This damand clearly indicated the change that had taken place in the temple entry restrictions. However, the response in the sample for this question had been half-hearted on the part of the participants in this group as also in the case of the Harijans where only 20 responded to this query. This is because of the unwillingness on the part of these castes to comit themselves unequivocally on this point which is quite understandable under the prevailing circumstances in the villages. None of the Harijan respondents put forth any claim for entrance into the *Garbhagudi*. Only 8 (40 per cent) of them claimed entry into the temple premises.

Even after more than a decade of legislation against discrimination among different castes with regard to entry into the temples, quite a substantial percentage (16.7 per cent) of people felt that restrictions on temple entry still existed. It was observed that least 163 (16.7 per cent) respondents out of 975 felt that some restrictions or the other existed for the various caste groups for admission into the different parts of the temple. All the respondents in the Brahman group (96) and Kshatriya group (25) thought that they would be allowed into all areas of the temple if they want. It may be a different matter that they may not themselves desire to enter the *Garbhagudi*. Among the Vaishya group. 5 (10.4 per cent) respondents felt that they would not be permitted into the innermost parts of the temple, but other 43 (89.6 per cent) did not take this aspect into consideration. Among the upper caste non-Brahmans, 33 (8.6 per cent) of the 384 respondents felt that they could be allowed admission into the temple only upto *Garbhagudi* and so was the case with 8 (5.9 per cent) respondents among the Serviec castes group. But among the Harijans, 104 (73.2 per cent) of the 142 respondents felt that they were denied admission into the temples through indirect methods for open refusal of entry was punishable by law. So also 12 (16.2 per cent) among 74 respondents belonging to Detribalized castes and others had no access to the temples. However, 38 (26.8 per cent) respondents among the Harijans claimed that they had asserted their right to enter the temples for worship. This only indicated the increasing trend towards improvement in the social status of the lowly placed castes in the society.

Apart from the restrictions imposed upon some castes about the extent to which they may be admitted into the temple, some castes prohibit their members from entering into some temples whose premises are considered by them as impure. As it has already been stated, the Shrivaishnavas among the Brahmans refuse to enter the Shaiva temple, and quite a few among this sub-caste adhere to this practice even today. This is reminiscent of the great rivalry that once existed between the Shrivaishnava and Veerashaiva cults. So also orthodox among the Jangamas refuse to enter the Vaishnava temples. This is because each of the castes considers the other and the deity it worships as inferior to their own. Besides this, there are some Christian converts in different castes. These converts have accepted the caste principles and caste restrictions in all functions such as marriage etc., except in their attitude towards religion and worship and generally do not like to go to Hindu temples. Further Dakkalas, the priests among Madigas, also desire not to visit any caste Hindu temples and restrict themselves to their own temples. This attitude on the part of Dakkalas also underlies their fear of losing their superior status within their caste rules. Among 96 Brahman group respondents, 7 (7.3 per cent) had reservations about their visiting some temples. These seven respondents invariably bslonged to Shrivaishnavas and Jangamas. There were 41 (28.7 per cent) Harijan respondents who would not like to visit Hindu temples. This constituted those Christian converts who by religious conviction did not want to pay a visit to Hindu temples and also some Hindu Harijans who did not like to offend the upper caste people by going to the caste Hindu temples (*Savarna* temples), lest it might prove detrimental to their livelihood and existence in the villages. Other 102 (71.3 per cent) Harijan respondents desired to visit Hindu temples freely. The 12 (15.4 per cent) respondents among the detribalized castes and others, mostly constituted the Muslims included in this category, who by religous belief did not wish to go to temples, and a couple of others who were treated as untouchables from among this category and who did not like to go against the wishes of the upper caste people in the villages.

In the foregoing pages it is seen how the pollution concept plays an effective role in regulating the admission for different castes into the temples. These restrictions also reflect the differences in social status enjoyed by these castes in the society. Till recent past, thus, there was a close correspondence between the ritual status enjoyed by a caste and its social status in the villages. It was, in fact, the ritualistic purity of a caste which placed the caste at a particular position in the social hierarchy.

Considerations of purity and impurity enter also into the estimation in which different occupations and means of livelihood are held. Naturally, those which involve dirtier repulsive work, such as scavenging and washing are regarded as impure and the castes which follow them as debased. Anything to do with dead bodies whether human or animal, is held to be particularly degrading. When death occurs in a house, the family is regarded as impure for a certain period which ends with a ceremony of purification. Those who handle corpses for the purposes of cremation are regarded as dregs of the population and even Brahmans who officiate at such cremations rank below other Brahmans. The Madigas (the untouchables) who skin dead animals and dress their hides, are of the lowest castes and the Muchikis, the cobblers, who handle the dressed leather, though superior to the Madigas, are also among the very low. But there is one exception to this general rule. The low castes who are patronized by the Brahmans rank higher than the castes which are unable to secure the patronage of the latter.

"Sometimes the Brahmans may minister to certain of the clean castes which is denied for others. Thus one of the measuring rods for the social status has been that of the availability and the willingness on the part of the Brahman by the clean caste."[2]

Much also depends on the extent to which the different castes follow Brahmanical teaching and observe the orthodox tenets of Hinduism and it must be remembered that many of the lower castes though they recognize the great Hindu deities, have animistic beliefs and worship different deities unknown to Brahmanism. In the great majority of castes, the religious rites are conducted by non-Brahmans; Brahmans neither officiate at the domestic ceremonies nor act as their religious preceptors, and they live in ignorance of Brahmanical doctrines. For some of the lower castes, the Satanis (Chattada Srivaishnavas) act as the priests. They conduct all ceremonies like birth, death and menstruation etc. The Brahmans refuse to officiate in their ceremonies. So also the Boyas have their own priests who are drawn from among them and are called Dasaris. The Dasaris sub-sects of some of the middle order castes also officiate for them. Brahmans generally do not agree to supervise their functions because they, are considered to be quite inferior in social status. Brahmans also do not officiate in the functions of Chakalis, Mangalis and other service castes. The Lingayats and Jangames have Jangamas as their priests. Not only that the Bryhmans do not like to officiate in their ceremonies; on their part they also do not require the services of Brahmans for they do not recongnize the superior position of the latter. Thus Brahmans officiate as priests at ceremonies of only some selected non-Brahman upper castes, Kshatriyas and Vaishyas.

Equally rigorous are the restrictions on drinking water. As in the case of commensal taboo, many restrictions are imposed with regard to drinking water. But here the question centres round the vessel in which the water is contained. An upper caste man may allow a lower caste person to fill his vessel for him with water but he will refrain from drinking water from the vessel belonging to the lower caste person. In the former case he performs certain ablutions before he takes the vessel filled by the lower caste man into his possession. "It is often stated that the test of a 'clean caste', that is to say a caste of respectability and non-polluting status, lies in whether or not a Brahman can accept drinking water at its hands."[3]

It will be worthwhile to note that clean Sudras or Sat-Sudras (upper caste Non-Brahmans) like Reddis, Kammas and

Balijas (Naidus) engage some of the lowly Sudra castes like Kummaris and Manchi Yanadis to cook food in their homes, but they refuse to dine with their cooks in their (cooks') homes in common dining, and thereby assert their superiority. Anyhow, these restrictions are not as rigorous with Kummaris as in the case of Manchi Yanadis.

In deciding the position of a caste in the ritual hierarchy, the principle that a caste is equal or inferior if it takes food from a particular caste and that it is equal or superior to it if it does not accept food from a particular caste, is adopted. O'Malley remarks: "In South India, however, there appears to be no general ban on members of different sub-castes within the same caste having meals in common."[4] But this contention is not wholly true. Largely it may apply to many of the sub-castes of a caste, yet it is not a general phenomenon. For instance, Srivaishnavites among Barhmans will have nothing in common with Smarthas, Madhvas or Aradhyas, some of the other Brahman sub-castes. An antogonism, almost verging on hatred and ill-will, prevails among these sub-castes. Kalinga Komatis are looked down upon by Arya Vaishyas in Srikakulam and Visakhapatnam areas but Kalinga Komatis are found only in those areas bordering Orissa.

Applying the above principles, the caste which is ritually most pure, *viz.*, Brahmans, is at the apex of the caste organization[5] and the untouchables like Malas and Madigas, whose presence or shadow even pollutes the upper castes form the base of this organisation. O'Malley states that "Next to the rules regarding inter-marriage and commensality, perhaps the most distinctive feature of the caste system is the way in which different castes are ranked in an order of social dignity. There is a graduated scale culminating in the Brahman and descending to what are known as the untouchables or depressed classes. There is no detailed warrant of precedence in which each individual caste has an assigned place but rather a social stratification in which castes are grouped in different layers."[6]

Pollution, Karma and Dharma are the trinity (trident)

which reflects and determines the hierarchical philosophy of Indian society. The different castes rank as high or low according to the degree of honour in which they are held by the Hindus as a whole, subject to the preeminence of the Brahmans, who form as it were, the apex of a pyramid in which other castes are superimposed in layers one upon another. A man, except in rare cases, remains till death in the caste in which he is born. The social position of each individual is fixed by ritual purity and not by material conditions. Differences of status are justified by the religious doctrines of *Karma* and the transmigration of soul. The doctrine of *karma* enjoins upon the members of different castes strictly to adhere to *Swadharma* (their rightful duties) and while doing so to follow a path of righteousness which will bestow upon them a better status in the next life. The role and status enjoyed by an individual, having been born into a particular caste, is the result of the life he or she has led in the previous birth and of the actions in that life.[7]

It must however be pointed out that ritual purity alone is not the correct indicator of one's rank in the social hierarchy. For instance, the Pancha Brahma group or Viswa Brahman Group in Andhra enjoys a unique status in the society. People belonging to this caste refuse either to dine with or drink water from the Brahmans; and at the same time, even the Panchamas or Untouchables refrain from taking anything from those people. Their food or water is taboo for all sections of the society. Nevertheless they are placed higher up in the hierarchical order. The story, as it runs, has been nerrated by one of the informants. According to him, in the remote past, there was a Brahman family. It was joint family of two brothers. Once they were performing some ceremony. During the ritual, a stray dog entered the house and touched the food heaped for the worship. Unmindful of it the elder brother took the food defiled by the touch of a stray dog. Thereupon the younger brother and a majority of Brahmans found fault with it and excommunicated the elder brother and those who were associated with him. These, who exhibited greater toleration and lesser orthodoxy, were known later as Viswa Brahmans. But the restrictions imposed on them and taboos that were observed, were so great that this group became totally hostile towards Brahmans and forbade all commensal relations with them. But the influence of Brahmans over the rest of the society was so great that they succeeded in completely isolating the Viswa Brahmans from others. This anecdote indicates the relative importance accorded to purity and difilement, in determining one's status within the caste system.

Thus status within the caste in the past, remote and recent, meant ritual status. Gradually the principle of ritual purity has been replaced by other factors like economic position, numerical strength of the castes and so forth.

With the gradual ascendence of the economic supremacy, there had been a tendency for the economic factors to play a decisive role in determining the social status of a particular caste. Wealth has assumed such importance that one who possesses it is at a decided advantage over others who do not possess it. This has helped the rich in elevating their privileged rank over the poor. Ritualistically speaking, Brahmans still occupy a prominent place in the villages but they have become inferior in rank to the castes which have economic superiority within the rural setting. Thus the question of subordination and superordination changes according to the social situation with which we are dealing. Reddis, who sometimes claim to belong to Kshatriya group. undoubtedly belong to the fourth Varna of the original Hindu social stratification. But this is the dominant caste in many of the districts of Andhra Pradesh; and so is the caste with Kammas, Velmas (Naidu) and Telagas (Naidu) and other great Sudra castes which are major social groups in several districts. In the villages these castes are placed on the top for all the vital matters concerning the village festivals and village development activities. They preside over the deliberations of the *Grama Chavadis* or informal village councils. In these village councils, the Brahmans play a subordinate role. They are co-opted to councils and participate in their deliberations. They are also a party to the verdict, but they generally play an ineffective role in arriving at the decisions except in some extra-ordinary cases. How is that these great Non-Brahman castes have overridden the traditional upper castes like Twice-Borns (Dwijas) in the social precedence? A close scrutiny of the socio-economic conditions of these castes reveal that the deciding factor in their favour is their superior economic position. Mostly they are engaged in agriculture and belong to the landed gentry.

Closely associated with the economic factor is the numerical strength of that caste. More often than not, it is seen that the relative position of a caste in the village invariably depends upon the strength of the household of that caste in it. A caste, which is rated relatively inferior in a region where it is in a minority position, may be considered superior in those where it is numerically strong. Thus due to the majority of its population also, a caste furthers its position upwards in the social ladder. Velamas (Naidus) and Gavaras, two of the agricultural castes, have a low status in lower Andhra but they are held in high esteem in upper Andhra. Generally one of these Sat Sudras or clean sudras happens to be the majority caste in most regions of Andhra. Numerical strength is nevertheless, not a very powerful factor in establishing the social precedence of a caste. It only helps a caste to emerge as a dominant caste. Curious as it may appear only such castes, which are numerically strong and have at the same time a strong financial position, control the socio-political affairs of the rural society. This is amply illustrated by the fact that some castes like Panchamas or Malas and Madigas could not attain higher status though they form a substantial and sizeable proportion among the population because of their financial backwardness and traditional lowliness.

Sometimes the adoption of a particular occupation by a group of people in a caste also results in the change of the social position of that group both within the caste and also outside it. This often leads to the formation of new sub-caste or caste. Radhakamal Mukerji points to the same fact when he states that "in some cases the adoption of a degrading occupation by certain families has spelt social disaster for that section, and, though still retaining the caste name, they are compelled to marry amongst themselves and thus form a sub-caste. In other instances the converse is the case, and a group that abandons a disreputable occupation or commands social respect by adoption of the customs (and restructions) of higher castes itself attains in time to a higher social grade."[8]

The ideas as to what are honourable and what are dis-honourable occupations are so extraordinarily different that they can be reduced to no one common factor. One idea which is generally prevalent and which has its roots in the remote past, is that industrial occupations and labourers' manual work are base pursuits. There is no conception of the dignity of labour in India. The higher castes despise manual work and consider it beneath their dignity to follow such work. In Andhra, there are two major sub-sections among Brahmans, namely Vaidikis and Niyogis. The former are those who are continuing with priestly functions and other liberal pursuits, whereas the latter are those who have taken up the position of village officers like *Karnams*. They are scribes by vocation. Since these Niyogis have deviated from their traditional priestly functions and have taken up more mundane positions, they are treated as having inferior status as compared to the Vaidkis and are condemned as worldly-wise people. Likewise, among Reddis, Patna Reddis are a poorer class of people and live by manual labour. Therefore, they are regarded as inferior by most of the other Reddi sub-castes. The same is the case with the Illuvellani and Campa Kammas or sometimes also referred to as Pedda Kamma and Chinna Kamma. As the nomenclature itself indicates, those of such families, which have taken to manual work in their agricultural pursuits, namely the Gampa Kamma or Chinna Kamma, are considered as inferior in status by those sub-castes which spurn manual work. Similarly Gazula Balijas (Bangle sellers among Naidus) of the Telega (Balija) caste are looked down upon by others because of their profession. This alone largely accounts for the growth of absentee landlordism among different castes, more so in the case of Brahmans, in the rural areas.

With socio-political awakening, there has developed an urge for higher education among the various sections of the society. People who had been content for ages with the traditional caste occupations and depended upon the Brahmans and other educated classes for knowledge have shaken off their old lethargy and are craving for more and more benefits of modern education. This education, for various reasons, evolved a hierarchy of its own based upon the 'achievement'. In consequence, it is found that there is a tilting in the balance of traditional social ranking. Castes which sensed ths necessity of higher education earlier and initiated their children into western education are emerging with improved social position. But this transformation in the attitude of the people has yet not become all-embracing and far-reaching.

The various factors mentioned above weigh with the rural people in the fixation of social status of individuals as well as of caste groups. While the traditional factors like status by birth and ritual purity still account for high social status, modern factors like wealth, social and political position and numerical strength of a particular caste-group also are responsible for the superior social status of certain castes in the rural areas. While birth and ritual purity still play a prominent role in determining the social status of individuals, they have nevertheless lost much of their significance. On the other hand, social and political position is now considered more important. Asked to indicate their preferences among different factors, most of the caste groups laid emphasis on 'social and political position', 'birth', 'wealth' and 'economic conditions'. Out of 96 Brahman group respondents, 36 or 37.5 per cent emphasized birth and 26 or 27 per cent emphasized social and political position. But in their second preference they emphasized wealth and economic conditions (26 or 27 per cent) and social and political positions (23 or 24 per cent). The Kshatriya group in its first preference stressed birth (7 or 50 per cent) and social and political positions (4 or 28.5 per cent) and in the 2nd preference, social and political positions (6 or 43 per cent) and numerical strength of a caste (4 or 28.5 per cent). In the Vaishya group, 20 or 38.4 per cent feel that birth accounted for a low or high social status, 12 or 23 per cent thought that numerical strength of a caste was more important than other considerations and 11 or 21 per cent felt that social and political positions were the main bases of social status. In the second performance, 17 or 23 per cent of the Vaishya group gave importance to social and political positions and 10 or 19.2 per cent to wealth and economic position. Upper caste non-Brahmans considered social and political positions (141 or 37.4 per cent) and birth (122 or 32.3 per cent) as equally responsible for high status, and in the second preference, 114 or 30.2 per cent accepted social and political positions, 69 or 18.3 per cent accepted the numerical strength of a caste, and 62 or 16.4 per cent birth as determinants of social status in the villages. The Artisan castes gave importance to birth (29 or 40.8) per cent) and social and political position (18 or 25.3 per cent) while the service caste group gave importance to social and political positions (61 or 46.9 per cent) to birth (30 or 23 per cent), and to the numerical strength of a caste (25 or 19.2 per cent). Both the Harijans and Detribalized castes accept social and political positions and birth, as contributory factors for social status in the rural areas. Thus social and political position, and birth are largely considered responsible for social status in the society.

So far we have confined ourselves to the analysis of the factors responsible for the high or low social status of groups and individuals within the caste hierarchy. It is worthwhile knowing whether different caste groups accept the existence of such graduations among different sections within their castes.

It was found that almost half of the respondents (44.6 per cent) thought that gradations in social status did exist within their castes. In fact, a large percentage (57.3 per cent) among Brahman group thought that there are gradations in their castes. Among them, people following priestly functions (14 out of 15 or 93.3 per cent), agriculture (26 out of 43 or 60.4 per cent) and other caste professions (5 out of 8 or 62.5 per cent) were emphatic about the existence of gradations. So was the case with the Kshatriya group, Vaishya group and service castes groups, for 55.6 per cent (15 out of 27), 52.3 per cent (23 out of 44) and 50.8 per cent (69 out of 136) of them respectively accepted the existence of gradations within their castes. In these caste groups also, people following traditional occupations like caste professions, business and agriculture accepted the gradation in their respective castes.

But in the case of Upper Caste non-Brahmans, Artisan castes, Harijans and Detribalized castes and others, larger percentage of respondents refused to accept any gradations in their castes. Even among these castes, there were some who did accept the existence of gradations within their castes which could be seen from the fact that 45.6 per cent (173 out of 379), 33.3 per cent (21 out of 63), 33.3 per cent (45 out of 135), 31.3 per cent (20 out of 64) respectively among the upper caste non-Brahmans, artisan castes. Harijans and Detribalized castes and others accepted graduations within their castes, sub-castes and sub-groups. Most of these people belonged to traditional occupations such as caste professions and agriculture. On the other hand, those who refused to accept the presence of such social gradations belonged to other occupations such as technical and non-technical services and coolies etc.

It is evident from what has been said above that while the traditional principles of stratification are still operative in the villages, new principles such as achievement, wealth and political power are also emerging side by side, and gradually gaining ascendency over the traditional principles. The rate of change from the traditional to the modern, however, seems very slow. Sometimes the new social forces have gone a way towards reinforcing the traditional values, but by and large the stranglehold of tradition has been declining.

REFERENCES

1. A.M. Hocart. *Caste*, Methuen, London, 150, *Passim.*
2. L. S. S. O'Mally, *The Indian Caste Customs*, Cambridge University Press, 1932, p. 14.
3. J.H. Hutton, *Caste in India*, Oxford, 1946, p. 71.
4. L.S.S. O'Malley, *Indian's Social Heritage*, Oxford, 1943, p. 16.
5. S.V. Ketkar, *History of Caste*, Ithaca, N.Y.
6. L.S.S. O'Malley, *The Indian Caste Customs*, *op. cit.*
7. L.S.S. O'Malley, *India's Sacial Heritage*, *op. cit.*
8. Radhakamal Mukerji, *Principles of Comparative Economics*, P.S. Kink & Son Ltd., Vol. 2., p. 8.

Appendix IV

RELIGION, REACTION AND CHANGE

Every religion knows different "sects" or "schools". By introducing changes and thereby provoking reactions they usually play an important role within the development of the religious system. Though this may be—roughly speaking—the role of sects in all religions, there are in the different systems considerable differences in the way changes are or may be introduced, the way reactions can take place and generally in the relation between change and reaction and their valuation.

Particularly in Hinduism the very specific and vital role of sects within the continuous formation and reshaping of tradition is not always estimated as it should be. For one is often inclined to look at Hinduism as a closed, some how static system, unsympathetic to changes and developments.

The task of analysing the way sects can introduce changes into a religious system is closely connected with another topic which was suggested for this conference, namely the problem of religious structures and institutions. If, as stated in the "*Report of the exploratory meeting on international economic justice in Asia*"[1] strategies for action should involve existing

Paper by E. A. Charlote.

groups and institutions of the different religions, some historic knowledge on these structures might prove to be helpful.

"The term "sect" is a Christian one. Though applied to other religions, it tends—as will be seen—still to retain some of its original meaning. This shows a general problem of comparative religion, which, being a rather young discipline, could not help making use of Christian terms, often without being yet able to redefine them as much as necessary.

It therefore seems advisable to start by giving a glimpse of what sect means within Christianity, especially as the Christian type of sect also plays a part in the modernization of Hinduism.

I

Sect is the Latin translation of the Greak term '*Hairesis*'. The literary meaning is "choice", and originally in the Greek context the term denoted any philosophical school or religious community one might choose to belong to. Being used by Jews and Christians the term definitely acquired a negative connotation, designating opinions, schools or communities whose tenets were not only considered to be deviating, but to be altogether wrong. The word was already used in connection with the definition of the canon of holy scriptures completed in A.D. 367. Congregations which did not agree to the contents of this canon, wanting either to include more scriptures, or, like Marcion, to drop some, were called heretics. With the development of the Latin and the Byzantine churches and their growing power, the notion of heresy became more important. Not only was a false doctrine resented and fought as such, it was moreover considered as a sinful contradiction against the established dogma and confession of the orthodox chruch, this church being considered to be the only steward of the means of redemption. Moreover, through the connection between Church and secular state, heresy was considered to be not only a spiritual aberration but a real crime, punishable by authority. Hence the institution of the Inquisition.

The term "sect", as already mentioned, took up this thoroughly negative meaning specifying it: sect means the community which sticks to heretical tenets condemend by the orthodox church, having thereby "cut off" itself from orthodoxy. It was because of this meaning that the etymology of the word "sect" was reinterpreted: being really derived from the Latin verb *sequi* ("to follow") it was later on considered to be a form of *secare* ("to cut").

The word "sect" in this meaning was also adopted by Protestantism, being itself a sect in the view of Catholicism, a church in its own view. After the Reformation those Protestant communities which differed from the established Protestant confessions and, most important, were not supported by political authority or even rebelled against it, like the Baptists or the Tomas Muntzer movement, were called "sects", as well as any further splittings from the established churches ("*Landeskirchen*").

This very brief survey shows that, within Christianity, "sect" is always opposed to "church". It was the great theologist and historian Ernst Froeltsch (1865-1923) who, being influenced by Max Weber, took up these concepts systematically. He considered the ideas of church, sect, and mysticism as the three constituent elements of Christianity, which, its fundations being present already in the Gospels, determined the whole development of Christianity "Church" he defined as the broad institution administrating the means of grace and of redemption. Relying more on the objective character of these means than on the subjective sanctification of the individual, the Church is able to admit masses as well as to adapt itself to the world. The sect is the opposite: according to Troeltsch it is a free union of serious, from and conscious Christians, separating themselves from the world and remaining confined to small followings. They stress the commandment instead of the grace, trying to establish the Christian regimen more or less radically whilst waiting for the coming Kingdom of God thereby often experimenting in social reform. As the third constituent element of Christianity Troeltsch has described mysticism as being an individual realization and inward intensification of the concepts of cult and dogma. The social organisation in accordance with mysticism woule be a floating one, depending on personal relations and characters. Troeltsch stressed the point that the needs and aims of this type were, for a long time, taken up and so to speak neutralized by the monastic orders.[2]

These definitions of Troeltsch are ideal types, *i.e.* he defines the pure concepts generally linked with the respective structures in forms which can of course, as he clearly says, also be influenced at different degress by the other concepts. Combinations will be more and more frequent, the more history advances. Especially in the last centuries, the task to distinguish clearly between Church and sect has become rather difficult. It is complicated even more by the situation in the USA, where no particular Church is linked with the political authority and where different sects acquired a specific church character, and were called "free churches".

One has to distinguish between the pure concepts of sect and Church as defined by Troeltsch, and the "pragmatic types",[3] *i.e.* the historically grown actual Churches and sects.

Within the "pragmatic" Protestant Churches the typological concept of sect made a new and slightly changed appearance. Setting out on educational, social and missionary activities, pietism and awakening developed special forms of subsidiary organisations which bridged in a way the different necessities of Church and sect. The religious societies, the well known Society for the propagation of Christian Knowledge, the Young Men's Christian Association (YMCA) and the Salvation Army are some of the most famous ones. Their aim is to penetrate the Church from within by creating specific organisations for different purposes and for different classes, ages and ranges of people, these organisations bear many typological features of sect. They consist of comparatively small congregations, and emphasise ethical strictness. Membership is attained by choice and mostly conveys the feeling of belonging to an elite. Thus they show even features of the typical antagonism between sect and Church, but as they mostly do not aim at introducing doctrinal changes, there is usually no segregation.

These subsidiary organisations played and still play a considerable part in development. Not only were most of the actions towards social welfare and general education in the last two centuries accomplished through this type of institution which spread also into other religions, but it is also this very development of the Christian sect-idea, which is at the bottom of the concept of Abrahmic Minorities often referred to during this conference as one of the most important, if not the only means of religion taking an active part in the struggle for justice and liberation.

The fundamental role of Christian sects, as dissenting separately organised communities, is obvious. By protesting against the prevalent tradition, and going back to the sources which they set out to reinterpret, the sects are continuously introducing elements of reform and, through the means of interpreting the Scriptures anew, sometimes even radical changes. The very formation of the sect—*i.e.* the expulsion from the main Church—is the reaction of the main tradition against the change introduced by the sect. Though officially rejected at first, the changes advocated by the sect on the long run influence the main stream of tradition: the Church has to adapt itself to the claims advocated by the sect, it has to remedy the abuses criticised by the sect etc. But even if the abuses which originally led to the schism are completely removed, the sect remains a separated body, usually—up to very recently *i.e.* the foundation of the ecumenical movement—unreconciled. That is to say, and this point I would like to stress, in Christianity the introduction of religious changes is possible only to a quite limited degree within the fold of orthodox tradition, Whenever the changes become too radical, they lead to the formation of new organisations, threatening each other as heretic, and claiming to be the only path to redemption.

Modern Sociology of Religion has tried to define the term "sect" in such a way as to be more easily applied to the "pragmatic" types within Christianity as well as to similar structures in other religions. Whereas "Church" is just understood to be the broader organisation, covering a whole region, "sect" is determined as a relatively small community being only one isolated section. Its characteristics are a spirit of protest and criticism against the institutional means of redemption, voluntary joining, ethical strictness and a feeling of being an elite [4]. Still this definition clearly reflects the Christian origin of the term and its indebtedness to Troeltsch. All its characteristics can only be understood out of the basic confrontation with the concept of Church and will hardly apply to religions where there is no Church-like organisation.

II

In Hinduism the term "sect" was introduced by analogy. Western scholars of the nineteenth century, like for instance Wilson, thus named the various religious communities distinguished from each other by a tradition and scriptures of their own, by worship of certain gods and often the founder as well, and by special rituals; these names have persisted ever since.

But the similarity is just a superficial one: these groups have a very different function and position than sects in Christianity. As a matter of fact there is practically no Sanskrit word meaning "sect" in the sense of a heterodox community. On the contrary, the term usually translated as sect, *sampradaya*, is a word for "orthodoxy"! It literally means "what is handed over", *i.e.* "tradition", and has in modern Indian languages also become an equivalent of "religion" (Hindu-sampradaya for instance). What does constitute a Hindu sect is not the fact of being rejected by a central authoritative institution. It is the tradition founded by a "sage" or "saint" (a *carya, guru*).

So for instance the school founded by Sankaracarya, generally considered to be one of the most venerable and orthodox manifestations of Hinduism, is called *sampradaya* as well as dissenting and protesting communities like for instance *Virasaivism*. The latter "radical sampradayas" as one might call them, introduced not only doctrinal changes, but are or at least were, advocates of considerable social changes. They challenged orthodoxy, by for instance not admitting image worship or by not recognizing and even deliberately trespassing caste-barriers.

It was probably Joachim Wach who first pointed out the unique character of the sampradaya and called it a problem to to the sociology of religion [5]. But still he did not point out that the sampradaya has a specific form of social organization. Unlike a Christian sect, it does not mainly rely on a close community of lay men. Instead the very cores are the centres, where the tradition is handed down, namely the *asharams* and *mathas* and in general the monastic orders initiated by the founder. The lay community is in most cases not strictly defined, only very few groups, like *Virasaivism* or the *Manbhaus* do have a special initiation ceremony for all lay members.

The extraordinary position of the sampradaya emerges from three special features distinguishing Hinduism from all other world-religions. The first and perhaps most striking of these features is the absence of any centralised institution which could control orthodoxy. There are institutions defining and supervising orthodoxy, but—and this makes all the difference, they are of consequence only within a certain place or region and are usually linked with a certain caste. Moreover the subject of their definitions are mostly not doctrinal. It is mainly in the realm of ritual and social behaviour that orthodoxy has to be proved, an orthodoxy not generally defined but qualified by caste and by region.

The concept of qualified orthodoxy allows Hinduism its famous tolerance and openness. And this concept also explains, why, with the exception of an attempt to invest to invest the *mathas* founded by *Sankara* with a sort of pontifical dignity, which in practice did not acquire great authority, Hinduism never developed any Churchlike institution. It was, so to speak, not necessary because of caste being able to perform many of the functions usually assigned to Churches. For instance the selection and training of priests—one of the most important prerogatives of Churches-could be lift to the family tradition of the Brahmins. Accordingly there was no need for the political authority to establish an unified state Church: the installation of a Brahmanical state cult at Court would be sufficient.

Caste and Church as defined by Troeltsch have striking similarities: the power to excommunicate or outcast rebels—the trusteeship of "objective" sacraments like marriage, admission by birth and the connection with political authority.

Caste being in some way the equivalent of a Church, it is natural that it should be also the counterpart of the sect. But whereas the Christian Churches have, as pointed out above, to reject the sects and their attempts to introduce changes, thereby splitting up and diminishing more and more, caste and sampradaya are basically supplementary. This is possible because of a second special feature of Hinduism, the institution of the *guru*.

The words of a spiritual teacher, or *guru*, are to be considered as direct revelations. His teachings may be objected by other schools, but can never, because of the lack of a central institution, definitely be ruled out. Moreover a guru is considered by his disciples as a god incarnate. It is said to be easier to obtain the forgiveness of a god than of one's guru. In spite of this exalted position, neither to become nor to follow a certain guru is in any way limited to certain castes or persons. Everybody can become an ascetic, a *yogi* or *sanyasi*, and potentially a guru, thereby overcoming the barries of caste. Everybody is equally free to follow whatever school or guru he likes, as long as he fulfils the basic ritual and social requirements of his caste. In traditional Hinduism redemption is considered to be an individual affair: though socially determined by birth, spiritually the individual is free to choose his own way of redemption, the guru to be followed and even the god to be worshipped.

Even if, like in the radical sampradayas, the new elements introduced by a guru strongly oppose the caste-system, they may yet be assimiliated by this very system. What happens, if a new sect arises and declares for instance the non-validity of caste, and in practice tries to overcome it? Up to the present day there is more or less the same variety of possibilities. The members of the new sect may be outcasted and, being subject to social and economic boycott, eventually give up their new creed. On the other hand this is by no means bound to happen. The newly established sect can also, in spite of its doctrines, not really touch the caste organisation. Its members may for instance once a year dine together, but nevertheless continue to marry within their own castes. Examples of both these possible reactions against the introduction of changes can for instance be observed in the history of the *Mahima Dharma* movement in Orissa.

But a radical sampradaya can also—on the long run—develop into a newly recognised caste which may or may not remain "open", *i.e.* accept members from all castes, and may even as has happened in Virasaivism, develop subcastes of its own. The role of sects in traditional Hinduism is to continually keep in motion the doctrinal as well as the social, and to some extent also, the ritual tradition. They may not fundamentally attempt to change the traditional system, because, as Prof. Rao has pointed out in his paper, of the forces operating in wider society, but they are the guarantees, that this system can never become completely closed.

The Sociology of religion has, since Max Weber, acknowledged the role of sects, *i.e.*, radical sampradayas, as agents of social mobility[6]. What is more seldom appreciated is the general doctrinal development enforced by them, a development which mostly leads to renewed and reinforced attempts at social change. This is possible because of the third peculiar feature favouring the introduction of changes, the nature of the Hindu canon.

We have seen that in Christianity the first reason for the formation of sects was the definition of the canon. The general acceptance of a canon, as we find it in most religions accepting holy scriptures, does limit the possibilities of change very much. Not only are all other, *i.e.*, all later scriptures minor in authority, changes can only be introduced by the means of translating and interpreting these very scriptures.

The Hindu canon consists of two *parts* the second of which-astonishing enough—is still unfinished. *Sruti*, literally "what is heard", is considered to be the immediate, literal revelation and contains the *Vedas*, *Brahmanas* and *Upanishads*. "*Smriti*", literally "what is remembered", is considered to be the revelation not literally taken down but only "remembered" by the *Rishis* (sages). *Smriti* includes the two great epics *Ramayana* and *Mahabharata*, the *Puranas*, the law books etc., texts which like for example the *Bhagavadgita*, have partly become much more important for the actual practic of Hinduism as the vedic ones. In theory smriti must go back to some element of the sruti. So the orthodoxy or validity of some smriti text can be questioned and opposed. But, as already noted in connection with the teachings of a guru, such an objection may be maintained by certain groups, but can never be generally enforced.

On the contrary, the contents of the smriti not being strictly defined, new texts may arise. It is stated for instance in the *Mahabharata* that the question of *dharma* and *adharma i.e.*, religion and non-religion, or right and non-right, "are both subject to the limitations of country and time [7]. It is therefore not astonishing, that the religious texts written in the regional languages have as a matter of fact become an ever-growing extension of the smriti. This gives to Hindu tradition an enormous freedom. Commenting on recognized sacred texts and translating them is only one way of introducing new elements and thoughts, which may also express themselves in new texts.

One of the most important texts of the smriti literature, the *Bhagavata Purana*, for instance, is in itself a product of such a process of change and reaction as well as a step in its further radicalization. There is in this text a criticism on the position of Brahmins and on the efficiency of rites. *Bhakti*, the pure devotion, poverty and low birth are considered to be better for attaining salvation. As van Buitenen has shown, the literary expression of such views, raised strong reactions from the side of the smarta Brahmins. Texts like *Yamunas Agamapramanya* show how the Brahmins strongly criticised the *Bhagavata* as not corresponding to the sruti and smriti, and struggled against the recognition of Bhagavata priests,[8] but with no lasting effect. The text, obviously being the expression of a large popular movement, became generally recognized more and more. Its importance reached a new stage, when, in the sixteenth century it was translated into Oriya and became a sort of "Bible" of the whole region. The translation was done by a member of the *Pancasakha* School. This movement had very unorthodox views: It denounced the position of the Brahmins, and was against all idolatry, temple cult, pilgrimage etc. stating that the true worship is only found within one's soul, true pilgrimage is the *yoga* which reaches the *tirthas* (sacred places) within one's body etc.

What it important is that, in order to prove their views, they could already rely on a text like the *Bhagavata Purana*, which had been recognized in the meantime. By being able to do so the *Pancasakha* could now go one step further. In their own scriptures they announced the imminent victory of this true worship over the current Brahmanical one. Of course there was again a strong reaction from the side of the Brahmanical orthodoxy, but nevertheless the writings of the *Pancasakha* spread all over Orissa and were in the long run accepted nearly by everybody. Again these scriptures once having themselves been the expression of a new movement, are now considered as traditional proofs (*pramana*) by another, later and more radical movement. The *Mahima Dharma* sect, founded in the nineteenth century, declares itself to be the fulfilment of the prophecies (*malikas*) of the *Pancasakha*, and again radicalizes the changes. What originally was considered to be a secret doctrine is converted by them into rules and regulations. For instance the doubt of the superiority of the Brahmins has developed into the prohibition to enter their houses or to eat their food. The condemnation of image-worship also a secret doctrine with the *Pancasakha* is externalised and radicalized to the extent that it was attempted by members of the sect to burn the famous image of Lord Jagannatha in Puri of course with a strong reaction following.

Coming back to the definitions of sect seen in the first paragraph, I think it is obvious they do not apply to the Hindu sampradaya. As the opposition church—sect is not present in Hinduism-the main features of the more recent definitions, the spirit of protest and the consciousness of being an elite are not important for the sampradaya. The spirit of protest will soon be assimilated, the feeling of being the "chosen people" will not develop strongly, as redemption is considered to be an individual affair.

Thinking along the lines of Troeltsch the sampradaya has elements of the mysticism-type, especially as it is linked to the institution of monastic orders. But the sampradaya is more for it does develop definite doctrinal as well as ritual traditions. It is a structure of its own, where the institution of an ascetic order, associated by Troeltsch with the mysticism-type, becomes the centre of a ritual, doctrinal and even social tradition which is clearly distinct and yet stays within the main stream of orthodox tradition. This tradition is, a process whereby originally new and unorthodox changes can be assimilated and integrated, more easily than in other religions. In the process of integration the originally heterodox, "revolutionary" movements and tenets undergo two opposite developments:

they become more and more generally respected and respectable on the one side and in the same time more and more radical, and may lead or at least support new outbursts of change.

III

Within the frame of the present seminar one has now to ask which part this role of sects in traditional Hinduism did or does play in the confrontation between Hinduism and modernity. It is an astonishing fact that radical sampradayas did not for quite a long time play any role in Hindu modernism at all. Not only was the fundamental openness of the Hindu tradition not at all considered—even tenets coinciding with the aims of modern thought were at first not taken up.

Hindu modernism may be defined as an attempt to reconcile the traditional religion with the modern materialistic and rationalistic "*Weltanchaung*." All modernistic movements especially wanted to introduce social consciousness and social reforms in their religious programme. A reference to the changes and social claims advocated by the radical sampradayas would have served the purpose very well. Curiously enough such references occurred rather late. The reason is, that Hindu-modernism set out not only, as it is natural that it should, against tradition, but so to speak, completely without tradition.

Ram Mohan Roy, the founder of modern Hinduism, in theory rejected nearly everything that was essential in Hinduism. His was a deistic concept of a "natural religion" completely in accordance with reason. As Voltaire, he saw this natural religion as the true source and basis of humanity to which an enlightened mankind must return. In the historical formations and appearances of the single religions he saw nothing but depravations of that original pure idea. A similar static conception of religion was present with Dayananda Sarasvati, the founder of the *Arya Samaj*, who tried to restore what he believed to be the original teaching of the *Veda* and in the same the foundation of all religions.

Both the great movements of *Brahma Samaj* and *Arya Samaj* were fundamentally opposed to the living Hindu tradition, and wanted to replace it. They took over to a considerable degree all the Christian misunderstandings and prejudices of the time, and therefore, tried to abolish all that was absolete to them. The scriptures to be read or accepted were strictly limited, new forms of ritual and cult with only some Hindu elements in it were introduced and there were attempts to overcome the caste system.

In spite of the deep differences between Arya and Brahma Samaj they are quite similar in structure: they both tried to establish Hindu churches according to the model of the Protestant churches of the time. Like Protestant 'churches the Samajes organized themselves as broad institutions relying on laymen and on specially selected, trained and supported "ministers."

Hindu modernism also took over the forms of subsidiary organisations developed by Protestantism. The samajes had their own Young Men's Associations, their societies, medical missions, educational societies etc. A great deal of social work, especially amongst the tribes and scheduled castes was accomplished through these organisations. Brahma and Arya Samaj both had been founded, to become Hindu churches, embracing and unifying the whole of the Indian nation. Though of considerable success for a certain time, these movements could not, of course, accomplish such a large task. What happened was the opposite of what had happened in Europe and America, where sects had become churches: what was meant to be a church became most definitely a sect. Criticism of the institutional means of salvation namely the cult, ethical strictness and the feeling of being an elite is present in the samajes as well as an unusually strong reaction and repulsion of the orthodoxy. For, to counteract modernism some parts of Hinduism while consciously remaining traditional in their tenets, for instance emphasizing caste and image worship, adopted modern organisational structures which considerably reinforced their reaction. Especially the different forms of subsidiary organisations taken up by newly founded anti-modernistic leagues like the *Bharata Mahamandala*, which thereby also took over ideas connected with these structures, namely missionary clan and social commitment.

But the development of Hindu modernism and the interactions with Christianity do not end here. Evidently, the current of modernisation could not, on the long run, leave aside the living Hindu tradition. It was extensively taken up in two different ways; One was by means of literary work and literary movements. The starting point of this literary modernism was the first modern comment on the *Bhagavadgita*, written in 1866 by Bankim Chandra Chattopadyaya. Modern interpretations of Hindu scriptures, especially the *Bhagavadgita*, proved to be of considerable influence by giving to the English educated people a new and acceptable approach to their own tradition. These interpretations as given for instance in the works of S. Radhakrishnan, tend to become widely recognized being even quoted by the Supreme Court of India, and seem to signalise the development of a new general concept of orthodoxy in Hinduism no longer qualified by caste and region.

While referring more and more to its own tradition, modern Hinduism also rediscovered the sampradaya. It was Swami Vivekananda who first took it up again in organizing the Ramakrishna Mission. This movement no longer tried to replace Hinduism by a new type of organization, as the samajes had done, but set out to spread the teachings of their guru Ramakrishna and the school founded by his disciple Vivekananda. Exactly like a traditional sampradaya the movement does not primarily rely on a congregation of laymen, but on a monastic order. All subsequent modern Hindu movements, the Aurobindo as well as the Ghandian movement, were organized in the same way: a relatively small centre, an ashram, a monastic order or a community of very devoted persons around which the most different classes and types of men can gather in different ways and without the necessity of any formal initiation.

Also the most recent movements like the Society for Krishna-Consciousness, which are no longer concerned with social or national problems, and have an increasing success in the West are organised along these lines. It is striking to see how, after the Christian concepts of Church and sect had been introduced into Hinduism in the nineteenth century, it is now the Hindu sampradaya, which spreads into the realm of Christianity.

The organisational structure of sampradaya proved to be equally fitted for the purpose of mission abroad as for the purpose of spreading modernism in India. The reason is, that it allows everybody an access of his own: the individual may adopt a new way of life, but he may as well continue his traditional way of life, taking up only new interpretations.

It was therefore this form of institution which, along with the literary movements, succeeded best increating a new and modernized religious identity and thereby laid the foundations to the national identity of modern India. The attempt to build Hindu-churches could not fulfil that task and was therefore not further developed. But the forms of subsidiary organisations taken over from Protestantism persisted, being adopted also by later modern movements like the Ramakrishna mission, and introduced into Hinduism a specific type of missionary and social work.

Contemporary Hinduism still contains all the different forms of change and reaction dealt with in this survey. Traditional forms of radical sampradayas still continue to exist. They nowadays meet not only with an orthodox reaction of the traditional type, but also with the different types of modernization—the samajes, the various modern sampradayas and the general orthodoxy of modern interpretations, thereby creating new complexes of change and reaction.

RELIGIOUS MOVEMENTS AND SOCIAL TRANSFORMATION IN INDIA*

While religion has been studied in terms of providing the basis for social cohesion and solidarity, its role in bringing about social change is not sufficiently stressed. This paper focuses its attention on the latter, in the context of certain 19th and 20th Century religious and sectarian movements in India.

A movement is an organized effort on the part of a section of society to bring about a change in any or all its aspects, and a religious movement is concerned with the system of religious beliefs, rituals, symbols and world view as providing an ideology for change. It is necessary to distinguish two types of religious movements. On the one hand there are religious and sectarian movements which are concerned almost entirely with bringing about changes in the existing religious beliefs, doctrines, rituals and practices, and they have little or remote impact on other areas of life. Certain *Bhakti* or devotional movements provide examples of this kind. On the other, certain religious movements have far-reaching social consequences in the nature of social reform and transformation. Arya Samaj and other sectarian movements exemplify this kind. This paper is largely concerned with the second type of religious movement where religion provides an ideology for social transformation. Such movements in fact are commonly known as socio-religious movements.

Three more preliminary points need to be noted. Throughout this paper I do not distinguish between religious and sectarian movements, as the latter are subsumed under the former. Secondly, I do not have space to deal with religious movements among the tribes and non-Hindu religious groups. Thirdly, I use the term social transformation to designate middle level

* This section comprises of a paper written by M.S. Rao.

structural and organizational changes between reform on the one hand and revolution on the other. Reform signifies a low key of social change while revolution refers to rapid and radical structural changes.

During British rule several socio-religious movements emerged in different regions, and these movements differed in respect of aims, scale of organization and consequences. While at the all-India level there arose such movements as Brahmo Samaj, Arya Samaj and Ramakrishna Mission, at the regional level there were such movements as Sangh Sabha movement in Punjab and Sri Narayana Dharma Paripalana movement in Kerala. All these were characterized by a spirit of revolt and protest. It may be asked whether there are any differences between these movements and those that emerged in ancient and medieval India. For instance, Buddhism, Jainism and several *Bhakti* or devotional movements. Veerasaivism and Sikhism were characterized in one way or the other by the element of protest. Buddhism made a frontal attack on the supremacy of the Brahmins. It repudiated the Vedas as the source of spiritual knowledge on the metaphysical plane and placed the Kshatrias at the top of the caste hierarchy instead of the Brahmins, on the empirical plane. The medieval saints like Ramananda and Kabir attacked once again Brahmanical supremacy and created a movement in favour of devotion as the basis of salvation and replaced the Sanskritic texts by the vernacular ones. This enabled the masses to take part in the worship, rituals and practices which were once the preserve of the Brahmins. Veerasaivism which emerged in the 12th Century Karnataka provides a singular example of a militant attack against the Brahmins and the caste system. Led by Basaveswara, the Veerasaiva movement acquired a militant spirit. It created a set of religious institutions parallel to that of the Brahmins, and in many places its followers came in physical conflict with the Brahmins.

All these myvements in pre-British India had important social consequences. They revolted against the ritual supremacy of the Brahmins and the basic principle of birth underlying the caste system. The devotional path was emphasized as the means of attaining salvation, and this was easily accessible to all without consideration of caste. Bhakti movements helped undermine, to a great extent, the monopoly of the Brahmins in their access to scriptures and their emphasis on the path of knowledge as the only means to salvation. They overlooked the principle of birth to a great extent in the recruitment of individuals to the sect, thereby overcoming the limitations of the caste system.

In spite of such liberalizing consequences the protest movements did not result in any far-reaching changes in the value system underlying the caste system, because of certain forces that operated in the wider society. The economic system was still largely associated with land and the caste system, although some occupations such as agriculture and trade were not exactly caste bound. The two legitimizing principles the king (political authority) and the priest (ritual authority) were effective in upholding the values behind the caste system which remained the only avenue for social mobility.

During British rule, however, significant structural changes occurred in the wider social content. Recruitment to jobs in administration and factories was not based on caste. Administration of justice was not related to caste hierarchy. Introduction of law courts undermined the legitimacy of caste and village councils to a great extent. English education introduced liberal and egalitarian ideas which challenged the hierarchical aspects of the caste system and the underlying ideas of purity and pollution. British rule allowed political democracy to function in different degrees, and this acted as a check against the sovereignty of kings. All these forces significantly undermined the two sources of legitimacy—the king and the priest—and opened up fresh avenues of social mobility, in addition to caste and sect, based on modern occupation, English education, polititical power and modern styles of life which included dress, speech, house and equipment and membership of clubs.

Religious and sectarian movements that emerged during British rule acquired a new dimension. The element of revolt and protest in them got reinforced by those egalitarian secular forces mentioned above, yielding significant results. I shall discuss three religious movements (Brahmo Samaj, Arya Samaj and Sri Narayana Dharma Paripalana) which emerged during British rule with a view to outlining their features and the nature of social transformation that they have brought about.

II

Brahmo Samaj[9] was established in 1828 by Raja Ram Mohan Roy. It attacked the idolatrous practices of Hinduism and devised a different set of rituals for its followers. In addition to a new system of beliefs, rituals, and symbols the movement revolted against the social and religious practices such as burning of widows (sati), child marriage, polygamy and the problem of widow re-marriage. Raja Ram Mohan Roy also laid the foundation of English education and journalism to spread his liberal ideas. The movement was later led by Debendranath Tagore, Keshab Chandra Sen others.

Brahmo Samaj had an impact outside Bengal. In Bombay Prarthana Samij came to be established, as a variant, under the leadership of M.G. Ranade, R. Bhanderkar and N.G. Chandavarkar. In Madras a theistic society was started in 1864 under the name of the Veda Samaj which later became the Brahmo Samaj of the South. R. Venkata Ratnam was one of the leaders of this Samaj.

Brahmo Samaj was largely an elite movement having its followers from the upper strata of society who were English-educated and westernized. The movement not only provided a mechanism of upward social mobility but also an ideology for reformation of the undesirable religious beliefs and practices and social customs. However, it mainly addressed itself to such problems of the upper castes as *sati*, widow re-marriage, child marriage and kulinism. It established may widow houses and worked for the emancipation of women and spread of liberal education.

It may be noted that the Samaj also had a programme for the depressed classes although very few among the latter became Brahmos. The programme mainly consisted of opening schools for them and supporting their amelioration. In this the movement reached the masses and worked, although in a small way, towards egalitarisnism and transformation of the hierarchical basis of the caste system.

From the point of view of far reaching structural changes, Arya Samaj[10] achieved a greater degree of success. It was established in 1875 in Bombay and in 1877 in Lahore. It aimed religious reformation of orthodox Hinduism Swami Dayananda Saraswati, the founder of Arya Samaj upheld the values of Vedic Hinduism, without idolatry. He made the Vedas and the fire sacrifice accessible to all irrespective of caste and sex. The wearing of the sacred thread was made essential, and the rites of the life cycle ceremonies had five-sacrifice as the central focus. The Arya Samaj built its own temples and trained a category of priests to conduct the newly formulated rites. It established a network of educational institutions combining English with Sanskrit. All these enabled the spread of Arya Samaj ideas.

Arya Samaj recruited people from all strata— upper, middle and lower. It sponsored a special programme of a *Suddhi* movement starting from 1909 which aimed at two things: getting new recruits from lower classes especially the untouchables and tribes who were outside the castefold, and re-converting the Christian and Muslim converts. This was in reaction to the evangelical efforts of the Christian missionaries. Lala Lajpat Rai gave a new dimension to the *Suddhi* movement. He admitted a number of untouchables and Domes into Arya Samaj and ate food cooked by them. Many low castes accepted Arya Samaj faith as they acquired the prestigious symbols of sacred thread, the *gayatri* hymn and the performance of fire sacrifice. This enabled them to break the monopoly of the Brahmins and assert their claims to a share in the use of ritual goods and services of High Hinduism.

There was another programme of Arya Samaj which involved the peasants in the rural areas, namely, the cow protection movement. Under the influence of Arya Samaj peasants opened *goshalas*, meant fore the care and protection of cattle especially cows. This movement was a direct reaction to the Muslim's cow slaughtering. The *goshala* movement banned selling of calves to persons whose credentials were doubtful. Further, it banned wearing of footwear made of calf leather.

Thus the set of beliefs, rituals and symbols of Arya Samaj developed into an ideology motivating its followers to action. Interest articulation is an essential element in the transformation of a set of religious beliefs and rituals into an ideology which motivates peopte to act, The followers perceive interests in the new faith, identify their interest with those of the community and get organised for 'political' action, against opposition by the orthodox Hindus, especially the orthodox Brahmins.

Arya Samaj had far reaching social consequences. It supported egalitarianism in the acquisition of ritual goods and services of Brahmanical Hinduism, irrespective of sex and caste. The women who were debarred from muttering vedic hymns and performing fire-sacrifices were allowed these rights. Similarly, low castes too acquired these rights in the teeth of opposition by the upper caste orthodox Hindus. It promoted and legitimized inter-caste marriages which undermined the edogamous aspect of caste. It also encouraged widow re-marriages reforming the orthodox Brahmanical practices. Thus it brought about both reform and transformation in the sense of equalization of opportunities in the use of ritual goods and services of Brahmanical Hinduism, attacking the hierarchical aspects of caste society.

Sri Narayana Dharma Paripalana Movement emerged among the Izhavas, who were traditionally today tappers, of Kerala, in the last decade of the 19th Century. The movement was started by the followers of Sri Narayana Guru Swamy for the propagation of his new religion and world view. Sri Swamy was born on 28th August, 1855, in a village near Trivandrum in a lower middle class Izhava family. He had his early training in secular Sanskrit, Malayalam, Tamil, Astrology and Ayurveda. During his adolescence, he escaped into the wilderness and came in contact with a teacher from whom he learnt Vedas, Vedanta and Yoga. Swamy returned to his village in 1890 and built a smalll monastery. He propounded a new religion with the central theme of one God, one religion and one caste. Re-interpreting the Vedantic position of Sri Shankracharya, he asserted that everyone irrespective of caste could study Vedas and Vedanta. He established a number of temples and installed idols. The Temple became the centre of community activities with programmes of education and as a place for conducting marriages. He created an order of priests and monks. He also established a chain of monasteries, and founded Sri Narayana Dharma Paripala Sangha at Shivgiri which manages all the monasteries and some schools. He formulated simple marriage rituals using both Sanskrit and Malayalam. He asked his followers to give up producing, selling and consuming liquor, and urged them to give up worshipping spirits and lesser duties, and the practice of animal sacrifice.

The set of beliefs, rituals and symbols expounded by the Swamy formed the basis of a new ideology motivating his followers to formulate a programme of action. Izhavas were considered unapproachables and they suffered from many religious and civic disabilities. They were not allowed to enter or walk near the temples of the upper castes, were prevented from worshipping Brahmanical deities, and were not permitted to study the Vedas. They could not use the tanks of the upper castes and the public roads and bridges. Their women were not allowed to cover their breasts. Thus their position on the scale of relative deprivation was very low.

Swamy's attempt to re-interpret Hinduism and to establish a set of religious institutions, rituals and symbols parallel to the upper castes expressed an element of revolt through isolation and self organization. Swamy was constantly arguing with and challenging in his mind the Nambutiri Brahmins. He demonstrated how Izhava and Pulaya boys could recite Vedas as good as and even better than the Brahmins. SNDP temples were cleaner than the upper caste ones and the SNDP priests were not corrupt in comparison to the Brahmin priests.

The impact of Swamy's teachings was felt in every nook and corner of Kerala. Numerous small associations sprang up which propagated the new outlook and world view given by the Swamy. A number of disciples hailed Swamy as the beacon light of wisdom and undertook to work for the spread of his ideas. Swamy himself toured all over Kerala, visited Sri Lanka and Madras establishing monasteries there. He was acclaimed as the charismatic leader in every sense of the term. He had healing powers too.

The essence of Swamy's teachings was egalitarianism, attacking the ritual monopoly of the Brahmins and Nayars. His teachings provided the motivating force for political mobilization. Palpu, a doctor from the Izvaha community, came in contact with the Swamy, and being influenced by his teachings established the SNDP Yogam in 1903 with Kumaran Asan, the famous Malaydalam lyric poet as its secretary. The Yogam led many agitations to fight for their basic civic rights and equality of opportunities. Under leadership of Kumaran Asan, in the first and second decades of the 20th Century, the Yogam fought for rights of admission of Izhava and other polluting castes to schools and colleges. In some places the agitators came into open physical conflict with the Nayars who opposed them.

Around 1917, Sahodaran Aryappan, a prominent leader of the Izhavas started a programme of inter-dining with the

Pulayas, a caste below the Izhavas, with a view to breaking rules of pollution. In order to promote this programme he established brotherhood associations in different parts of Kerala. Swamy was very happy with this. In fact, he made it a point to appoint only the Pulayas as cooks in the monasteries which he established. This was a move to equalize by pulling the bottom up.

The next major programme was the fight against unapproachability, under the leadership of T.K. Mydhavan. In 1919 he organized an agitation demanding the equality of job opportunities mobilizing not only Izhavas but also Christians and Muslims. He organized the famous Vaikom Satyagraha in 1924. This became a national event as Mahatma Gandhi participated in it. The Satyagraha was also blessed by the Swamy. The temple entry movement was a direct attack on the monopolistic rights of the upper castes to places of worship. In the 1930's all the temples were thrown open to the low and untouchable castes.

Under the leadership of C. Keshavan the Yogam led a successful agitation for communal representation in the Assemblies. In the 'forties and fifties' the Yogam concentrated its attention on creating facilities for higher education. Under the leadership of R. Shankar a separate S.N. Trust was founded and it established about 12 colleges, several hostels, and a hospitals. All these activities formed part of the SNDP movement. While the Yogam became the organization fighting mainly for specular benefits the SNDP Sangha has remained largely a religious body maintaining *mutts*, some temples and schools, training priests and propagators, and running a school for teaching the philosophy of the Swamy.

Swamy died in 1928 at Shivgiri where a marble statue of him has been installed. Shivgiri has become a place of pilgrimage and once a year a large congregation gathers there.

The SNDP movement in its religious and philosophical

aspects has acquired an international dimension thanks to the efforts of Sri Nataraja Guru, a close disciple of the Swamy. The Guru was the son of Dr. Palpu and he did his Ph.D. in philosophy from France. On his return to Kerala, he expected that he would be the natural successor to Swamy. But he got disappointed and started a splinter movement called the Gurukula movement. He established an ashram at Nilgiri and other ashrams in Shivgiri. Bangalore, Sri Lanka, Belgium, Geneva and U.S.A. The main aim of the Gurukula movement has been to propagate the philosophy of Swamy to peoples in different parts of the World. The Guru interpreted Swamy's universal philosophy in the language of Western philosophy thus making intelligible to the wider audience all over the world. However, Nataraja Guru's impact has remained at the level of founding a different but allied system of beliefs and organisation. Nataraja Guru believed in the personal communication of spiritual knowledge by the teacher to the student. The Gurukula movement, unlike the SNDP did not become a mass movement.

The SNDP movement, which is still active, has had many far reaching social consequences, during a period of about seventy years. Narayana Guru Swamy was able to bring about a total transformation in the attitude, outlook, would view and the value system of the Izhavas in particular and of Kerala society in general. He revolted against the Brahmins and the value system underlying the caste system. He challenged the ritual supremacy of the Brahmins and gave his followers complete opportunity for participating in the religious and cultural system of the upper castes, from which they were kept out for centuries. While the Swamy withdrew and created a set of parallel institutions, the leaders of the SNDP Yogam agitated for rights of entering the temple of the upper castes and successfully broke then monopoly in the use of places of worship, tanks, roads and bridges.

The SNDP movement not only made fuller participation in the religious system of the Brahmins possible but also secured the basic civic rights of women to cover their breasts, of admission to schools and colleges, of recruitment to Government jobs and of representation on various political bodies.

The movement thus transformed the position of the Izhavas in the Kerala society, to that of a better status. While they were included in the Depressed Caste Category in the 'thirties, they are now part of the other backward classes. Izhavas wield considerable political power in the State, some of them having been the Chief Ministers. There is an all round development of various types of elite—the professional, administrative and business. The religious ideology of the Swamy provided a rational ethic for the pursuit of modern economic activities. Swamy encouraged holding of industrial exhibitions in the temples. He considered temples of workshops imparting new skills. In his own ashram he had looms on which his students worked for a living.

The movement also transformed the nature of the caste system attacking the basic principles of purity and pollution. It ushered in a programme of egalitarianism in various spheres—religious, economic, educational and political. The movement, being the first one of its kind in Kerala, had an impact on the other castes such as the Nambutiris, the Nayars and the Pulayas who later started organizing themselves to reform their caste customs.

III

In conclusion, let me briefly summarize a few points made earlier with a view to describing the general features of the Religious Movement in relation to social transformation. Different kinds of religious and sectarian movements emerged in various regions and at different periods of time. While some movements were confined to the establishment of a different set of beliefs, rituals and symbols, others involved social mobilization on a large scale to bring about changes in different spheres of social life. In a sense all religious movements started off as a protest against the existing situations, but a few of them attacked the Brahmanical Hinduism in a radical manner. Such movements in pre-British India, which were characterized by protest ended up forming another sect, largely, leaving the overall system only relatively modified, because the only two sources of legitimization—the Brahmin priest and the King—remained effective. During British rule, however, several forces were released which undermined, to a great extent, the legitimacy of the Brahmin and the King. A liberal and egalitarian ideology that began to find expression in the institutions of Law, education employment and politics undermined the value system of the caste and provided a source of social mobility outside the caste system. The religious movements that emerged under such social and cultural conditions acquired a new spirit of challenge, protest and revolt, and they were also able to counteract the opposition from the upper castes as the traditional sanctions had become weak.

It is necessary to emphasize that it is only when a set of religious beliefs, rituals and symbols develop into an ideology that a religious movement becomes the basis of social mobilization. Interest articulation provides the link between a set of beliefs and action. When people perceive interest in the new faith it develops into an ideology motivating people to evolve a programme of action. Religious also provides the basis of establishing identity. For instance, Brahmo Samaj provided a style of life which served as a factor of identify. The Arya Samaj established identity on the basis of certain symbols such as fire sacrifice and absence of idol worship, wearing of sacred thread and uttering the *gayatri* hymn. Samajists were distinguished from others—the Sanatanist in this regard. Their opposition groups also included the Muslims and the Christians. The SNDP movement established identity on the basis of new philosophy and rituals provided by the Swamy and membership of related associations in opposition to the Nayars in the secular field and the Nambutiris in the ritual area.

Leadership in a religious movement is crucial in social

mobilization. Brahmo Samaj, Arya Samaj and SNDP were led by charismatic leaders. The movement attracted able leaders at different levels. These were English educated westernized professionals and intellectuals who brought new skills of organization and new techniques of agitation to bear upon the movement. Organization is part of the mobilization process. SNDP Yogam which was the association at the Kerala level, had many unions at the Taluka level and branches at the village level. Democratic processes were adopted in running the association at various levels. The federal structures of these associations enabled a programme of action extended at the village level. Some of the programmes included dismantling the Izhava shrines meant for the worship of lesser deities, preventing people from singing obsence songs at the fairs of Bhagvati, stopping animal sacrifice and banning consumption of alcohol. There were also such positive progrgmmes of action as building a temple, promoting inter-dining with the Pulayas conducting Satyagraha for entering caste Hindu temples, and adopting the new marriage ritual given by the Swamy.

Agitation was one of the main means of organized action and this often led to conflict which groups which opposed the efforts of agitators. For instance, in the temple entry agitation the Izhavas and other low castes were opposed by the Nayars and Nambutiris. The latter had the support of the Travancore Maharajah. Whereas the British Administration favoured a liberal policy, the State adopted a conservative policy in many matters regarding admission of Izhavas in schools and their recruitment to government jobs.

The nature of social transformation that the religious movements have achieved varies from one to the other. With the Brahmos the change was in the nature of reforms in the orthodox Hinduism and the changes in the orthodox customs like *sati*, child marriage and window re-marriages. Thus it addressed itself mainly to the problems of the upper castes and it never became a mass movement. On the contrary Arya Samaj became a mass movement with its programmes of

Suddhi and cow protection. It was an egalitarian religion and the low castes quickly perceived in it advantages of upward social mobility. The Arya Samaj brought about significant changes in the nature of the caste system by undermining the traditional rules of purity and pollution. Similarly, the SNDP movement not only provided an avenue for social mobility but it changed the character of caste society by successfully challenging the monopolistic rights of the upper castes in several spheres—religion, education, employment and politics. Through social mobilization the movement widened the boundaries of identity from local endogamous caste units to caste or sect as a large ethnic unit at the level of the State vis-a-vis other ethnic groups like the Christians, Muslims and Nayars. The emergence of Izhavas, as an ethnic group was the result of social transformation brought about the SNDP movement. The ideology of Arya Samaj and SNDP movements was essentially egalitarian in nature. It provided the motive force, for the relatively deprived sections society to fight not only for the equalization of religious opportunities but also equalization of educational, economic and political opportunities.

REFERENCES

1. *Report of the Exploratory Meeting on International Economic Justice in Asia*—Bangkok 5-7 March 1973 (mimeographed copy) p. 9.

2. Ernst Troeltsch: "*Die Saziallehren der christlichen Kirchen and Gruppen*" Tubingen 1912, p. 967.

3. This differentiation was introduced by S. Morberg, "*Potential Uses of the Church—Sect Typology, in Comparative Religious Research*" in "*International Journal of Comparative Sociology*" No. 2.

4. These characteristics are given by G. Mensching, "*Soziologie der Religion*" Bonn 1968, pp. 240-244. It is interesting how, in order to be able to apply the term sect to Hinduism, Mensching tries to somehow reinterpret the element of splitting typical of the Christian sect: "Das kann sowohl bedeuten, dass die Sekte sich aue einer grooseren organisatorischen Einheit absplittert und dabei zugleich aus dem Abstammungskomplex dieser Gross-gemeinschaft einzelne

Elemente heraushebt und einseitig in den Mittelpunkt stellt, als auch, dass die einzenne Sekte mit anderen Sekten ein Ganzes bildet, wahrend es keinen eigentlichen Religionsorganismus gibt, von dem sie sich gelost hatte," (p. 238).

5. Joaehim Wach: "*Religionssoziologie*," Tubingen 1951, p. 143 ff.

6. For instance David G. Mandelbaum: "*Society in India*," Vol. II "*Change and Continuity*," Berkeley 1970, p. 543 f. "Jati mobility has bene one adaptive process in this social system, the rise had of sectarian groups may be another. Once a sectarian rise and been accomplished, the new group continued in the common pattern jati mobility."

7. P.V. Kane: "*History of Dharmasastra*" Vol. V, part II, Poons 1962, p. 1629 f·

8. J.A.B. van Buitenen: "On the Archaism of the Bhagavata Purana," in: "*Krsna*: *Myths, Rites and Attitudes*" ed. by Milton Singer Chicago 1966, p. 31 ff.

9. See for detailed description. C.H. Heimsath, *Indian Nationalism and Hindu* Reforms. Princeton: Princeton University Press, 1960; Kopt D., "The Brahmo Samaj Intelligentsia and Bengal Renaissance" in R. 1. Crane (ed.), *Transition in South Asia*: *Problems of modernization*. Durham, Duke University, 1970.

10. For a detailed account see C.H. Heimsath. *op. cit.*, 1969, Lajpat Rai. *The Arya Samaj*, London, Longmans Green, 1985.

Appendix V

INTER-CASTE RELATIONS

The caste system is one of the more rigid forms of social stratification. It is generally assumed by most people that with the advent of industrialisation, the hold of the caste system is becoming much less rigid. There is, however, little empirical data cn the situation. The present chapter discusses the prevailing relationship and the attitudes toward these relationships. Knowledge existing inter-caste relations is essential for understanding the rural society as well as for starting a community development programme.

A generally accepted definition of the caste is given. Through this, it would be possible to indicate some of the features of the caste system, and make it easier to understand the data pertaining to inter-caste relations. Caste is defined as follows by Blunt:

> "An endogamous group, or collection of endogamous groups bearing a common name, membership of which is hereditary, arising from birth slone, imposing upon its members certain restriction in the matter of social intercourse either:
>
> 1. a common traditional occupation or
> 2. claiming a common origin or

3. both following such an occupation and claiming such an origin and generally regarded as forming a single homogeneous community."

From the definition and other descriptions, the following factors can be considered as the major features of caste system:

(a) Hereditary status,

(b) Hereditary occupation,

(c) Restrictions of food (with whom to eat and what to eat),

(d) Endogamous marriage, and

(e) Other social restrictions (visiting, borrowing, smoking, residence, etc.)

The caste system is essentially a feature of Hindu society. However, the influence of the system is apparent among Muslims and Christians as well. In Sarangapur there was hardly and evidence of a "caste" among Muslims.

Next to the family, the caste system is the most important social institution. Caste is a dominating and a determining factor in many aspects of the life of the village. The influence of caste on occupations and organization has already been discussed. Other areas where the social relationships are more direct are discussed in this chapter.

Invities

A question was asked as to whom they would invite if there was a ceremony in their house.

The Brahmins said that they would invite all their relatives, however far they lived. They would also invite the members of their own caste from nearby villages (within a four to five mile radius). The invitation would be restricted to their own ub-caste and to those who had not participated in any function or a party of any members of an alien faction. Further, the invitation would be extended to the Panch Praja (literally translated, it means "five subjects"), that is, those who work for them, barber, carpenter, washerman, tailor, and sweeper. A number of them said that they would invite the whole village for some ceremonies-particularly for marriage. The number to be invited and the area of the spread of their invitations was governed to a very large extent by the economic status of the individual. In the case of death, as in the age of the dead person, caste has an influence on the number of people invited for ceremonies connected with death.

In the B group the invitations would be confined to their own sub-caste in the nearby villages. The people who worked for them would also be invited.

It must be pointed out that although the higher castes would invite the lower castes, they were not allowed inside the house and were not seated with the members of the higher caste.

The C group usually invited people from their own hamlet, and one of two nearby villages.

The Muslims invited their relatives, those who worked for them, and friend, regardless of caste and religion. The major restriction for them was the sect. There two seats among the Muslims. Inter-relations between them are not cordial.

Smoking

The Brahmins are not allowed to smoke, so a question concerning those with whom they would share their hookah (water pipe) did not apply.

The sharing of the hookah is an indication in other castes of the nature of social relations. The B group share it only with those who belong to the same that within the sub-caste.

The C group also shared it only with those of the that.

It may be mentioned here that both the "leather workers" the "pig keepers" had seven sub-castes each. Even within the caste itself there was a status hierarchy based on the sub-castes.

The Muslims have no particular objection to sharing their hookah with anybody. In practice, however, there is some indication that they did not share it with the lower caste people.

Borrowing of Things

Among the restrictions placed on the members of a caste is one with regard to the borrowing of certain things, particularly vegetables, fruits that are cut, and salt. There are few restrictions in borrowing uncooked food grains, whole vegetables and whole fruits.

Actually, however, very little borrowing seems to take place among the village population. A few in fact said that they never borrow anything from others because most of the things needed are available in nearby shops. They prefer to buy rather than borrow.

To the question as to whom they would borrow from if there was need, all the Brahmins said that they would borrow food grains, vegetables, salt sugar, and pickles only from their own caste and within their own faction.

While the majority of the B group said that they would confine the borrowing to their own caste, some said they had no objection to borrowing from the Brahmins.

Temple Entry of Harijans

One of the social laws passed after Independence is that all people should be allowed to enter all temples. Until this law was passed, the temples were open generally only for higher castes. Two questions were asked of the people with regard to this:

1. Are Harijans allowed to enter temples?

2. Should they be allowed to enter?

Of the total population, fifty-one per cent said that Harijans were allowed to enter the temple and forty-six per cent felt that they were forbidden. Three fourths (seventy-five per cent) of the C group felt that they were forbidden, A very large percentage of the B group also felt the same, whereas only one third of the Brahmins said that the Harijans were not allowed to enter temples (see Table).

To the question as to whether they should be allowed sixty per cent of the population said that they should be and forty per cent said that they should not be allowed.

TABLE V.1

Percentage Distribution of Population According to Whether They Think Harijans are Allowed to Enter Temples and by Caste

Opinion	*Caste Group*				
	A	*B*	*C*	*D*	*Total*
Yes	62	24	25	83	51
No	36	67	75	13	46
Don't Know	2	9	—	4	3
Total	100	100	100	100	100
N	52	22	28	23	125

All the Muslims said that they should be allowed to enter the temples. They have no objections to non-Muslims entering their mosques. Among B group, seventy-two per cent said that they should not be allowed, whereas among the Brahmins only forty-two per cent said so. Among the C group, thirty-six per cent said that they should not be allowed. When questioned further, they said that they had not entered the

TABLE V.2

Percentage Distribution of Population as to whether They cousider Harijans should be allowed to Enter Temples and by Caste

Opinion	*Caste Group*				
	A	*B*	*C*	*D*	*Total*
Yes	58	28	64	100	60
No	42	72	36	—	40
Don't know	—	—	—	—	—
Total	100	100	100	100	100
N	52	22	28	23	125

temples until now and that they would not know how to behave. They seemed to indicate a sense of insecurity in doing something which they had not done before.

Among all who said that people should not be allowed to enter temples said that God is the God to all and so there should be no discrimination.

Those who said that the Harijans should nor be allowed gave the reasons listed below. (They are listed according to highest number of mentions in descending order.)

1. Harijans eat meat.
2. Harijans are not clean.
3. Harijans have not entered the temples up to this time.
4. It is against the religion.
5. They are low caste people.

The next two tables given an analysis of this opinion according to whether Harijans are allowed to enter temple or should be, on the basis of age differential.

According to age-wise analysis little difference was found

in the percentage of people below thirty years and over thirty years who thought Harijans are allowed to enter the temple and those who think that they should be allowed.

TABLE 5.3

Percentage Distribution of Population According to Whether They think Harijans are Allowed to Enter Temples and by Age

Opinion	*Thirty and Below*	*Thirty-one and Over*	*Total*
Yes	48	53	51
No	46	47	46
Don't know	6	—	3
Total	100	100	100

TABLE V.4

Percentage Distribution of Population According to Whether they Think Harijans should be Allowed to Enter Temples and by Age

Opinion	*Thirty and Below*	*Thirty-one and Over*	*Total*
Yes	57	62	60
No	43	38	40
Total	100	100	100

"Usefull" Caste of the Village

There are two questions asked regarding the usefulness of castes. The first question had reference to the caste most useful to the village, the second question was; "Which caste is most useful to You?" Tables give an analysis of the answers.

TABLE V.5

Percentage Distribution of Population According to which Caste is Most Useful to the Village

Most Useful Caste to the Village	*Caste Group* *A*	*B*	*C*	*D*	*Total*
Brahmins(A)	15	17	64	17	26
Harijans(C)	100	46	18	57	64
Muslims(D)	—	—	—	—	—
All Castes	4	27	18	13	13
Others	2	—	—	22	5
No response	—	—	—	—	—
(Totals more than 100 as some mentioned more than one caste)					
N	52	22	28	23	125

TABLE V.6

Percentage Distribution of Population According to the Caste Most Useful to Oneself and by Caste

Most Useful Daste to Oneself	*Caste Group* *A*	*B*	*C*	*D*	*Total*
Brahmins (A)	2	24	64	13	22
Harijans (C)	88	31	7	65	56
Muslims (D)	—	—	11	—	2
All Castes	4	31	11	22	14
Others	6	9	—	9	6
No response	—	5	7	—	2
Total	100	100	100		
(Totals more than 100 as some mentioned more than one caste)					
N	52	22	28	23	125

Sixty-four per cent of all the villagers felt that Harijans were the most useful caste of the village. The most important reason given for this opinion was that they were labourers and without them agricultural work could not be carried on. A few said that they were useful because of sanitation, particular reference being to pig rearers and sweepers.

About one fourth (twenty-six per cent) thought that the Brahmins were the most useful for the village. The reason that C group gave was that the Brahmins gave employment. Other reasons given were that they were rich, gave loans, and educated. Two or three people said that they were useful as they were necessary for performing rituals.

All castes were considered useful for the village by thirteen per cent of the population. Those that were employed by different caste people considered that particular caste most useful.

No one indicated that Muslims were the most useful for the village. This probably was due to the fact that Muslims are not a "caste" and are not an integral part of the caste system. An other factor may be that they were in a hamlet by themselves and hence isolated.

With reference to the caste most useful to oneself, eighty-nine per cent of the Brahmins said that the Harijans were the most useful to them, whereas sixty-four per cent of the Harijans (C group) said that Brahmins were most useful to them. The reciprocal relationship can be explained by the fact that there is an employer-employee relationship between them.

The opinion among the B group as to which caste was most useful for them was rather spread out among the various groups. They had their own land and worked on it themselves. They had no direct relation with any particular caste. This probably explains the opinion regarding the "most useful caste to oneself" being widely divided.

While sixty-three per cent of the Muslims considered

Harijans the most useful, only eleven per cent of the Harijans considered them most useful to themselves. There was no mutual relationship as was seen between the Harijans and the Brahmins.

CASTE DISCIPLINE

Among the Hindus, the caste is rigid and the behaviour of individuals is guided by the norms and standards set by the caste.

A further list of forms of behaviour was given which defy the regulations: the question put to the subjects concerned the course of action they would take if

1. a member of the family, and
2. a member of the caste behaved in some of the ways listed in the questionnaire.

Within the caste, the only action that can be taken is to ostacize the person from the caste. If a member of the caste were ostracized and if any other member had any form of contact with him, then he too would be ostracized.

In Table an analysis is given of the actions that people would take against their family members for behaving in certain ways. Those who said that they would not take action against the family also said that they would not take action against the members of the caste either.

To the question as to what action would be taken if a person took food outside the caste, forty-three per cent of the total population said that no action would be taken. This is a sense is misleading because there is no particular restriction for the Muslims regarding eating with others. When a look at the other caste is taken, it is noted that a larger per cent of the Brahmins than of the B and C groups would not take action. Only a very low per cent among the C group would not take action.

TABLE V.6

Percentage Distribution of Population by Type of Punishment to be Meted Out if Members of Family Behaved According to the Way Indicated

Form of Behaviour	*Scold*	*Beat*	*Out of House*	*Purifying Ceremony*	*Others*	*No Action*
Food outside caste	4	10	20	2	19	43
Water outside caste	14	12	13	5	16	45
Married outside caste	1	6	49	2	16	23
Married a widow	4	1	20	1	6	60
Married a person of low morals	26	13	29	13	10	14
Take food not approved	4	6	41	6	17	17
Joint other religion	2	7	40	2	6	17
Occupation not of caste	6	3	5	3	4	75
Smoke outside caste	1	3	6	7	15	21

The pattern is similar for anyone taking water with people not of the same caste.

The changes in attitude-or the tolerance of either members of family or of caste are probably due to the fact that a number of them are working in military service, railways, or factories where they are forced to eat with others. In educational institutions, too, they have to eat with other caste groups since there are no exclusive arrangements for different castes. In travelling, people have begun to use hotels more freely and very rarely is the caste of the owner or of the cook known. All this has led to a relaxation of regulations.

If a person married outside the caste, nearly a fourth of the population said that they would not take action. Nearly Half (forty-nine per cent) would turn the family member out of the house. Sixteen per cent said they would not allow them to share the "hubble Bubble" with members of the caste or the family, but they would maintain speaking relations.

Two of the Brahmins in the village have wives (by common law) whose caste is not known. The villagers have very little social intercourse with them. Only a few villagers talk to them, but no borrowing or visitation by the other Brahmins occurs. During the observance of the Holi festival when a group went singing from house to house, their houses were by-passed. However, the two Brahmins do not seem to be too bothered because they work in railway and do not spend much time in the village. They are financially well off, have probably the best houses in the village, and own about ten acres of land.

Among the B, C, and D groups there are no strong restrictions against widow remarriage; however, it is not a particularly approved form of behaviour. Among the Brahmins, widow remarriage is forbidden, yet fifty per cent of them said that they would not take any action. There seems to be some relaxation with regard to the idea of widow remarriage, particularly if the girl is young and more so if the marriage had not been consummated. In Sarangaput there was a Brahmin girl who was quite young (about twenty years) who husband had died when she was about ten years old. The author was tole that many attempts had been made by villagers to have her marry again, but the girl herself took the view that she must put with her fate.

Only fourteen per cent said that they would not take action if an individual married a person known to have low morals. If both were from the same caste, the caste could not take action. Even in the family no serious action could be taken through, this would be resented, and although twenty-nine per cent said that they would turn them out of the house, the remaining said they would take some mino taction. In another study which the author made, character was indicated as the primary factor to be considered in looking for a bride.

Every caste has certain restrictions as to the type of food people within it should take, Muslims are forbidden to take liquor or pork. Eating forbidden food seems a serious matter in view of the fact that forty-one per cent said that they would turn an offender out of the house. The person would be automatically ostracized from the caste. Seventeen per cent said that they would not take action. A larger per cent of the Muslims than of A, B, and C groups said that they would not take action; actually, among the Muslims, the restrictions are not strong except for taking pork.

One Brahmin was seen preparing "egg nog" for his brother who was sick. When questioned as to how a Brahmin could take egg, it was explained that the egg and milk were ordered by the doctor. Any diet suggested by a doctor is considered a medicine, and regardless of what it contains, it can be taken without offending caste rules.

As for joining another religious group, people generally felt that no action would be necessary since any person changing his religion would automatically go out of the house and the caste. However, forty per cent did indicate that they would turn their family members out of the house. Seventeen per cent said that they would not take any action. Most felt it would not be necessary. If a member of a family or caste were to change religion and other were to have any relations with the individual, then they too would be ostracized.

Three fourths of the population (seventy-five per cent) said that they would not take any action if either a member of the family or of the caste engaged in some occupation not followed by the caste. In the C and D groups few people would take action. This is probably due to the fact that the C group usually have very lowly jobs and the Muslims have no traditional jobs. Among the A group, seventy per cent said that they would not take any action because they too do not seem now to have any "traditional" occupation as not all of them can be priests. In B group, which is the artisan group, the tendancy seems to be greater to hold on to traditional occupations: a little less than half the population (forty-five per cent) said they would take some action if a person talk a job not in keeping with caste tradition. On the whole there seems to be little reaction to the forms of occupation persons engage in.

The research assistant at the end of the survey wanted to take a job as a night watchman in a factory because he could not get any other work. His father prevented this, feeling that it was neither in keeping with the jobs that his son had earlier nor with the dignity of the caste and family.

The Brahmins do not smoke and so they did not answer any questions on the action they would take if a person smoked the water pipe with members of some other caste. The Muslims have no restriction, only the B and C groups replied in terms of traditional restriction. Two types of action would be taken:

1. To make the person undergo a purifying ceremony and
2. to prevent the individuals sharing the water pipe with other members of the caste. This is in a sense as serious as being ostracized from the caste.

Appendix VI

DRIVE AGAINST CASTEISM

Casteism is one of the prime evils of Indian Society, but he drive or movement against it has been effective or successful so far. Morarji expressed his doubts about the eradication of the caste system through by legislation alone. Nor could the incentives or bans which Mr. Charan Singh suggested to Jawaharlal Nehru long ago be of much use. The present suggestion is that, apart from examples of reform like inter-caste marriages and dining, caste appellations should be dropped from the names of individuals and institutions. This would be one more reforming step, though it is doubtful how far Reddys, Singhs Agarwals and Yadavs would disappears, through newspaper headlines, for the sake of convenience, even now make Mr. Charan of Mr. Charan Singh. The origins of caste and of its long course in India are not exactly known, but a caste has been usually defined as "an endogamous and hereditary sub-division of an ethnic unit occupying a position of superior or inferior rank of social esteem in comparison with other such sub-divisions". It resembles the clan in some respects and differs from it in others. There is caste in most countries. Jews and gypsies are *de facto* castes even in modern Europe. Apart from the varna or colour theory, caste may have originated from class and is here and there breaking out into class. While caste is a special from of social class, it has become rigid and petrified and allows little of social mobility.

This is its greatest weakness. Caste has degraded the status that Harijans and low castes in general are allowed to attain, carrying many economic, if not legal, disabilities. Religion became embedded in social division when Hinduism became largely Brahminism. Yet conditions vary. In the South, the Brahmin is in a minority, sticking to ancient priestly functions and learning, apart from taking the first advantage of the benefits of modern civilization; in the North, the Brahmins are in some regions the largest minority, almost counted as a majority. The Ambedkar approach to the Harijan problem was to provide them with all facilities, education and jobs, while Gandhi cast the responsibility for eradicating untouchability, as a kind of penance, on the higher castes. As it is, the caste system is net easily amenable to any analysis, Marxist or otherwise, and no political party has attacked it.

The place of caste in a highly industrialised society gives rise to hope, though old habits persist also in the present highly industrialised societies. The Hindu caste system, apart from the more mobile caste systems of other religions, is bound up with Karma and Dharma and ideas of purity and pollution. As long as an occupation like scavenging is forced only on the Harijans, the Harijans will remain where they are. There are also washerman, barbers, and midwives. As long as the idea of pollution lasts and there are rules about it, there would be restrictions, through groups can change their status in several generations by changing their behaviour to conform to these rules. It is easy to accept invitatious from Harijan ministers for food but not so easy at the common level. Among the working classes too, caste is not breaking down, though it is less rigid in factories than in the field. The struggle for status and opportunity for occupation will go on, and there are reasons why, even Brahmins sometimes think that they might have better opportunities as Harijans. Caste will require an attack from all sides. Even now it is too flexible and adaptable to changing conditions. There should be a more exact study than is possible for politicians with their pet theories. It is not a question of Karan Singh becoming Karan or Charan Singh becoming Charan. Those who oppose increasing industrialisation are not eradicating caste but working for its preservation. Surely, industrialisation, which no country can now avoid, is one way, and agriculture at its best has to be treated as an industry. Fortunately, Gandhi succeeded in fighting separate electorates for Harijans; if he had failed, there would have a demand for a Harijan version of Pakistan by Dr. Ambedkar and others. Politically caste is playing its part even in Janata Party circles. Unless these trends are fought, the caste system and, along with it, untouchability cannot be fought. Caste may not wither away soon but casteism at least should.

Castes and Outcastes

In the recent State Assembly elections in Andhra Pradesh, Karnataka and Tripura, almost every party was accusing every other party of exploiting caste and thus indulging in casteism for the sake of securing the vote. It is not only for votecatching but for many other purposes that many Indians, including their leaders, indulge in caste appeal. Caste means subcaste.

As long as the caste system exists, there are bound to be outcastes, said Dr Ambedker, that embittered but wise man. To the problem of caste has been added the problem of Harijans or Scheduled Castes, who were so called because the British had put them in some schedule. "Harijans", which Gandhi popularished on some body's suggestion is also not a happy word, through it elevated them nominally without reconciling them to Hindu society.

Dr. Ambedker believed that Harijans could be emancipated only if they acquired political and economic power and position. The position of the Negroes has improved with their economic betterment, some of them being Negro millionaires owing Cadillacs, but that has not made segregation disppear in the North or in the South, Gandhi believed that it was the duty of caste Hindus to do penance by devoting themselves to the task of Harijan emancipation. He was thinking of the Harijans remaining permanently a part of the Hindu fold.

The lot of Harijans has not politically or economically improved as a whole, though some Harijans have achieved good positions in politics and the services. No Harijan has yet becomes a President, Vice-President or Prime Minister, though it is but one test of political and social equality. Jagjivan Ram was nearer to achieving that supreme position, but he has been missing all chances, for which he has to blame mostly himself.

Vested Interest

If Gandhi had not succeeded in getting separate electorates for Harijans scrapped in 1932, by his fast into death against the Communal Award, which seemed irrational to many at that time, there may have been a demand for a notional Pakistan of their own, as there would have been a demand for a Pakistan inside the country if separate electorates for Muslims had remained after Independence.

The result after all these years of Harijan uplift seems to be that the Harijans have devoloped a vested interest in remaining Harijans with reservations and that caste Hindus have developed a vested interest in Harijans remaining Harijans. Caste Hindus, like others, require Harijans for scavenging and other dirty purposes.

Unless man becomes his own scavenger with the help of modern sanitary methods, he will need Harijans, and while some Harijans may become ministers and other enter the services, most remain scavengers. The over-all problem will remain, as Dr. Ambedker envisaged that till caste is abolished or casteism disappears, there will be outcastes, and all types of dirty work remain for them.

This writer has tried to discuss with sociologists, historians, political scientist, philosophers and others what Hindu society would be without caste, assuming that people want caste to disappear. No satisfactory answer has been forthcoming, a feeble answer being that Hindus without caste would be like Buddhists. It is for experts in religion and sociology, including the Sankaracharyas, to ponder. The Marxist might say that class will re-emerge from caste, under increasing economic absorption, and that it is already re-emerging. It takes us back to the origins of caste.

Brahminised

It is now broadly agreed that caste developed from varnas, or classes based on occupations. The Portuguese who first used the word caste found, when they arrived in India in the sixteenth century. Hindu society divided into separate groups, and they called them castes, meaning tribes, classes or families. There is no end to the number of castes and sub-castes but the main castes have remained four, and these and more have remained among Muslims and Christians after their conversion from Hinduism. The priest, the warrior, the peasant and the serf could be found in ancient Persia also.

In India, the rigidity with which the caste system developed may have been due to the Brahminisation of Hinduism. The Brahmins achieving great power through their ascendancy and ritualised everything, including law, till law also became a fetter on progress, as reformers of Hindu law found. The occupational base became systematised as Brahminism developed exclusiveness. A member of one caste could not reach a higher caste. Economic change was slow and social change did not seem possible.

Rene Guenon, in his "Introduction To The Doctrine of Hindu Doctrines", says: "Caste which the Hindus describe indifferently by one or other of the two words jat and varna is a social function determined by the particular nature of each human being." This links caste to the idea of dharma, and it was in this sense that even Gandhi talked of varashram dharma. Dharma, the model of the caste system, which does not stand modern tests, raises the question how a natural model of human society assumes the form of a social stratification based on birth and ritual.

Besides, the caste system to in conflict with the modern idea of individual freedom. It is possible to defend traditional theories in terms of tradition, but they do not fit into modern society or its functioning and cannot deserve the support of modern sociology.

Persisting

Thus it can be argued that from any point of view, caste should go. But it is not easy to make it go. Inter-caste and inter-State marriages are on the increase but these have not been enough to make caste disintegrate. In times of crisis, it is showing its stub-bornness and comparative indestructibility. At the time of elections, it is still a powerful factor. Why should there be always Reddys and why should there be always Kammas, taking Andhra as an example where caste has built its citadels.

Panikkar held that if land cellings were impossed strictly, the power of the Riddys would go. But no ceilings were imposed strictly under the successive Reddy regimes and their power remains. As long as market economy remains as it is, the Kammas flourish with their capacity for capital accumulation through domestic economy and their spirit of adventure and enterprise. The examples can be multiplied from all states. The origin of the Jats is not clear, but they will not disintegrate.

The economic aspect can provide a new answer to caste and its disintegration. There are signs that class can reemerge from caste. But while class conflicis are inevitable, there is yet no powerful operation of them even at election time. Class is far more dynamic than caste. It will not become a system, though the attempts to achieve classlessness are not shining successes.

The greater the impact of economic change, the greater will be social change, and then caste may start losing its rigidity. What it will means to Hinduism and to Hindu society, it is yet difficult to say, Hinduism is now like a federation of faiths bound together by steel hoops of caste.

Caste Remains an Abrasive in Indian Society

Few days pass in India without the newspapers reporting fresh manifestations of caste conflict. Beating, shooting, rape and mutilation are added almost daily to a dismal catalogue. Caste is part of the framework of Indian society and also one of its enduring abrasives.

The present eruption of violence in the western state of Gujarat, which has so far cost 25 lives and appears to be growing more bitter, is a caste conflict rooted in a government policy which attempts, in a well-meaning egalitarian spirit, to confront one of the central issues and enigmas of Indian life.

The costitution says: "The state shall promote with special care the education and economic interests of the weaker sections of the people". Since independence these words have been translated into action through the policy of reserving places in colleges and government offices for Harijans (Mahatma Gandhi's name for Untouchables) and for tribal people, who make up about a sixth of the population.

But according to a growing body of opinion the quota system is getting out of hand. It is argued that the noble purpose enshrined in the constitution, which outlawed untouchability, has become distorted in practice and that the contradictions in the policy sharpen rather than mitigate caste differences.

Critics contend that caste has become one of the important commodities in the political market, with politicians promising larger job quotas in exchange for votes. Positive discrimination creates resentment where people are given jobs on caste grounds rather than on merit, and causes trouble in cases where well-off harijans are allotted places and jobs at the expense of poor upper-caste people whose need is evidently greater.

A harijan is not always at the botton of the economic heap. Anger has grown among those in the upper castes who believe it is now they who are victimized on caste grounds.

In Gujarat the quota system is being fiercely attacked and stoutly defended. Until recently a quarter of post-graduate places in medical colleges were held for harijans and others of what are called the backward classes. But gradually the allotment has been increased to half. In a few specializations even more places are held for the backward classes.

Anti-quota agitation by upper caste medical students and counter demonstration by Harijans have brought turmoil to several parts of the state. Police have fired on rioters and the Army has been called in to help keep order. More than 60 textile mills have been closed by striking Harijan workers protesting against the students' campaign.

Caste has been for more than 3,000 years a central and powerful force in Hindu society and to a considerable extent still determines a man's place in society.

It is part and parcel of Hindu ideas of life, rebirth and predestination, and clearly has a stabilizing or ordering effect in society. But for the lower orders it is also an instrument of repression and is therefore a cause of violence.

The system had its origins in four castes, broadly speaking the priests, soldiers, farmers and artisans. The rest were the untouchables. Now there are said to be 3,000 castes, with numerous sub-castes.

Modern conditions and influences, especially the growth of education, travel and the development of urban societies, have gone some way to eroding traditional caste barriers. In cities a different style of life and enforced mixing and sharing in public transport, restaurants and cinemas have helped to make caste less important.

Most caste strife originates in the countryside. Harijans tend to be confined to their traditional menial tasks, live separately in villages and draw water from different wells. Belief that Untouchables contaminate leads to the practising of an apartheid extraordinarily complex in its detail.

Ill-treatment of Harijans has been commonplace for centuries. Atrocities in which Harijans and tribal people are victims have increased threefold in three years according to the Commissioner for Scheduled Castes.

Much of the trouble in rural India today is caused by land feuds as peasants, mostly Harijans and low castes, try to claim their rights, and become the victims of landlords who resort to murder and maiming to resist the pressure.

Prejudice is not a one-way affair. A few days ago Harijan villagers cut off the nose of a Harijan girl who had offended by marrying into a higher caste. Marriage is still a sensitive and important area where caste lines are concerned.

In more educated circles prejudice and superstition are still there, even if more convert. After a reception in Delhi the host ordered the crockery to be smashed because it had been used, and so defiled, by a guest who was an Untouchable.

When a former deputy prime minister, a Harijan, unveiled a statue two years ago, high caste Hindus gave it a wash after he had gone, because he had touched it.

Recently a Harijan presented an idol worth £2,700 to a temple, but priests stopped him entering the temple because his presence would have polluted it.

In the generation since independence India has made huge strides in agriculture, industry and education, and living standards have been raised remarkably. But improvement has been offset by large growth in population, so that in spite of all the advances more than two-fifths of the people live below the poverty level. Pressure on land has grown, and this is one of the factors in caste conflict.

Many Indians are anxious to find ways of lessening tensions while bettering the lives of those traditionally kept under the heel. But the caste structure itself is a part of India that cannot be eradicated.

Fighting Casteism

The simple reply of a young boy to the puzzle: "How do you shorten a line without touching it?" is well known. "By drawing a longer line beside it", he said.

There can be no better illustration of the wisdom imbedded in this approach than its application of the solution to the challenge of casteism. The bigger line of Hindu appeal shortens and gradually overshadows the smaller lines of several caste-loyalties to such an extent that ultimately the latter vanish altogether. The Hindu Resurgence movement in Tamil Nadu, gathering momentum day-by-day, is mainly directed towards this end.

The Naidupuram area in Kodaikanal, the famous hill resort of Tamil Nadu, is a telling instance in point. That 7000 ft. high beautiful township, nestling in the lap of the Sahyadri ranges, draws the jolly holidayers from all over the country and more so from abroad. But it has also become the happy hunting ground for instant-rich Muslim petro-dollar-wallahs who are busy cornering plots and buildings. The Christian church too is busy trying to buy up the poor and the ignorant among the Hindus through their well known modes of inducement.

The RSS workers there decided to mend matters. They did

not, however, start crying themselves hoarse against the Muslim and Christian machinations. They knew better. The present plight of Hindus stems from their own sins of omission and commission. Corrosive elements like caste-rivalries and untouchability have rendered them weak and made an easy prey to others. The smaller lines of divisive loyalties could be dissolved only by the call of a broader vision. The Sangh leaders began making a systematic personal approach to the leaders of all sections of Hindu society and appealed to their higher Hindu conscience. The result was the birth of a united Hindu platform—the Hindu Munnani—on which every single community, big and small, has joined.

Naidupuram took the lead in giving a practical shape and content to these ideas. The area comprises roughly 400 hours. Its special feature is that family is the unit of membership, not the individual—thus emphasising a basic element of the Hindu polity. The member in whose name the membership of Re. 1 is collected is a representative of his family. The members of a street elect a street representative. The Munnani Committee of 16 represents all the 400 and odd families in the 6 divisions of Naidupuram. It has in turn elected a President. A minimum programme for ensuring the continuity of the spirit of unity has been formulated. Every family, on the appointed day and time of every week, should depute one of its members for the get-together. For the first time in the history of that township, one sees all the various caste-groups, rubbing shoulders with each other in the common bond of Hindu brotherhood. Bhajans, patriotic songs, discourses, discussions on the problems facing the Hindu society go on. Special religious programmes are planned and they afford an opportunity for the women-folk to mingle and rub off their coste-inhibitions.

The weekly gathering over, the Committee sits to resolve the individual cases of friction and dispute. Both parties agree to abide by the Committee's decision. In fact, all the members are firm on one promise—that they shall not go to police or to the courts for redress. Gradually, the Committee's verdict is becoming the law and all the member-families feel intensely relieved from the bitter wranglings getting aggravated among neighbours and the heavy expenditure they were incurring whenevere they went to the police or courts. A Christian, who had observed the smooth and inexpensive way of resolving their disputes among his Hindu neighbours, also appealed to the Committee seeking justice. Although the respondent was a Hindu, the Committee gave its decision in favour of the Christian. The Hindu, who was patently at fault, bowed to the decision. No wonder, the common run of Christians have come to look upon the Committee with a new eye of respect for its justice and fairplay.

The Munnani, from its very start, has been consciously applying itself to pulling down the barriers of caste. One of the rules it has framed for all its 400 and odd family members is that in case of death in any family every one has to subscribe one rupee each, to lighten the economic burden of the bereaved family. The affected family—even if it be affluent—should not refuse that contribution, for that is a symbol of fraternity of the entire community. A member or two from each family of that locality also makes it a point to come and console the bereaved family with words of solace and comfort.

Some time back, death occurred in the house of a Harijan. Every Hindu family of Naidupuram hastened to that home to express their condolence. The President of the Munnani, Parangari, and Vice-President O.K.A. Thevar were also, of course among them.

All over Tamil Nadu, the two castes, the Thevars and Harijans, have been especially at loggerheads. Even physical conflicts are not uncommon. That day, Thevarji, had an urgent work to attend to in another town. But he knew his absence in Naidupuram that day would definitely be misunderstood. He, the Vice-President of Munnani himself, would lose credibility in the eyes of all his members. That would deal a very severe blow to the noble purpose with which they had launched the movement. Without a second thought, Thevarji cancelled all his other engagements and stayed back to participate in the funeral ceremony of the Harijan resident of the locality.

The School and Hospital started in Kodaikanal by the Hindu Mission are also the offshoots of the Hindu Awakening. The old and so-far neglected temple is now humming with religious activity. A community hall is also coming up to house the growing activities of social functions and cultural and art programmes. A devoted worker of RSS who works as the full-timer for the Hindu Mission, is the moving spirit behind all these activities.

Tenkasi is yet another place where a similar direction is being given to the Hindu Awakening. As elsewhere, here too are the cleavages between various castes. Meenkshipuram is in this very Tehsil, of Kadayanallur, the notorious hotbed of Muslim smugglers and inflow of petrodollars for conversion is just nearby. The RSS Sanghachalak of the Tehsil, Subrahmanya Raja, decided to take the initiative. He spoke to the leaders of nearly thirty important caste-groups in the town. And what a pleasant surprise it was for him to find that they too were equally anxious to mend matters! They decided to join in common endeavour to do away with their mutual frictions and put up a united Hindu Front. As a result, *Anaittu Hindu Samudaya Peravai* (Akhil Hindu Samaj Mahasabha) was born. For the first time in the history of the town the Hindus began to speak not in several discordant notes as caste-representatives, but in a single voice as Hindus.

And as a first step they resolved to settle their matual complaints through the Peravai and not seek the intervention of police or courts. And soon a long-standing labour dispute came up before it. Jyoti Fibres is a small factory employing a dozen workers. Both the proprietor and the workers bypassed the communist gentleman whose leadership rested on continuing the tension. They sought the Peravai's good offices. Both the parties agreed to eliminate the root cause. And both returned satisfied with the compromise arrived at. Now the factory is working as a happy fraternity.

The shocking news from Sri Lanka stirred the Peravai deeply. But what pained them more was the way the whole tragedy was painted everywhere. The one word which was on everybody's lips was 'Tamil', 'Tamil'. Every tragic reference such as the massacre, the atrocities, the refugees etc., referred to the 'Tamils'. All seemed to have simply forgotten that they are Hindus and are the flesh and blood of the 60 crore Hindu people in Bharat. It was natural that this kind of exclusive and separatist painting of the gruesome holocaust overtaking lakhs of their Hindu brethern left the 60 crores of Hindus in Bharat and even those abroad entirely cold. Peravai leaders of Tenkasi, in contrast to the 'Tamil' protest processions taken out elsewhere-decided to take out a 'Hindu' procession.

Shahul Hameed, the Muslim League MLA of Kadayanallur—the moving had behind the Meenakshipuram conversion and the engineering of Harijan-non-Harijan riots coupled with Muslim attacks at Puliangudi last year—began pestering the police that RSS was out to incite the Hindus against the Muslims and therefore the procession be banned. But the police, who knew Hameed through and through, curtly told him that they were quite capable of maintaining peace and he need not worry. For the first time in the history of the town all the 28 caste groups, including the Harijans and other so long neglected sections rubbed shoulders with each other. The papers put the figure of processionists at 7000, a number unheard of before in those parts.

There is another interesting off-shoot of this growing phenomenon of Hindus overcoming their caste prejudices and coming together as Hindus. The 'revolutionary' campaigners against caste, such as the communists who ought to have felt happy at this development have, on the contrary, begun to cry 'wolf.' They are crying that this upsurge of 'Hindu Communalism' would obliterate the existence of political parties and poses a threat to parliamentary democracy—thus admitting inadvertently that casteism and caste-animosities have been the chief hope for their policial future! The joining of communists in their anti-Hindu chorus with the rank Muslim and Christian communalists at every such place also proves the same point—that the internal caste-rivalries among the Hindus have been their main capital all along and now with the 'spectre' of Hindu unity becoming a reality, they feel like going pauper!

And this very outcry should serve as a warning to the Hindus—particularly the weaker and neglected sections—that the so-called champions of 'caste-war' of 'liberation theology', or of 'the oppressed and exploited', are in fact their worst exploiters and that their real redemption lies in standing up as Hindus, as equal and honoured partners of their colossal 60-crore entity imbued with the highest and noblest of cultural and spiritual values.

Caste Syndrome

Of late there has been a revival of the movement to do away with caste-based surnames. Though laudable, it is doubtful that the movement will be much of a success because most educated people cannot reconcile themselves to being addressed by their first names. Besides, doing away with surnames by itself is not going to make much of a difference. Few in the South are known by their surnames, but this does not make them less conscious of their castes.

Among the so-called higher castes, in particular, the sense of belonging to a superior order is deeply embedded in the subconscious, colouring their response to day to day, routine matters. It also creates a strange bond of oneness among people belonging to the same caste or sub-caste to the alienation of others. This is not healthy for the nation.

In a 44-page paper on "Castes, classes and parties in modern political development, with special reference to Kerala," the Marxist leader, Mr. E.M.S. Namboodiripad, has stated that the caste factor is taken into account by all political parties, including "the party of the working class with the most advanced ideology", while selecting their election candidates and making ministerial appointments.

Though other political leaders may not be so honest and forthright in admitting it, it is well known that caste and communal considerations are of paramount importance in politics at every level. That this should be the state of affairs after 30 years of Independence reveals how little our national leaders have cared to support the evils of casteism from society.

Frequently recurring incidents of violence and atrocities against Harijans and Adivasis are the most grim aspects, of casteism. The fact that the police often connive with the upper castes in punishing the "low born" is a matter of disgrace for all of us. Most local-level politicians, too, tend to take such offences lightly—thus encouraging the perpetrators of these offences.

Very recently a young Rajput of Bihar and his bride, a Harijan of the Dussadh sub-caste, were beaten and stripped for having committed the "crime" of contracting a perfectly legal civil marriage. While the wife was kept captive by the local landholders, all belonging to the upper castes, the husband was driven away with only a towel around his waist.

Such incidents should not be tolerated. And this calls not only for prompt action against the guilty but for scrupulous adherence to seculaism in terms of both religion and caste by all of us.

It is high time voluntary organisations and those who pride themselves as leaders of men started a meaningful and uncompromising movement againt the phenomenon of caste itself.

Appendix VII

CASTE, SAY DALIT POETESSES, IS "PERMANENT EMERGENCY"—Vipra

While Dalit men poets like Neerav Patel (whose poetical collection 'Burning from both the ends'' was reviewed in these columns recently) and Namdeo Dhasal (of Golpitha' fame) have expressed the innermost feeling of the social cast-away in a highly emotional and direct language, some talented Dalit women have not lagged behind in describing their sense of social segregation and deprivation in flaming poetry.

As the Dalit movement is mostly confined of Maharashtra, the Dalit Sahitya is mostly written in Marathi. It is mainly the product of the late seventies, and is now branching forth into what is called 'Buddha Sahitya' by some new lovers of the classical mould who think that not socio-economic change but conversion to Buddhism is the only way of abolishing the caste system.

Anyway, this Dalit and Buddhist literature is said to be based on three principles called 'Trisutri', which are—*Vigyan nishta* (scientific outlook), *Vidroha* (revolt) and *Nakaar* (negation). It is literature of the 'oppressed' in the true sense of the term and includes the social, economic an political dimensions of the problem it is not confined to poetry, but includes some beautiful short stories, novels and biographies as well.

Given hereonder is English rendering of representative poetry of some prominent Dalit women:

In a poem named Alyachar (Atrocities), Asha Manik says that the sufferings of some people during the Emergency pale into insignificance before the atrocities on the Harijans. They have been prisoners in their ghettos and suffered grave social disabilities for ages. It is like a permanent Emergency for them. As she puts it:

You have been greatly distressed
On account of the atrocities.
Of the nineteen months of the Emergency?
But we have suffered greater atrocities, and
Still suffering the pains of
Untouchability
Under MISA you were put behind the bars of the prison,
But were you not looked after as 'Rajbandis'?
We were imprisoned in the Maharwada, beyond the wall,
As Untouchables, and
There was no trace of any facilities for us.
Were your children prohibited from attending the schools?
Was your shadow polluting any one?
Did your mother-sister suffer any molestation?
While you were put behind the prison bars?
Were your kith and kin burnt while tied to the trees
For not bending while offering salutations?
Were the wells not open for you to draw water in the Emergency?

But our throats have dried in shouting for water after the Emergency?

Why did you not remember about individual liberty

When you kept us in chains for centuries?

This is no justification of the Emergency.

But the exposition of the reality and unreality.

The following lines from a poem named *Udrek* (Eruption) by Surekha Bhagat contain a dire warning that though the Dalits have taken to Buddhism, the silent volcano may erupt because their patience and peaceful protest have not had any impact on society:

We have reached the last limits of our patience

And the threads of peace are being unstitched;

To stitch them is needed the needle of Revolution

Which we could pick up any time at our will

But we are considerate,

And if you want to ascertain the truth,

You may inquire from Death.

Our minds have been greatly hurt

By humiligtions, hatred, jealousies.

And the awesome assaults of Untouchability,

And caste discrimination and atrocities,

And we have all been ignited fully

And how much time will the fire take to engulf the world

The volcano is bound to erupt add burst forth,

It is not afraid of the times.

It doesn't fear any one.

In the following lines Sugandha Shende, a retired Principal

and editor of a woman's magazine, wonders why the toilers of the land, most of whom belong to the scheduled castes, are denied integration with the rest of society:

> Among toilers, workers,
> The Untouchables are more numerous;
> The construct dams and reserviors of water,
> And take the pipe line to villages
> But···why should the same pipe have two taps
> One for the Savarna,
> The other for the Avarna
> If one thinks over it, one gets confounded.

Untouchability is like a bone-deep wound on the body of Hindu society; and a shame on religion, she says in a long poem 'Doctor':

> The wound of the Hindu culture
> Deepend into the bones,
> Like the black bees consume
> The beams of an old house.
> The ages of Treta, Dwapar have all gone by
> And came there the yug of Kali
> The saints and mystics are chanting mantras,
> And presenting herbs, or pills to cure it.
> The cultural unity has a deep wound in the bones
> That spreads the stinking odour of casteism.
> Alas, no cure could be effective for it,
> For the head-aches, but the feet are kept in plaster.
> The wound becomes septic and deepens,
> And starts gnawing at the heart

That raises cries of helplessness,
And deaths of the hungry occur.
The slave spoke to other slaves,
That he was angry and disgusted,
That his arms were vibrating to demand justice,
And to struggle for human rights.
Kindle the torches, to light ten dark road,
Shame on the religion!
That bars the way to humanism!

The following lines depict a Dalit sister's anguish at the ruin caused by the brother's drinking habit:

How long shall I tell you, my brother,
That you fail to understand,
That we are ruined
By your habit of drinking.
Our father had never touched liquor,
Nor had he every visited the liquor shop,
Nor he ever kept company with one who drank
How long should our mother earn for us?
How are we three to struggle helplessly
And lack necessities like chilly?
Alas, how should I live!
Will any one suggest any remedy to me!

Another leading Dalit poetess Heera Bansode echoes the *Farayad* (Cry for Justice) of a Dalit woman fallen a prey to sexual atrocities by hight caste men and calls upon conscientious people not to slt listiess like Pandavas:

My fellow countrymen, to your court,

I have brought a complaint.

May I expect justice at least from you ?

I have borne the deep wounds of humiliation on my person.

We are being dishonoured and molested,

On the fanatic platform of casteism.

Our character is burnt

On the pages of the scriptures.

While thousand of Draupadis are plundered of their clothes,

Brethren, do not sit like the Pandavas

With your head sunk low.

Now at least, you should remove the strip from your eyes.

To change this humiliating history.

In the following lines from the poem *Dankh* (Deep Sting), shesays that the sting of social discrimination has infected *every* religion and the bitter arsenic of casteism has poisoned human relations, so that every man looks down upon the one lower below in the social heirarchy:

Caste has stung man,

Religion has stung man.

Through the orthodox breaths

And the structure of traditions

All have been stung by caste,

All have been stung by religion

This sting has gone deep

Into the Bible of the Churches.

The Quran of the mosques.

Nay, it has stung even the wind, the stars
And every drop of water here,
And every morsel of food even,
Caste, and religion, could not escape.
This sting has bored into
Innocent and soft hearts.
Even friendship has been stung
With the bitter arsenic of casteism.
This sting has caused the towers of humanity to crumble.
This has destroyed the crusaders against casteism
On the cruel crosses of religious censors.
The priesthood has stung the Kshatriyas,
The Kshatriyas have stung the Vaishyas,
The Vaishyas have stung the Shudras
But whom did the shudra sting?
A cobra stings a man, but
A man never stings a cobra,
And therefore, the suffering Shudra,
Stings himself,
And dies as victim on the bloody altar
Of social tradition.

Another prominent Dalit poetess Jyoti Lanjewar says that her poems cannot adequately describe the poverty and misery of a Dalit ghetto which provides such a contrast to the villas of the high caste people. But the latter are full of moral stink and provides no poetic inspiration.

The darkness in the hut near the village gate is burning me;
The tears from the eyes of the hungry

Are sucking my life;
The grievances on their dry lips
Are treasured in my heart
Half-naked bodies with worn-out clothes
Raise a question mark in my eye
And now tell me, O builders
Of the wall of casteism,
How can I write a poem ?
In the fine gardens in ihe courtyards of
Your houses, on leaves and flowers,
And on the cruel beasts from this
Locality of the inhumans
How can I write a poem?

INDEX

Abrahmic Minorities, 245
Abrasive in Indian Society, 292
Adult Suffrage, 199
Adultery, 31
Aitusha, Kevasha, 119
Ambedkar, Dr. B.R., 164, 207
Angerson, C.A., 45
Anglo-Indians, 214
Anti-nationalism, 215
Anti social sprits, 184
Antyaja, 37, 121
Arabic traveller, 19
Arya Samaj ideals, 261

Bagehoti, Walter, 157
Bailey's study, 73
Barlley, F.G., 82
Bandhayana, 33
Bertrand, A.L., 56
Besant, D.R. Annie, 63
Bhakti moments, 258
Bhandarkar, R., 260
Bindney, David, 56
Bloch, Mare, 55
Blunt. E.A.H., 81
Bonnerji, W.C., 165
Boskoff, Alvin, 54
Brahmo Samaj, 260, 268
Braibanti, Ralph, 57
British cabinet system, 202
British Churches, 242
British North America Act, 221
British system of govt., 200
Byzantine churches, 242

Cahnman, Werner, 54, 57
Caste & class system, 59
Caste consciousness, 185
Caste discipline, 281
Caste in India, 17
Caste & out castes, 288
Caste syndrome, 300
Caste system, 60, 272
  Dr. Ambedkar, 138
Caste theory, 163
Ceremonial discriminations, 20
Chand, Tara, 137
Chandavarkar, N.G., 260
Chattopadhyaya, B.C., 255
Civil Rights Protection Act, 193
Commissioners annual report, 131
Communial Award, 170, 209
Communial majority, 210
Constitution of India, 70
Cooley, 55
Creation of norms, 51

Dalit movement, 302
Davidas, Rhys, 40
Dawson, 85
Deities temples, 226
Demand for Education, 115
Depressed classes, 205
Dharma, 34

Different varnas of court, 21
Distribution of population, 276t
entry by age, 278t
members family behaved, 282t
Doctrine of Hindu, 290
Doob, 85
Dreeben, R., 108
Drive against casteism, 286
Durkheim, 48
Dynamics of social status, 224

Economic privileges, 24
E 'ucational & economic interests, 65
Educational scene, 116
Electorates, 211
Employer-employee relationship, 280
Evolutionary perspectives, 56

Fallacy of functional consequences, 49
Fiction of majority, 214
Fighting casteism, 295
Final election, 211
Forms of modern behaviour, 98t
French-Canadian, 220
French republic, 97
Fundamental rights, 190, 196

Gandhi, Mahatma, 64, 81
Garbha, Guel, 226
Gabriel, Trade, 157
Gautama, 42
Geertz, Clifford, 57
Gemeinshaff-Gescllschaft, 53
Ghurye, G.S., 60, 81
Govt. of India act, 208
Government intervention, 123
Grama, Chavadis, 234
Greatman theory, 154
Group dynamics, 51
Guru, Natranja, 266

Hairesis, 242
Hagen, Everett, 54
Harijan castes & occupation, 124t-126t
Harijan population, 131
distribution of, 134t
Harijan Sewak Sangh, 64
Herberle, Rudolf, 53
Hield, Wayne, 56
Hindu's code of life, 219
Hindu mission, 298
Hindu psychology, 161
Hindu scheme of values, 62
Hocart, A.M., 240
Homans, George, 47, 56
Hoselitz, B.F., 56
Human Organisation, 49

Identifiable modern man, 85
Ill-treatment of Harijans, 294
Indian caste system. 224
Indian social system, 59
Indian Nationalism, 215
Individual modernization, 102
Industrial worker, 92t
Interactional concepts, 51
Inter caste relations, 272
Inkeles, Alex, 106

Kachcha Food, 225
Kahl, J.A., 106
Kane, P.V., 271
Keshan, C , 265
Ketkar, S.V., 150, 225, 240
Krishna-consciousness, 256
Kshatriya, 24
Kshatriya group, 239

Late socialization influences, 94t
Lauriston sharp thrilling theory, 50
Lerner, Daniel, 53
Lipset, S.M., 81

Mahima Dharma movement, 249
Majority party, 201
Malinowski, 46
Manava-dharma-shastra, 24
Manchi Yandis, 232
Marx's determinism, 104
Maunji bandhana ceremony, 18
Max Weber, 52

Mechanical relationships, 50
Micro-change, 47
Micro structural factor, 105
Moore, Wilber, 54
Morgan, L.H., 53
Mydhovan, T.K., 265

Namboodiripad, E.M.S., 301
Nambutiri Brahmins, 264
Nationalism, 221
Non-Brahmin population, 152, 231
Non-Hindu religious groups, 257
Non-scheduled caste organisations, 75
Non-sociologists in desperation, 54

Objective behaviour & clasm, 100t
Ogburn, W.F., 48
Old fashioned terms, 47
Origin of mechanism, 151

Pancasakha schools, 251
Parliamentary democracy, 197
Pollution concept, 228
Poona Pact, 208
Primary election, 21
Progress Phobia, 52
Psychosomatic symptosms test, 102
Punjab Land Alienation Act, 192

Quest for equality, 117

Radcliffe-Brown, 48
Ramakrishna Mission, 255
Ranade, M.G., 260
Religious discriminations, 20
Religious movements, 257, 260, 267
Residential segregation, 62
Rogers, Everett, 57
Roy, R.R,M., 63, 253

Sanskrit technical term, 147
Sarasvati, Dayanand, 253
Scheduled castes, 64
Scholary communications, 84
Sects, 24
Self imposed celibacy, 147
Sharma, B.N., 136
Sharma, R.S., 136
Sharp, Lauristen, 56
Shaw, P.G., 64, 81
Shudra-woman, 29
Shukrat-niti, 23
Singh, Charan, 286
Smith, D.H., 106
Social change, 49, 51
Social mobility, 66
Sociology of development, 54
Socioeconomic status, 67
Socio reform policy, 169
Sorokin, P.A., 81
Spengler, J.J., 48, 54
Spiethoft, Arthur, 55
Srinivas, M.N., 81
Status of harijans, 112
Steward, Julian, 55
Suddi movements, 261
Sutra, A.G., 41
Swamy, N.G., 263
SNDP Yogam, 264

Temple entry, 275
Theoretical implications, 66
Theoretical orientation, 45
Theory of purity & population, 18
Theosophical society, 63
Thomas, Watter, 136
Troeltsch, Ernst, 270

Untouchability Cases Under Act, 132t
Untouchables, 112, 218

Varna intercourse, 31
Varnabheda, 118
Vincents introduction, 51
Vishnu-smriti, 27, 42

Wach, Joaehim, 271
Weber, Max, 243
Wilson, H.H., 41
Wirtschaft stypen paper, 55

Yajnvalka, 42
Youngmen's association, 254

Zero order coorelations, 88